REBEL

GREEN

A Family Saga

Kate Foley

ISBN 978-1-913224-32-5

Cover design by Jared Shear

Discover other titles by PJ Skinner

<u>The Green Family Saga</u>

Africa Green (Book 2)

Fighting Green (Book 3) coming soon

<u>The Sam Harris Adventure Series</u>

Fool's Gold (Book 1)

Hitler's Finger (Book 2)

The Star of Simbako (Book 3)

The Pink Elephants (Book 4)

The Bonita Protocol (Book 5)

Digging Deeper (Book 6)

Concrete Jungle (Book 7)

Go to the PJ Skinner website for more info:
https://www.pjskinner.com

In Memory of an Irish Childhood

Chapter 1 – The Journey, July 1969

As soon as summer term ended, Bea Green packed her children's suitcases and sent them to stay at their grandparents' house. Liz, the eldest at twelve, had been looking forward to some lazy days in her family's sunny garden after the long school year, and took a dim view of their hurried move. She wondered if their departure was related to the whispered conversations between her parents, which tailed off when the children appeared. Neither of her younger siblings, Michael and Isabella, had managed to winkle a clue out of either their mother or their father.

'But why aren't you coming, mummy?' said Liz, as Grandpa Joe loaded their suitcases into the car, an ancient, racing-green Morris Minor, with semaphore indicators which raised out of the frame to indicate a right or left turn, a relic, even in nineteen-sixty-nine.

'Daddy and I have some things to organise first. Granny Ellen will take good care of you, sweetheart. We'll be there in a couple of days, and then we're going on holiday,' said Bea.

'Where are we going?' said Michael.

'I can't tell you. It's a surprise.'

'Did you tell Granny I don't like spinach?' asked Isabella.

'She knows,' said Bea.

Liz doubted her grandmother would be sympathetic to any food preferences from the feisty nine-year-old. The military discipline imposed by her grandfather included clean plates at mealtimes and absolutely no fussing. 'People are dying from starvation,' he said once, prompting Isabella to ask, 'So why don't they give my food to them?' They had sent her to bed without supper, but maybe that was what Isabella wanted. She could be quite sneaky.

'Can I take my football?' said Michael.

'Yes, but don't play inside. You know how much precious china Granny has.'

'She tells us all the time,' said Liz, sniffing. She didn't enjoy staying in her grandparents' house, which resembled a museum of breakable objects ruled by archaic guardians.

'Get into the car, please,' said their grandfather, unused to insubordination from his troops.

All three children clambered into the back seat and sat meekly while their grandfather took his leave of their mother. Bea fought back tears, and her father dabbed her eyes with his handkerchief, giving her a rare hug. Liz elbowed Michael and alerted him to the scene with a toss of her head, raising her eyebrows. There was something very odd about her mother's distress. Bea Green's emotions almost never showed above her parapet of patience and kindness.

Their grandfather got into the driver's seat, emitting a loud sigh as he started the engine.

'Why did you wipe mummy's eye?' said Isabella. 'Was she sad?'

'No, pet, she had dust in her eye.'

Liz and Michael exchanged glances. Their grandfather's neck went pink, a sure sign he had lied. The major couldn't lie to save his life.

Liz leaned over and hissed in Michael's ear. 'I told you something was going on.'

She would have liked to gossip about the mysterious happenings of the last few days, but she didn't want to get into trouble with her grandfather for talking in the car. Michael writhed with impatience. They travelled the rest of the way in silence.

Their grandmother hugged them on arrival and sent them up to the spare room with their bags.

'Granny never hugs us,' said Liz. 'Why is everyone being so weird?'

Despite their efforts, Michael and Liz couldn't find out the cause for the distress affecting the older generation of the family. Their grandparents tried to keep them occupied, and outside hearing distance for conversations with their daughter.

'What's the big secret, Granny?' said Michael.

'Never you mind. You'll find out soon enough,' said his grandfather, patting him on the head.

Later that evening, after their grandmother had turned the lights out and gone downstairs, the phone rang. Her grandmother answered it with a 'Hello, dear'. The only person her grandmother called dear was her daughter, Liz's mother.

Liz got out of bed and crept onto the landing, avoiding the board which creaked theatrically if trodden on. She sat on the top stair, straining to catch the conversation without being seen. A cold draught blew up the stairs, making her shiver and rub her feet. She did not make out many words, and the temperature soon drove her back to the spare room. Instead of getting into her bed, she slipped into Michael's. Her nylon nightdress sparked against the polyester sheets, causing her to giggle and squeak.

'Shh, they'll hear us,' said Michael.

'They're deaf. Budge up.'

'You're freezing.'

Michael moved sideways and had to grab Liz's arm to stop himself falling out of bed.

'Come here, silly,' said Liz, putting her arm over him. Of all things on earth, she loved him most. She often guessed what he was going to say before he said it.

'Where were you?' said Michael.

'On the stairs. The telephone rang and when Granny said 'Hello dear.' I guessed it might be mummy. I tried to listen to what they were saying.'

'What did they say?'

'Something about moving. Granny Ellen sounded sad. Do you think they are going away?'

'I don't know. Nobody tells me anything. They think I'm still a baby. It makes me so cross.'

'I haven't been told either, and I'm a year older than you. Maybe Mummy doesn't want to worry us.'

Michael snorted.

'Not telling us anything doesn't help,' he said, and turned his back on her.

Liz kept her arm draped over him and drifted off to sleep.

***

Three days later, Tom and Bea arrived, not long after dawn, to pick up their still sleeping children. The weak sunlight filtered through the drizzle and branches heavy with summer leaves, piercing the net curtains in the spare room which they entered brimming with false bonhomie.

'Rise and shine,' said Tom, pulling off the children's bed covers. 'We have to leave soon.'

'Don't forget anything,' said Bea.

4

'What's the big rush, Daddy?' said Michael, rubbing his eyes and scratching his stomach. 'Where are we going?'

Isabella planted her hands on her hips, and her body quivered with resentment.

'We're going already?' she said. 'But we've only just got here.'

'Why aren't we staying with Granny and Grandpa?' said Liz. 'What a pain. I bet we're going to the Lake District again. I hate camping.'

They had endured the interminable drive to the Lake District once before, controlling their bladders and their impatience as they obeyed their father's edict to keep quiet while he drove. Liz remembered the last trip there as a miserable sojourn in the pouring rain, filled with compulsory family fun in the soggy countryside.

Bleary-eyed, the three children put on their clothes. They gathered their things together, stuffing their pyjamas into the already overloaded suitcases. Liz rummaged through hers, tutting.

'What's up?' said Michael.

'Some holiday,' said Liz. 'I can't find my swimming costume or shorts in this bag.'

When they were ready to go, the children straggled out into the drizzle to find their father transferring their belongings into Grandpa Joe's ancient vehicle.

The children's suitcases wouldn't fit in the boot which was already stuffed to overflowing with their parent's luggage, and other random items.

'Hang on,' said Grandpa Joe. 'I've got a large plastic mattress bag in the garage. We can pack the children's suitcases into it, to keep them dry, and tie the whole bundle onto the roof rack.'

He shuffled off into the garage and soon came back, holding the neatly-folded, dusty mattress bag.

'Why are we taking Grandpa's car?' said Michael, as his father wrestled with the bag.

'Our car needs mending and has to go to the mechanic,' said Tom.

'It looks fine to me' said Liz, glancing at Michael, who rolled his eyes. 'Are we going on a long holiday?'

'All aboard,' said Tom, ignoring her.

Their grandparents waved them off with the minimum of fuss.

'Let us know when you arrive,' said Granny Ellen.

'As soon as we can,' said Bea.

Tom pulled out of the driveway as the children knelt on the squashy leather seat and waved out of the back window

'Okay, sit down,' said Bea. 'And no noise. Daddy's driving.'

'But I don't want to sit in the middle,' said Isabella. 'It's not fair, I always sit here.'

'Are we going far?' said Liz.

'Yes, quite far,' said Bea.

'Okay, then I'll sit beside Michael so I can play with him,' said Liz. 'We can swap when I get uncomfortable.'

'That's not fair,' said Isabella, pouting and shaking her unruly curls. 'I want to play with Michael.'

Liz snorted. Isabella could be so irritating. People fawned over her as if she were a film star, and she had an attitude which matched her faux fame.

'Life isn't fair,' said their father. 'Let Liz sit in the middle and stop fussing.'

'I'm hungry,' said Michael.

'We'll eat on the way,' said Bea, raising a cheer from the children. 'But not much, we don't want anyone being sick.'

'I'm never sick,' said Liz, hoping for permission to grab a snack. *If life wasn't fair, how come she couldn't have breakfast? She didn't care if the others couldn't have any.*

'Enough talking,' said Tom. 'Count trees or something.'

'One, two, three,' said Isabella.

'In your head,' said Tom.

After a few hours on the road, made more tolerable by Bea passing around a tin of boiled sweets, they pulled into a service station on the M6 motorway to Liverpool.

'You can have some toast or cereals,' said Bea. 'And get milk to drink.'

'But, mummy, I want sausages,' said Liz.

'No, darling, I don't have enough cash. I need to go to the bank to change a cheque later.'

Liz sighed. Her mother always had money in her bag. Just as she never ran out of tea or loo roll. *Holidays were the harbingers of treats and extra spending. What on earth had changed this?*

After their frugal meal, Bea took the girls into the women's toilet and Michael followed Tom into the men's. Bladders emptied, they regrouped at the car. Tom lit a cigarette and took a long leisurely drag, to the agitation of Bea, who kept looking at her watch. He ran his eyes over his wife, a slim, tall, straight-backed woman with brown eyes and auburn hair, and smiled at her seductively. She blushed and pretended to be cross.

'You know how I hate to be late,' she said. 'We should have left earlier.'

'We've got plenty of time, darling,' said Tom, stroking the worry from her face. 'Don't fret.'

'Easy for you to say,' said Bea. 'What if there's an accident up ahead?'

'We're still going to make it, even if they have to resurface the road first,'

'Make what?' said Michael, listening from the car.

'You'll see.'

They pulled into Liverpool docks about an hour before the ship sailed and queued up to board the ferry.

'We're going on a boat?' said Isabella. 'But I'll be sick.'

'Me too,' said Michael.

'We're going to Ireland,' said Bea. 'It'll be an adventure. You'll see.'

'Ireland?' said Liz. 'Why are we going there?'

'That's not much of a secret,' said Michael, frowning. 'I thought we were going to France, or Spain.'

'Are there beaches in Ireland?' said Isabella.

'Of course, darling. It's an island,' said Tom.

Liz sighed and rolled her eyes. *All that whispering over a trip to Ireland? She couldn't believe it.*

Tom parked the car in the bowels of the ship and the family headed for the steps to the upper decks.

'Did you get that car in a museum?' said one sailor, winking at Bea, who ignored him.

The family sat in a lounge with plastic seats on a carpet with a swirly pattern which didn't disguise the black greasy blobs of ingrained filth.

'Off we go,' said Tom, as the foghorn sounded.

Soon they were out at sea, rolling with the waves in a mild south-westerly. The ferry had only been sailing for a short time before Isabella turned green. Bea trotted her to the toilets where she vomited up the remains of a sausage, stolen from Tom's plate when he wasn't looking. Bea wiped Isabella's face and took her hand to go back to the seats, but Michael burst in at the same moment and dry heaved into a basin.

'I'm never going on a boat again,' he said.

'I'm sorry, darling. It's the only way to get there.'

'Why didn't we go on a plane? I've been dying to fly for ages.'

'We need a car in Ireland, so this was the only way.'

'I can't understand why we don't just hire one,' said Michael, and heaved again.

Bea ruffled his hair. Their comfortable life had just disappeared, but she couldn't bring herself to tell the children. Not yet.

The ferry arrived at Dun Laoghaire after a fraught journey where everyone vomited except Liz and Bea. The pouring rain and the mixed emotions of the family members made the afternoon even gloomier. The fishy smell of the docks percolated into the car, forcing them to shut the windows.

'Ew, I'll be sick again,' said Isabella.

'Is that even possible?' said Liz.

Tom lit a cigarette which made them open the windows again.

'Daddy, don't smoke in the car,' said Liz. 'It's blowing right into my eyes.'

Tom sighed and flicked the cigarette into the oily puddles on the dockside, watching the dying ember as he waited for the queue of cars to move forward.

'I'm hungry,' said Isabella. 'Are we going to eat soon?'

'We'll stop on the way and buy some snacks.'

Bea handed round the tin of boiled sweets.

'Suck them, they'll last longer.'

The sharp taste of the sweet caught Liz in the jawbone as she gazed through the rivulets of rain coursing down the glass at the bleak concrete wasteland of customs sheds with their corrugated iron roofs. Her gut told her their lives had undergone a fundamental change. *What were they doing in Ireland? Why did they have so much luggage?*

They drove between the piles of pallets and rusty shipping containers and entered the massive customs shed, driving down the wrong lane, and ending up with the lorries. Tom sighed and reversed out again before they got trapped. The lane for private vehicles moved along at a good pace and they approached the line of trestle tables where an official signalled for them to stop. Tom brought the car to a halt and wound down the window.

'Soft day, thank God,' said the official.

The light drizzle had soaked his boiled wool jacket, which looked as if it might reek when damp. He showed no interest in the contents of their car, except for its female occupants.

'Well, haven't you three lovely daughters altogether, sir?' he said to Tom, with a wink at Bea.

She coloured and pretended she hadn't heard, tying her headscarf tighter on her head.

'I'm not a girl,' retorted Michael from the back of the car, but the man did not notice his rebuttal.

'He didn't mean you,' said Liz, patting his leg.

'Do you have any contraband?' said the man. 'Besides the smuggling of beautiful women?'

Tom Green did not show his annoyance at the man's cheeky references to his wife.

'No, just them,' he said, forcing a grin and clearing his throat. 'Could you tell me how I can get out of Dun Laoghaire, please? I'm driving south to Kilkenny.'

'No problem. Turn left at the junction down there. If you use that route, it will take you through Dalkey and

Killiney. Just follow the signposts to Bray and on southwards from there.'

'Thanks.'

The customs man waved them on with a smile. Tom followed his directions, navigating through streets lined with pebble dashed houses until they emerged from the suburbs out onto the road to the southern counties of Ireland. Notwithstanding the sedate pace at which Tom tackled the narrow roads, the towns soon petered out, and they entered countryside smothered in bright green grass with ancient oak and beech trees growing in massive unkempt hazel hedges.

'I'm starving,' said Liz. 'Please can I have something to eat?'

'I'm sorry, you'll just have to wait. I don't want the others vomiting in the car,' said Tom.

So, don't give them anything Liz thought.

'Look, there's a pheasant,' said Bea. 'You don't see them in Reading.'

The same mizzle which coated the windows of the car gave the scenery its lush appearance and dripped into the ditches on the side of the roads from the dark branches of the chestnut trees. Emerald grass hid perilous boggy verges, deep enough to trap the unwary.

'They must be saving money on signposts,' said Tom, as he took yet another wrong turning on their route. Each time they asked for directions, an endless supply of cheerful locals, who seemed bemused that anyone wouldn't know the way already, pointed out their error and sent them down the correct road.

'I wouldn't start from here if I were you,' said one, sending them back into town and out the other side.

'Where are we going, Daddy?' asked Liz, after several hours of this.

'Kilkenny,' said Tom, as if that explained everything, and with a tone that didn't brook any further questions.

Chapter 2 – Dunbell Farm, July 1969

The Greens' car arrived on the outskirts of Kilkenny on its last drops of fuel. The cathedral's round tower stood out on the horizon in the dusky light of the summer's evening. As they motored through the quiet suburbs, Bea noticed new bungalows with neat flower beds lining the roads. She wondered if it looked as good in the daylight. They would soon find out.

Tom searched fruitlessly for a petrol station in the gloom. A light drizzle coated the roofs of the houses and the canopies of the chestnut trees, making them gleam in the streetlights. A crescent moon poked out from behind the spire of the cathedral, only to be swallowed by the darkness as a cloud hid it from view. The children peered out of the windows into the Stygian night.

'Don't they have petrol stations in Ireland, Daddy?' said Michael. 'This country is stupid.'

'I'm sure we're the stupid ones. There must be one around here somewhere.'

Bea scanned the town through the windscreen, leaning forward in her seat until her nose almost touched it.

'There's one,' she said.

'Where? I can't see it,' said Tom.

'Above the roofs on the left. Can you see it? A Shell sign.'

'No, oh, yes, I can. I'll head there now.'

The petrol station loomed out of the darkness, its neon lights contrasting with the dim emissions from terrace houses whose thick curtains shielded their windows. A sleepy teenage lad emerged from the payment booth and held out his hand for the car keys. He filled the car with petrol while Bea used the toilet at the back of the station. She took a moment to straighten her hair in the mirror and caught the pain in her eyes in her reflection. *How do I hide it? What on earth are we going to do?*

She pasted a fake smile on her face and emerged straightening her skirt.

'Thank goodness,' she said. 'I couldn't hold out any longer.'

Despite getting explicit instructions from the teenager at the station, Tom took another forty minutes to find the correct route out to Mrs O'Reilly's farmhouse, down the minor winding roads with their tight packed hedges. Bea hid her anxiety by pointing out local landmarks like the concrete platform at the crossroads built to hold milk churns for delivery and collection. Several rabbits blundered across the road in the headlights, temporarily blinded in the light. Tom braked to avoid the less agile.

'These boreens are death traps,' he remarked to Bea, as a car speeding the other way almost forced them into the ditch.

'What's a boreen, Daddy?' said Isabella, who woke as she slid across the back seat into a grumpy Liz, and blinked into the darkness.

'It's a narrow road,' said Tom.

'More like boring,' said Liz.

'Are we nearly there yet?' asked Michael, who had come to the end of his tether and found it hard to keep his temper.

'Any minute now,' said Bea, turning to smile at her miserable offspring. 'Or they'll eat each other,' she whispered to Tom.

'Ah, here we are, at last,' said Tom.

A tired cheer rose from the back seat, and the children wound down the windows to get a better look. Two square concrete posts with balls on top marked the entrance to a driveway pock-marked with potholes. A plaque on one of them read Dunbell farmhouse, but there were two houses at the end of the long straight drive lined with tall beech trees.

'We've travelled all day to come to a farm?' said Liz. 'What sort of holiday is this?'

A closed gate barred the entrance to the parking area in front of the houses.

'Can you open the gate, please Michael?' said Tom.

Michael sighed and jumped out. He had to wiggle the bolt to loosen it and slide it back, pinching his finger in the process. He sucked it to reduce the pain. Bea noticed and gave him a sympathetic smile. She held her forearms in her hand and hugged them to her body for comfort. *No going back now. The die had been cast.*

Tom drove into the front yard and parked the car beside a stone wall with a cattle trough in it. He got out, looking around at the houses and the trees in the driveway, followed by his weary family, who slid out of the doors with sighs of relief. A tall, plump woman emerged out of the front door of the house on the left, and walked directly to the yard gate to shut it again.

'Shut the gate every time you open it, or the cattle will escape,' she said coming towards them beaming.

'Oh, what lovely children! Aren't they only gorgeous, Mickey?'

A small wizen man wearing a flat cap loitered at the cattle trough near the side of the first farmhouse. He took off the cap and twisted it in his hands, nodding his head in agreement. The children blushed and hid behind their father and mother. The woman did not seem to notice their reticence.

'You must be Tom and Bea,' she said. 'You're welcome to Dunbell Farm. I'm Jacinta, Jacinta O'Reilly, Lee Kennedy's friend. God rest her soul. And this young fella is Mickey who works for me on the farm.'

'Thank you, Mrs O'Reilly. We miss Lee dreadfully. She would have been so happy to know we'll be living on your farm,' said Tom.

'Which house is ours?' said Bea.

'The one on the right. I live on the left. If you need anything, you can come to me. I've put some essentials in your kitchen for breakfast, but you'll need to go shopping tomorrow. I'll come with you and show you the town.'

Bea felt her shoulders relax as she took in the kind intent behind the bossy air which emanated from her. Twinkling blue eyes in Mrs O'Reilly's weather-beaten face peered at the family over the top of some reading glasses held together with sticky tape at the nose. She carried her considerable bulk upholstered in a large tweed skirt and jacket of industrial strength wool. Racehorses decorated the silk headscarf tied under her chin in a severe knot, but a light brown curl had escaped and hung down on her forehead.

'The journey must have tired you out. Let's get indoors,' she said.

Mrs O'Reilly led the family up the garden path across the front lawn into the plain L-shaped farmhouse with its grey slate roof. The red front door had recently been repainted and evidence of at least two or three previous incarnations had splashed on the doorstep. The heavy door swung open to reveal an oak staircase with turned wooden bannisters and a well-worn rail, which looked perfect for sliding. Bea ran her hand along it as she examined the entrance, taking comfort from its warm smoothness. She looked around, trying to quell her feeling of panic as she took in the dimensions. *Beggars can't be choosers.*

A small sitting room sat on the right with vintage matching sofa and chairs. Bookshelves languished empty and some heavy velvet drapes sealed out any light. The dining room on the left had an air of neglect, its empty table in shadow surrounded by high-backed chairs with tapestry upholstered seats. A second door led through to the spacious kitchen, the biggest room in the house. It had a low ceiling and a floor of battered red tiles in various states of repair. A large oak table and six wooden spindle chairs with curved backs took pride of place in the middle of the room. Someone had stuffed a folded piece of cardboard under one table leg to stop it wobbling. An ancient-looking Aga occupied one wall with a blackened pot rack hanging over it. Bea looked around but could see no fridge or washing machine. She fought to keep the disappointment off her face.

A deep sink with a wooden washing board on the drainer sat under a window with a view of the back yard where an ancient mangle had pride of place. Bea sighed as she mourned her brand-new twin tub back in England. Tom caught her sigh and looked over at her for reassurance, receiving a tired smile from his wife.

The family moved upstairs to look at the bedrooms, three of them, each smaller than the last. The bathroom on the landing had a sink, and a toilet, and a rather stained bathtub with lion's feet.

'There aren't enough bedrooms,' said Michael. 'How are we going to fit in?'

'We must share for now,' said Bea, dreading the inevitable tantrums.

'You and I can take the double room at the end,' said Tom, oblivious to the coming storm.

'Liz and Isabella can share the middle room, and Michael may have the small bedroom at the far end over the little sitting room,' said Bea.

Liz's face turned purple with fury and she stamped her foot.

'I don't want to share with Isabella,' she said. 'Why does Michael get his own room? I'm the oldest. Why should I share with the baby?'

'I'm not a baby' retorted Isabella.

Liz ignored her.

'Why can't I share with Michael? We're almost the same age.'

'We'll see,' said Bea. 'Let's try it like this tonight and then we'll talk about it in the morning.'

No such discussion would take place, and Bea anticipated a terrible sulk from Liz, who often complained about the special privileges awarded to boys she didn't understand. But Bea was thinking of the future. Liz would soon go through puberty and might not appreciate sharing with a boy. She needed to pre-empt the situation as they could not afford to rent a bigger house.

They returned downstairs to the kitchen.

'There's a back boiler behind the Aga,' said Mrs O'Reilly. 'If you keep the Aga lit, you'll have hot water. The turf's out in the back yard.'

What on earth is turf? But Bea decided not to ask. It would keep.

While Tom and Mickey staggered up and down the stairs with the suitcases, Mrs O'Reilly fed the children in her own kitchen.

'I know a child on its last legs when I see one,' she said, taking Isabella by the hand and leading them into her house. 'What's your name, lovely?'

After a supper of fried sausages and colcannon, Mrs O'Reilly returned the children to their new home. Bea sent them straight upstairs where she had made the beds and put hot-water bottles in them.

'Your pyjamas are on your beds,' she said. 'I'll be up in a minute.'

She turned away so they wouldn't see the tears that leaked from her eyes despite her best efforts. Mrs O'Reilly patted her shoulder.

'George told me you about your troubles,' she said. 'I'm here if you need anything. Lee would expect it.'

'How did you know her?' said Bea.

'Oh, her Mammy and I were childhood friends. She grew up nearby,' said Mrs O'Reilly.

'Dear old Lee. Poor Tom misses her still, almost as much as George.'

'God love him. That poor man will never be same. Lee was his entire life.' She sighed and pointed to the Aga. 'I've left you some supper in the warming drawer.'

Bea looked around the kitchen after Mrs O'Reilly had left. She stood sobbing while Tom finished emptying the car, oblivious to her distress. Then she blew her nose and washed her face with cold water.

Why had this happened to them? She kicked the Aga in frustration.

Meanwhile, the children had gathered on the landing upstairs for a hissed conversation.

'There's something funny going on,' said Michael. 'This doesn't feel like a holiday to me.'

'It's probably just another of Daddy's mad adventures. At least you have your own bedroom,' said Liz.

'I don't want to share with you either,' said Isabella.

The children put on their pyjamas and sat in their beds until Bea came to kiss them goodnight. Isabella hugged her rag doll and avoided talking to Liz, who glared at her from the other side of the room.

'How long we going to stay here, mummy?' said Liz.

A good question. One which she had to answer sooner or later.

'This is our new home,' said Bea, trying to sound happy. 'We are going to live in Ireland now.'

Liz took this in. She went bright red and burst into tears.

'Our new home? I don't want to live here in this horrible tiny house. Where are all my toys and books? I don't want to share with Isabella. I want my bedroom back.'

'It's a lovely house, darling. You'll have a marvellous time in Ireland and make lots of new friends.'

'But I didn't say goodbye to my old friends. What about my gym club? I should be on the team next term. I don't want to live here. I want to go home.'

Tears cascaded down her cheeks as she wailed in misery. Isabella started sobbing in sympathy. Bea smoothed down Liz's rebellious black locks with a calming hand.

'Now, darling, don't work yourself up into a state. It'll be all right. You'll see.'

Michael appeared at the door in his pyjamas.

'We're going to live in Ireland?' he said. 'I don't believe it. There aren't any petrol stations here, and the people speak funny. Anyway, what about Daddy's shop?'

'Daddy will open a nice new shop here. Go to bed now, we're all exhausted. Tomorrow we can have a nice talk.'

'Ireland is stupid. I'll never like it here,' said Michael, and stomped off to his room.

Bea kissed the still-sniffling girls goodnight and, having looked in at Michael, who refused to kiss her, she descended the wooden staircase and went into the kitchen.

'Oh dear,' she said to her husband, 'Would it be easier if we told them the truth about why we are here?'

'They wouldn't understand the truth.'

'But is it fair to lie to them?'

'Is it fair? Do you think it's fair on you or me? It's not, but we don't have any choice in the matter. That bastard ruined us, but we can start again, and we'll make it work. It'll be all right, I promise.'

He stood up and took his wife in his arms.

'How could we not be all right? It's still you and me. No-one can keep us down if we are together, chicken,'.

Bea allowed herself to feel comforted, despite the view she had of the godforsaken mangle out in the yard, bleak like their future.

Chapter 3 – Bea, August 1969

The first weeks in Ireland passed in a blur of fresh sights and sounds. Tom's conviction that Ireland would be identical to England, but with different accents, turned out to be far off the mark. The horse and donkey-drawn carts clipping down the lanes, the groups of nuns and priests swathed in black in the streets of Kilkenny, and the men in their flat caps and tweed jackets walking fleets of greyhounds in the boreens enraptured the family with their novelty.

Bea wondered if she had gone through a time warp to a parallel universe. Unlike her husband, who had fitted in like a local from the moment they landed in Dun Laoghaire, she found it hard to adapt. The variety of Irish accents and references to mysterious customs and clichés made her head spin. She tried not to dwell on their lost life in suburbia: the carefully matched cushions, a luxury from Habitat; the beautiful mahogany Philco radio console with its Bakelite dials.

'Second hand, but first class,' said Tom, as he replaced a valve.

She mourned her Silver Cross coach-built pram, which had sheltered consecutive babies from the weather during their daily hour outside in the back garden. Tom had splashed out for the best make with impeccable logic.

'It's got to last us for at least four babies,' he said.

They stopped at three. Bea had suffered a miscarriage after Michael and before Isabella, and they had not tried again after she appeared. The pram stayed in England, sitting abandoned in the utility room with Bea's precious washing machine.

Now, piles of dirty washing taunted her with the loss of her twin tub, and the wind blew through the cracks of the double door to the back yard. Bea watched out of the kitchen window as Mrs O'Reilly got Mickey to oil the mangle and string a washing line across a corner of the back yard. Bea scrubbed the family's clothes in the large stone sink, dropping them into a metal bucket ready for the mangle. Her hands were red raw with effort and she added rubber gloves to the list of shopping in her head. She picked up the bucket and staggered over to the mangle, swearing under her breath as some water slopped into her shoe. Mrs O'Reilly watched her, hands on hips as Bea tried to wind the handle herself. She snorted.

'Mickey, you're in charge of the mangle,' she said. 'Bea, leave it to him, you can hang the clothes up instead.'

Micky appeared pleased with his additional responsibility, puffing out his chest and striding to take over the duties. Bea soon decked the line in flapping shirts and multicoloured children's clothes.

'Thanks, Mickey. You're a great help,' said Bea, beaming.

Despite Bea's efforts. Mickey took his time to warm to her. He hung around in the yard and helped her with the mangle until she hung all the washing out to dry. But Bea had to lure him into the kitchen with the promise of a Marietta biscuit. After a cup of sugary tea, he let slip his concern about them renting the farmhouse.

'I don't think it's safe at all, at all,' he said, wiping drips from his stubbly chin with a sleeve of his filthy jacket.

'Why do you think that?' said Bea, without turning from the Aga where she was frying onions. 'Are you concerned about us being English?'

'Oh God love ye, no, no that's not it at all,' said Mickey. 'I'm worried about the children on account of the dynamite mine they're opening up past Gogan's farm.'

Bea spun around, startled.

'A dynamite mine? Are you sure?'

'Oh yes, that's what they told me at the crossroads.'

A dynamite mine. Wouldn't that be dangerous? Bea feigned indifference, but alarm bells rang in her head as the onions browned and shrivelled in the pan. *What sort of place had they moved to?*

Later, she asked Mrs O'Reilly about the mine as casually as she could.

'Oh no dear, don't mind him. Old Mickey is away with the fairies. I heard they opened a dolomite mine. Maybe that's what he meant.'

Bea's kitchen had been her refuge in England, but it became a challenging island of unseen peril at Dunbell. Apart from the lack of a fridge or washing machine, learning to use the Aga became her biggest challenge. Tears sprang unbidden to her eyes as the hotplates followed their own rhythm, heating, and cooling at random, causing havoc with her cooking. *I never asked for this, it's just not fair*, she thought as she threw away some burnt mashed potatoes.

Mrs O'Reilly, who burst into the kitchen most mornings, like a friendly heifer with no ceremony or warning, caught Bea crying in frustration.

'What on earth's the matter?' she said.

'It's the Aga. I can't make head or tail of it. It keeps going out despite my efforts to keep it fed, and the lack of dials is driving me crazy. Everything either burns or doesn't cook at all.'

'It can't be that bad,' said Mrs O'Reilly.

'Yesterday, I put a casserole in the warming oven by mistake, and it was still raw when I took it out for supper. We had to have Spam fritters,' said Bea. 'And a couple of days ago I found some cremated scones in the hot oven after I forgot to take them out. No smells seep out of the ovens to remind you something's cooking. I feel like an amateur again.'

'Spam? Oh, dear,' said Mrs O'Reilly, smirking. 'It's a bit tricky, but I'll help if you want me to.'

'How do you cope?' said Bea, smiling despite herself. 'I tried kicking it, but I just hurt my toe.'

'You need to coax the meals out of it. Think of the Aga as a cat, whereas gas stoves are like a dog.'

Bea raised an eyebrow.

'You'll have to explain that one.'

'Well, if you tell a dog to sit, it sits. If you feed it, it wags its tail. You know where you are with a dog. A cat will just look at you if you ask it to sit. It does whatever it wants and you have to adapt to the cat and not vice versa.'

And how does that help? I just want to turn the heat up and down.

'I don't understand,' said Mrs O'Reilly.

'Well, a normal stove has dials which you use to regulate the heat. If you turn it up hot, it heats, if you turn it down, and so on.'

Mrs O'Reilly shook her head.

'An Aga only has one setting; on or off. You need to learn where on the hotplates to put your saucepans and to move your meals around so they don't overcook.'

'No chance of setting a timer then?' said Bea.

'Oh no, if you put the kettle on the hotplate, the oven cools down and takes longer. It's an art, not a science.'

Bea sighed. At least the Aga heated the hot water and warmed the kitchen, a property which would come in useful in the winter months. Cooking would take an age to master, but she could imagine the Aga would soon become the centre of the household because of its use in water heating, clothes-drying, and the boiling of constant kettles for cups of tea. Bea set up the clothes airers in a fence around it, to fend off children, who tried to taste whatever she cooked on the range.

Thanks to Mrs O'Reilly's bush telegraph, the Greens' neighbours had been briefed about the new family in the area. Having learned of the family's financial difficulties, they were ready with boxes of second-hand toys and clothes to smooth the transition from strangers into residents. Bea had a constant stream of visitors bringing gifts of outgrown clothes and spare furniture and linen.

When the first woman arrived at the back door with a box of used toys, Bea almost sent her away.

'It's so embarrassing,' she said to Tom. 'I feel like a charity case. Are they only coming to mock us? The stuck-up English family down on our luck?'

'Why would you say that?' said Tom. 'I've found them to be friendly and sociable. They'd be mortified if they knew what you thought of their generosity.'

Her husband's tone made Bea feel awful. *Was she looking a gift horse in the mouth because she thought she was too good for them?*

'I don't mean it like that,' said Bea. 'Of course, they're just being kind, but their gestures have made me realise how far we've fallen. I'm not accustomed to receiving charity. I've spent my life baking cakes for fêtes and sifting through the children's old clothes to give to worse-off families, and now we're one of them. It makes me feel so ashamed.'

Tom frowned, and a shadow passed over his face.

'I'm sorry, darling. I had no idea Henry was such a bastard. How do I make it up to you? I'm doing everything I can.'

'Oh, sweetheart, it's not your fault. I'm not blaming you. I'm just feeling fragile and needy. The local women are only trying to make us feel at home, but I'm not used to supportive people. The girls at my school were snobby about my subsidised place, and my father's low army pay, and I didn't have any real girlfriends. I guess I don't have any practice at trusting people,' said Bea.

'I don't want you to feel guilty either. We're here now and we have to make the best of it. I promise things will get better when I open my shop, but meanwhile we need help. Don't feel beholden. As soon as we have money, we'll reciprocate.'

Bea sighed.

'You're right, of course. I feel so lost here.'

'It's a colossal blow for any family, but we can see it through. The children are already settling in. We just have to follow their lead. I'm off to help Mickey lift a few hay bales.'

Bea bit her tongue and sorted through the clothes and toys. She pretended it was Christmas, and that she had opened her present drawer to select gifts for everyone. To her amazement, she found a few exact replacements for favourite books and games among the boxes, and she put them in the children's rooms. *Perhaps they would make the children feel more at home.* Someone had included a stack of women's magazines, which Bea left in the little sitting room. A tweed hat attracted her attention. It had a hole in it, but she knew Tom would love it, anyway. *Maybe they could make this work.*

Mrs O'Reilly laughed when Bea confessed her aversion to being treated like a charity case.

'Have you never heard of the black babies in Biafra?' she said. 'The nuns are obsessed with them. Anyway, doing good deeds is top priority for Catholics who want to get to heaven. It's a points system. Those women are all mounting up their points so they can get in. Helping the black babies and poor English families earns them points. That's why they go to confession all the time, in case a bus runs them down. They want a load of points and a spotless soul.'

Bea laughed.

'That's a bit mean. I'm sure they are helping out of the goodness of their hearts. I feel terrible about resenting their help. It's just that we scrimped and saved for ten years to have a successful business and a lovely home. It's like a ghastly game of Snakes and Ladders. We've slid all the way back to the beginning.'

'When Mr O ran away, he left me alone with the children. I had to pretend he had died while abroad on a business trip, so people wouldn't see me as the poor old bitch who got abandoned.'

Well, I never.

'Is he still alive?' said Bea.

'I doubt it. Some jealous husband probably stabbed him years ago. Now get that bacon joint out of the cold room and I'll show you how to cook it on the Aga.'

Chapter 4 – Neighbours, August 1969

The farm provided an idyllic setting for the children to play in, with its many outbuildings and storage sheds. Their tantrums about leaving England had almost dissipated, replaced by ecstasy, as adventure beckoned around every corner. Having come from a town, they soon discovered the joy of being free to roam the fields. They disappeared for hours to make houses with straw bales in the barn, or watch Mickey do the milking. Even Michael stopped sulking for long enough to enjoy his freedom.

Soon the children plucked up courage to visit the neighbouring farms and made friends with local children. The Green children's origins in England made them exotic and prized as friends amongst the rural children, and they spent long hours away from home. Bea became nervous about them exploring by themselves and mortified by them visiting without an invitation.

'We don't stand on ceremony around here,' said Mrs O'Reilly. 'It's not like England.'

'But they keep coming home saying they're not hungry,' said Bea.

'Oh, don't worry about that,' said Mrs O'Reilly. 'The neighbours' children will soon invade your house too. It's always like this during the school holidays.'

Sean and Nuala O'Connor, from the farm up the lane, were similar ages to Michael and Isabella. Nuala was almost a year older than Isabella but she acted much younger. They were soon a constant feature in the Green household. Sean's fascination with soccer won Michael over when he extolled the virtues of the English football team that won the world cup.

'Is the Irish football team any good?' said Michael.

'No. We're better at hurling. Kilkenny are the All-Ireland Champions.'

'What's hurling?'

'You play it with a stick and a ball.'

'Like hockey?'

'Not really.'

Liz took a jaundiced view of Michael's budding friendship with Sean.

'It's not fair. Michael never wants to play with me any more. I'm Michael's best friend, not Sean,' she complained to Bea.

'Darling, Michael still loves you, but he'll be going to the same school as Sean in September, so it's nice for him to have a friend in his year,' said Bea.

'But why can't Michael come to the convent with us?' said Liz.

'Mrs O'Reilly told me that boys have to go to the Christian Brothers after they are ten,' said Bea.

'Ireland is stupid,' said Liz.

'It's not stupid, it's just different.'

'Why did we come here?'

How could she explain? After all their work to build up a business, it disappeared overnight when Tom's business partner bankrupted the business with his gambling. The shock of learning they had lost it all had almost finished her. *Thank goodness for George, their white knight, saving them from ruin. How lucky the bankruptcy laws didn't apply in Ireland*

'I'll tell you one day, I promise, but you'll make Daddy sad if you keep hating Ireland. Try to get used to it.'

'I don't like it here. My friends in England will miss me. I want to go home.'

'This is home now, sweetheart. You need to make new friends.'

But there were no girls Liz's age who lived nearby. She read Malory Towers in her room rather than play with the younger children, spending hours shut away from the others.

'What's wrong with Liz?' said Tom.

'Michael is spending a lot of time with Sean O'Connor, and she feels left out,' said Bea.

'Should we talk to him?'

'No, I think it's for the best. She'll get her first period soon and her hormones will kick in. She's unlikely to want to hang out with Michael after that.'

'Already? But she's only a little girl.'

'Not for much longer. She'll be wanting to date soon,' said Bea.

'Over my dead body,' said Tom.

Bea made her first outing to the O'Connors' farmhouse, carrying freshly baked scones before her like soft warm tributes. The caws of rooks floated down from the rookery of twig-built nests in the trees lining the driveway to Dunbell. Soft clouds scudded overhead, driven by the summer breeze. She breathed in the cloying sweetness of honeysuckle and sucked the nectar out of a fuchsia flower. The shot of sweet liquid reduced her nerves. *Maeve O'Connor was just a mother like her.*

She completed the short walk along the lane and pushed open the wonky iron gate in the stone wall that divided the lawn from the scruffy tarmac. When a soft knock on the door did not produce any result, Bea skirted the farmhouse and entered the back yard. Maeve O'Connor stood outside talking to a tall, slim youth who had his back to Bea. When she saw Bea appear, she whispered something to him, and he hurried away in the other direction. He glanced back at Bea, and a sneer passed across his handsome boyish face.

Maeve wiped her hands on her apron as Bea approached, holding the tin of scones out in front of her. Her brows knitted together with worry.

'Hello,' said Bea. 'You must be Maeve. Mrs O'Reilly tells me you've been feeding my children.'

Maeve gave a nervous glance in the direction the adolescent had taken. He had disappeared, and her expression changed to one of welcome.

'I am, and you're Bea. My children are so happy to have neighbours their age. I hope they're not making a nuisance of themselves. I know it's hard to get settled in an unfamiliar area.'

'Not at all. They're very welcome. I just wanted to thank you for the potatoes you sent over from your harvest. I brought you these.'

Bea thrust the tin into Maeve's hands. Maeve lifted the corner and the aroma of freshly baked scones escaped.

'Mm. Those smell great. Will you come in for a cup of tea?' said Maeve.

'Yes, please,' said Bea.

She followed Maeve into the kitchen and sat down on one of the wooden chairs around the uneven oak table. Maeve put an aluminium kettle onto the gas hob of a cooker that had seen better days. An odour of sour milk permeated the air, making Bea wrinkle her nose, but the kitchen looked spotless. *Perhaps she had spilt some milk behind stove.*

The two women sipped their tea and chatted. Maeve moved her red hair away from her face, revealing a purple bruise on her temple. Bea registered the injury without comment, but Maeve noticed her quick glance and put a protective hand to her face.

'I'm such an eejit,' she said. 'I banged my head on an open cupboard door.'

'Oh, I do that all the time,' said Bea, which was true. 'Is Sean looking forward to going to the Christian Brothers?'

'He is putting on a good show, but I think he's nervous. Those priests beat the boys, you know.'

'I can't say I do, but there's no choice around here. I hope Michael will adapt. He's a sensitive boy.'

'Sean will look out for him. He just needs to keep his head down. Anyway, the junior class is not so bad. There's no pressure until they get into the exam sets. That's a whole other thing altogether.'

Bea nodded, trying not to show her alarm. *How could she let Michael go to that barbaric place?* Maeve checked her watch and a fleeting expression of panic crossed her features. She stood abruptly.

'Well, I've got to get on. The supper needs to be ready for himself when he gets in, or there'll be trouble down on the farm.'

Bea laughed.

'My Tom's a bit of a stickler for mealtimes,' she said.

But Tom never complained about anything, and Maeve's sudden nervous reaction to being late with Brian's dinner gave Bea an odd prickle up her spine.

When Mrs O'Reilly found out Bea had been to the O'Connor farmhouse, she pumped Bea for information about her visit.

'Was Brian there? I've heard he spends the family allowance at Byrne's pub. That man has a nasty reputation.'

'No, just Maeve--' Bea wavered under Mrs O'Reilly's inquiring glance. 'Well, I saw a young lad in the back yard. I thought he might be a farmhand.'

Mrs O'Reilly's beady eyes glinted.

'What did he look like?'

'Oh, I don't know. Thin, red-headed, pale, quite handsome. I didn't get a good look at him and he left just as I arrived.'

'Well, isn't Maeve a dark horse?' said Mrs O'Reilly.

Bea did not have a suitable reply. Maeve seemed to her to be a sad and frightened woman. The house had seethed with secrets and things unsaid.

'I'm willing to bet her son, Liam, paid her a visit.'

'But I thought she only had two children,' said Bea.

'With Brian. But she was already pregnant when she married him. Liam's actual father ran away, and Father Doherty tried to put her into St Joseph's.'

'What's that?'

Mrs O'Reilly ignored the question.

'Brian O'Connor had a tremendous crush on her. She hadn't been interested in him because he had a reputation as a drinker, even at that young age. Anyway, Brian found out she was pregnant, and he offered to marry her if she would give the baby away when it was born.'

'And she accepted?'

'Beggars can't be choosers. Maeve gave the baby to a female relative with a crippled husband, but she kept in touch with him against Brian's will. The poor boy is pretty screwed up. I heard he has an unhealthy interest in politics.'

She shrugged and pulled at her skirt, shaking her head.

'Liam shouldn't be going to the farm to see Maeve, though. Brian can be violent when he has drink taken.'

Bea blurted out before she could stop herself.

'Maeve had a bruise on her face.'

Her hand flew to her mouth. Mrs O'Reilly shook her head.

'Oh, don't worry, dear. It's no secret Brian uses her as a punchbag.'

'But why does she stay?'

'And where should she go with three children to care for? The government provides a children's allowance, but it wouldn't feed a mouse.'

'Couldn't she get divorced and find someone else? Why doesn't Liam's father help?'

'There is no divorce in Ireland, and nobody knows who Liam's father is. Maeve won't tell anyone. She can't leave.'

'She's trapped? How awful.'

Mrs O'Reilly patted her hand.

'It's the way things are here. Whatever you do, don't tell anyone you saw Liam at the farm, or Maeve might get a lot more than a bruise on the temple.'

Chapter 5 – Tom, August 1969

While Bea picked her way through local politics with the delicacy of a moorhen walking on waterlilies, Tom blundered into every new situation with a total ignorance of local decorum or habit. His accent gave him away as English, and local tolerance increased once the circumstances of the family became common knowledge.

'Isn't that foreign fella ignorant, lads? He was in Keogh's last night for over an hour, and he didn't buy a drink for anyone.'

'That's a bit harsh. It's not his fault he can't afford to buy a round. He's destitute.'

'I didn't know. What's the story then?'

'His best friend swindled him, and he went bankrupt. They had to sell everything to pay the banks. Don't quote me on this, but I heard they had to run away from Britain to escape prison.'

'Mary, mother of God, that's terrible.'

'They haven't two pennies to rub together. They're living on scraps and eat porridge for breakfast instead of a fry.'

'Have you seen that hat of his? It's as old as the hills.'

'I didn't know. I'll buy him a pint next time he wanders into the pub, the poor devil.'

'Did you see his wife?'

'Now, there's a fine-looking woman. I'd say she's a good ride.'

'You filthy fecker. Don't go getting ideas. He's a quiet man, but they can be the most dangerous.'

Oblivious to his perceived failings, Tom immersed himself into their new life in Ireland. Scenes from the idealised version of the country fed to him in his youth by Lee Kennedy came to life as he explored his surroundings. He roamed the countryside transfixed by childlike wonder, absorbing sights, sounds and smells with glee. *Lee would have loved this. How he missed her.*

His early childhood had not prepared him for his time with the Kennedy family. His own parents were so self-absorbed that they seldom spent time with him and did not make any allowances for his youth. They had done their duty by having a child and appeared bemused by the continuing commitment this required. Tom had left for prep school at seven followed by boarding school at eleven and hardly ever came home for the weekend. His parents had spent a lot of money sending him to boarding school and didn't understand why he needed to come home at all.

If he hadn't met Ben Kennedy and his family, Tom might have gone to his grave thinking all families were like his. Ben became Tom's best friend at university, his only close friend. They rowed in the same boat for the university club and sweated blood together through three seasons until they left university.

The first time Tom went home with Ben for the weekend, he experienced a profound culture shock. Ben's home did not resemble his in any way. Creepers covered in little white flowers grew all over the front of the house and draped the windows. As he stepped through the front door, the aromatic smell of curry entered his nostrils, making him breathe deeper to inhale more of it.

Unlike his mother, who had puritan leanings, Lee Kennedy, Ben's mother, had decorated her home in a riot of colour; camel bags jostled with paintings of flowers and rainbow-coloured ceramics. Lee bustled into view, her mop of red-brown hair poking out from under a green turban. Short and compact with a sea of freckles on the visible parts of her body, she embodied warmth and welcome. She clasped Tom's hand, unwilling to release it as she stared into his eyes with her piercing green ones.

'You must be Tom,' she said, her Irish accent still strong despite her years in England. You're very welcome. Ben has told us loads about you.'

'Thank you, Mrs Kennedy. It's nice of you to have me to stay.'

Lee snorted, making him blush.

'I won't have any of that formal stuff in this house, Tom. My name is Lee, and this is George. Will you have a cup of tea? I'm just making the supper. A nice leg of lamb. You like lamb? I got it from the butcher in the high street. He's a grand fellow.'

George was ten years older than Lee. His hair had already turned grey and his trousers strained over a newly developed paunch. Tom and Ben both towered over him, but he had fought at El Alamein, and his stature did not hide his resilience. He was no pushover.

'So how are the studies going, Tom? Ben tells me you are way too serious.'

'Oh, well, um, he's exaggerating. I don't work that hard,' said Tom.

'Do you have a girlfriend? I know Ben is keen on that Annie girl he's going out with.'

'No, I haven't met anyone special yet.'

'Ah, the one-woman man. One look and it's all over, eh?' said George, winking.

'I guess so.'

'And what's this about your rowing? They tell me that you won a bronze medal with Ben in the college championships. That's fantastic. Who's the best oarsman?'

'Oh, definitely Ben sir.'

'I'm sure you're both good and don't call me sir. I told you already. We are George and Lee.'

'Okay, George sir.'

George's eyes crinkled at the corners.

Tom had the foreign feeling of hot pride when he overheard George describing him to the neighbours.

'We've got that nice Tom Green staying with us. You know, I've told you about him. He rows with Ben at University. What? Yes, they won a medal. We're very proud.'

This weekend of love and attention blew Tom away. Lee had hugged him close when he left, perhaps guessing at his longing for human contact. The rush of emotion he experienced at being wrapped in the arms of love brought tears to his eyes, which he hid in shame. The Kennedys adopted him, to all intents and purposes, and his life changed forever.

Lee's death of cancer had robbed them all of her physical presence, but he carried his love for her with him everywhere. He explored Ireland with this love vibrating inside him, soothing the pain of the financial disaster that landed them on these shores. Every new wonder made him remember her more fondly.

On his walk, he spotted the Travellers' wooden caravans on the Bennettsbridge road being pulled by giant chestnut horses controlled by scruffy red-headed men perched on their front boards. They had made their camp in a layby near to the farm, and Tom found an excuse to make his way to their campsite, carrying an old cooking pot with a hole in it, borrowed from Mrs Reilly. She had been using it for geraniums, but he had a plan for engaging a traveller in conversation. She shook her head in mystification as he headed down the driveway, whistling and swinging the pot by its handle.

'Your husband is soft in the head,' she remarked to Bea, who laughed.

Pungent wood smoke assailed Tom's nostrils as he pushed his way through a gap in a beech hedge lining the layby and found himself surrounded by brightly coloured caravans with large wooden-spoked wheels. The arched roofs hid interiors lined in benches covered in coloured wool blankets and crocheted antimacassars on scruffy armchairs with patched reed seats. Copper pots hung from hooks in the ceilings, ready to clang against each other like an early warning system of the travellers' arrival.

There were several wild looking boys riding bareback on the coloured cobs in the fields near the travellers' camp, followed by packs of greyhounds and lurchers. A lurcher ran up and poked its nose into Tom's hand, the cold touch making him jump. He ran his hand over the coarse hair on its head and scratched behind its ears, inhaling the odour of damp dog that rose to meet his nose. Tom fancied buying a dog, but he was waiting for the right moment to broach the subject with Bea, who had expressed a preference for cats.

A little nervous at his flimsy excuse, Tom approached the patriarch of the Travellers as he sat on the steps of his caravan enjoying some spring sunshine.

'Grand day, sir,' said the man, looking him up and down with a twinkle in his eye. 'What can we do for you today?'

'I heard you fixed pots and pans when the need arose,' said Tom.

The man roared with laughter.

'Jaysus,' he said. 'I haven't mended anything for nearly twenty years.'

He gesticulated at some other men standing nearby. 'This English fella wants me to fix his pot.'

The men came over to investigate, surrounding Tom and laughing at him, speaking in a language he didn't understand. *This was not my best idea. What have I got myself into?*

He apologised, stuttering. 'I'm sorry, I didn't realise.'

'Oh, don't worry about it. We live by horse trading and breeding greyhounds for coursing these days.'

'You've some beautiful hounds,' said Tom. 'I'd love one as a pet.'

'A pet?' said the man. 'Those animals are thoroughbreds,'

'Oh yes. I, um…' Tom tailed off, embarrassed.

And now I've insulted him.

'We could sell you one,' said another man.

'Oh, I don't think my wife would like that,' said Tom.

'We'll give you a great price. The lurcher bitch just had a litter. Why don't you choose one?'

Money again. The one thing he didn't have enough of. The travellers would think he was an idiot.

'I'm afraid I only have a few shillings. I'm not working yet,' said Tom.

The atmosphere changed, and the men melted away as suddenly as they had appeared. The old man shook his head.

'Did I say something wrong?' said Tom.

'They thought they could make some money from you. Do you really want a dog?' said the patriarch.

'I've wanted one all my life. This is the first time I've lived somewhere it's feasible to have one.'

'Why don't you take the runt of the litter? I won't charge you for her. I'm not sure she'll survive, mind you.'

Tom rubbed his chin, stalling for time. *I should ask Bea first, but I can't risk insulting him now.*

'Let me give you two bob for a drink,' he said. 'I'd feel funny taking the puppy for free.'

'You're a fine gentleman, sir' said the man, eliciting a blush.

In the land of blarney, Tom stood out as an easy mark. No matter how many times they complimented him on his standing as a fine gentleman, Tom never linked the phrase with a swindle. He walked home with the puppy wrapped in his tweed jacket, oblivious to the jeers of the men in the Traveller camp. Her small warm body shook in his grasp and his excitement turned to doubt. *Should I subject the children to a surprise which might end in tragedy? Perhaps it will be a useful lesson, even if she dies.*

Crossing his fingers, he stepped into the kitchen, the aroma of a beef stew overwhelming him with hunger. The children were playing an elaborate game with pebbles of various sizes and what seemed like a shifting rule base to accommodate Isabella's tantrums. They looked up when he came in, their pink faces inquisitive. Isabella jumped and poked the bundle he carried with exaggerated care.

'What's that?'

'Don't touch,' her father said. 'I need to show your mother first.'

But the puppy's long hairy tail slipped out of his jacket and gave a feeble wag.

Liz gasped.

'It's a puppy. Let me see, Daddy. Please.'

Isabella screamed with glee, and Tom glanced at his wife for approval. Bea took one look at the bliss on his face and the excitement on the faces of her children and kept her opinions to herself. She nodded. Tom squatted down and surrounded by his excited offspring; he unwrapped the quivering animal.

'He's so beautiful,' said Liz. 'Why's he shivering?'

'It's she, darling, and she's the runt of the litter, so she hasn't been eating enough.'

'What does she eat?'

'Well, she needs a bottle of milk, but I'm not sure we have anything we can use.'

'I've got one,' said Isabella, her eyes shining. 'My dolly has a bottle just the right size.'

She dashed out of the kitchen and he could hear her heavy steps thundering up the stairs. Not for the first time, Tom wondered how such a small child could make so much noise. *She sounds like an elephant.*

The puppy broke everyone's resistance. Even Michael, who had been carrying on a one-man strike against their move to Ireland, became animated, lowering himself to the tiled floor to stick his nose in her fur.

'What's her name?' said Michael.

'You can choose one, if you want,' said Tom.

Michael stroked the grey fur which stuck to her small, sweaty body.

'Blue, let's call her Blue.'

'Don't get too attached to her. She may not survive. She's not strong,' said Tom, but Michael had fallen in love.

The next day, when Sean O'Connor turned up to play, Michael roped him in to help him nurse Blue.

'She's a grand colour,' said Sean. 'I wish my Dad would let me have a dog, but he'd only kick it.'

'You can share Blue with me.'

'If she lives.'

'Oh, she'll survive. I'll make her.'

And he did. Days after the rest of the family had forgotten the novelty and gone back to their usual interests, Michael tended to Blue and nursed her to full health. She ate huge amounts but kept the slim profile of a lurcher with greyhound ancestry. Her long tail whipped from side to side with pleasure whenever Michael came near. Soon she was causing havoc in the house, so Bea relegated her to the yard for most of the day, but Michael sneaked her up to his bed at night to stop her whining.

'I don't mind. He hasn't complained about Ireland once since Blue arrived,' said Bea.

'He'll be fine,' said Tom.

Chapter 6 – Bea, September 1969

As summer wore on, some gentle sunny days broke up the drizzle, drying the clothes flapping on the line. Bea soon learned to keep an eye out for rain and made mad dashes outside to rescue the dry clothes before they got soaked again.

'In Ireland,' proclaimed Mrs O'Reilly. 'There are three types of weather. It's raining, it has just rained, or it's about to rain.'

She's not kidding. It rains every day. Drives me mental, thought Bea, as she rushed outside yet again.

The lack of a fridge forced Bea to store the meat and dairy products in the cold pantry. In theory, the thick stone walls insulated the contents from outside temperatures, keeping food cool in the summer and stopping it from freezing in the winter. However, nothing stayed fresh in there for more than a day or two. The meat from the high street butcher came riddled with bluebottle eggs from which maggots hatched and then burrowed into the cheap stewing steak and mince. Their fat white bodies and black heads made her shudder.

'Mrs O'Reilly didn't mention the bluebottles when she told me about the butcher, and the other wonders of Kilkenny,' muttered Bea, as she picked them out.

'She's probably used to them,' said Tom. 'I promise I'll get you a fridge soon.'

Mrs O'Reilly loved to boast about Kilkenny, a medieval town of black limestone buildings founded by friars in the sixth century in honour of Saint Canice. The colourful high street ran south from the Protestant cathedral in Irishtown down to the castle. It paralleled the course of the river Nore, which cut through the town crossed by a series of picturesque stone bridges. Small pastel shopfronts, with shiny gloss-painted windows framing their displays, jostled with pubs and betting shops.

The Munster House, an all-purpose department store in the old style, occupied the prime real estate on the street opposite the Town Hall, selling everything from knickers to sofas, and perfumes to shoes. Bea compared it with John Lewis and found it wanting, but at least Kilkenny had a department store. Isabella dubbed it the Monster House, a nickname which stuck.

The town had one scruffy cinema where empty Guinness bottles rolled down the aisle while the Greens watched films. A colony of rats found rich pickings amongst the Tayto crisps which fell between the seats and scampered up the aisles during the movies. Bea, who took the children to The Sound of Music, christened the cinema Rats and Guinness.

'Honestly,' she said to Tom. 'I was so distracted by the rats, I missed half of the film. I'll have to go again.'

So, she watched it a second time, taking Mrs O' Reilly, who declared herself enchanted.

'You wouldn't catch our nuns singing like that,' she said. 'Father Doherty would have a conniption.'

As if it's any of his business, thought Bea.

If the failure of the Monster House to measure up to John Lewis proved disappointing to Bea, it representing an opening to Tom, who paced the town from end to end, scouting out the competition. Several of the multipurpose local shops had electric blankets or toasters or other exotic items for sale displayed on the top shelves or in the window, but he could not find an established electrical goods store. His heart beat faster as he realised that he could restart his business and get back on track.

Encouraged, he scoured the streets for a suitable locale. It didn't take him long to find two empty properties on the high street. One had broken glass and boarded-up windows, but the other looked as if a business had recently vacated it. On the afternoon that Bea and Mrs O'Reilly were being entertained by the Von Trapp family, word of mouth led Tom to the owner, nursing a pint in the nearest bar. Tom's total lack of guile shone out from his craggy face. A chance to make some easy money. After the minimum of negotiation, Tom shook hands and left, beaming, to meet the women in the car park.

'They have offered me a shop at the cathedral end of the high street for twenty pounds a week,' said Tom. 'What do you think, Jacinta?'

Mrs O'Reilly bristled with fury, threatening to burst out of her tweed jacket.

'How much? You must be codding me.'

'Twenty pounds,' said Tom.

'Is that expensive?' said Bea, startled by Mrs O'Reilly's reaction.

'It should have gold wallpaper at that price,' said Mrs O'Reilly, shaking with indignation. 'Who owns the shop?'

'Bill Quinn,' said Tom. 'Do you know him?'

'Know him? Oh, yes. I know him, the greedy fecker. He must have seen you coming. You leave it to me,

Tom, I'll not let those scoundrels charge you a penny over the odds.'

The redoubtable Mrs O got the rent reduced to ten pounds and six shillings a week and persuaded the owner to paint the interior dove-grey before handing it over to Tom. The unit already contained shelving, which Tom sanded down and painted with a white gloss. He telephoned a former supplier who gave him the contact details of a source in Ireland for electrical goods to stock the shelves.

While Tom got his premises ready for opening, Mrs O'Reilly took Bea to look at the local schools to prepare for the autumn term.

'Will the children will be okay in a convent?' said Bea.

'The nuns will love the challenge of having two children to convert.'

'I wish Michael could also go for a year or two.'

'He has to go to the Christian Brothers School,' said Mrs Reilly. 'Boys can't to go to the convent's junior school after the age of ten. The nuns like to keep them away from the girls after that. Anyway, the CBS is free, unlike the convent.'

'But Maeve O'Connor told me the priests beat the boys with a cane on the slightest pretext.'

'They have a heavy hand, but Michael's not a naughty boy, and he's resourceful.'

'Michael pretends to be tough,' said Bea. 'But within the bold exterior lurks an interior as soft as a marshmallow, and just as likely to turn to liquid fury if overheated. He has a temper like his father. I don't like to think what might happen if he gets upset.'

Mrs O Reilly shook her head.

'He'll just have to control himself,' she said. 'Lots of other boys Michael's age will enter at the same time.

Sean O'Connor will be in his class too. Michael must keep his head down and fit in with the rest of them. My boys all attended the CBS, and they survived.'

But Bea couldn't relax. *How could she send her little boy to that horrible place?* She confided her reservations to her husband.

'I'm worried about Michael going to the CBS,' she said. 'What if he loses his temper and gets into a fight? They may beat him.'

'He's only a little boy. They're unlikely to cane him. I think you're exaggerating,' said Tom.

'But all the mothers say the same thing. They can't all be making it up,' said Bea. 'I'll ring George Kennedy tonight and ask him for advice. We need to thank him for his loan anyway.'

Once the children had gone to bed, Bea booked a call to England with the operator. George's familiar voice came on the line.

'Hi George. It's Bea.'

'Bea! How are you? Has everyone settled in?'

'Ireland's different, but everyone's doing well. I'm learning how to bake soda bread with Mrs O'Reilly, and the children are making new friends.'

'That's great. It was a brave move to leave England, but a positive one, under the circumstances. Has Tom made any progress?'

'The shop will open in a week or two, thanks to your loan. It's so generous of you. I've got my fingers crossed, but Tom is convinced he'll be ready.'

'You're welcome. I'm confident I'll get my money back. Have you got something on your mind?'

'Michael worries me. He has no real self-confidence, and his move to Ireland has dented the little he possessed. He's become quite defensive and the other boys may tease him when he starts school.'

'I can imagine that. It's not easy being different, especially in a tough school where you can get picked on,' said George.

Good old George. She should have known he'd understand.

'Priests run the local state school for boys. It has a gruesome reputation for violence, and the large class sizes and rote learning won't suit him.'

'The CBS? It hasn't changed much since Lee's time,' said George. 'Look, he doesn't have to go there, you know. Lee's legacy fund for your children's education could stretch to sending Michael to a boarding school over here.'

'But he'd be so far away from us. He wouldn't be able to come home at weekends,' said Bea.

And she would miss him.

'What about Whittingham? I know it's not the biggest public school in England but it has an excellent reputation. And it's near enough for me to keep an eye on Michael for you,' said George.

There was a brief silence while Bea considered this suggestion. How would Michael cope so far away from his family? It was a solution, but not one she wanted to explore yet.

'That's a very generous offer, thank you. Let's see how he manages the CBS first. Is that okay with you?' said Bea.

'Okay. How much are the girls' school fees? I'll send you a cheque.'

'I hate to take more money from you after all your generosity.'

'Think nothing of it. Since Ben left for South Africa, you have been my family. Lee would approve.'

George sent the full amount, and included some extra money for books, claiming Lee would haunt him if he let them go short for the lack of a few pounds.

Bea bought knee-length pleated blue tunics and white nylon shirts for the girls, and for Michael, the same shirts with grey polyester shorts. To the chagrin of Liz, who had developed a style at twelve that did not involve baggy polyester tunics and rolled-up sleeves, thrifty Bea bought everything in a larger size than necessary.

'This is too big,' Liz said, pouting.

'You'll soon grow into it, darling. We can't buy extra uniforms every time you get taller,' said Bea.

How she wished she could buy Liz beautiful things. *My lovely daughter will have to dress in baggy clothes just to make them last longer.*

'Don't worry,' said Tom. 'The other girls won't notice.'

'Yes, they will,' said Liz and she stomped off to her room.

'It's not much fun being poor,' said Bea, struggling with a mountain of washing.

'I'll get you a twin tub washer with the first profits from the shop,' said Tom, giving her a squeeze.

'Don't forget my fridge,' said Bea.

And a television.

By the time Tom opened the shop to curious customers, he had become a firm favourite with the locals. Sales of the new-fangled electrical products lagged at first. Tom had to rely on the money lent to him by George.

'The locals are playing you,' said Bea. 'They've discovered that they can drop in for a cup of tea and a biscuit during their daily shop without buying anything.'

'You leave it to me,' said Mrs O'Reilly. 'I'll get them to open their wallets.'

Bea laughed. *My soft touch of a husband. He'll never make any money.*

When Mrs O'Reilly put out the word that she had ordered a television, competition replaced caution and sales picked up pace. The television which appeared in Mrs O'Reilly's sitting room caused great excitement amongst the Green children. It had a small screen and two big knobs; one for turning it on and off, and one for volume. There was only a single channel on Irish television, RTE, resulting in a restricted selection of programmes, but they hadn't had a television at their home in England, so they didn't know the difference.

Mrs O'Reilly let the children watch it whenever they wanted. They soon established family favourites such as Get Smart and I dream of Genie, which they watched with Mrs O'Reilly while they ate toasted Barm Brack with fresh butter and big mugs of scalding hot tea.

The children got most fun out of the Angelus. At six o'clock every evening, a picture of the Virgin Mary appeared on the screen and a bell pealed on the television at intervals of two seconds timed to coincide with the triple repetition of the Hail Mary prayer and other incantations. This ritual was a Catholic practice of devotion to gain indulgences or the forgiveness of sins. The children did not understand the significance. They stood in ridiculous poses, changing with the peals, the more bizarre the better, all the while shouting 'Bong' every time the bell sounded.

'Stop it, right now,' said Bea, the first time she witnessed this blasphemy. 'I'm so sorry Mrs O. I had no idea they were being so rude.'

'God love you. It doesn't worry me at all. I like to see them having fun. Mr O'Reilly was the religious one. He would've blown a gasket at such blasphemy.'

Bea wondered what kind of husband Mr O'Reilly had been. Mrs O'Reilly did not display any photographs of him around the house, and she only referred to him in negative terms. He sounded quite horrible.

'Has your husband been gone long?' she said.

'Not long enough,' said Mrs O'Reilly, crossing herself.

She soon became the surrogate grandmother to the children. They loved her cheery outlook and big warm tweedy hugs. Their own grandmothers had been short of the fairy tale ideal, so Bea encouraged them to confide in and appreciate their Irish granny.

Mrs O'Reilly adored her new family. The Greens had filled a gigantic hole in her life, and it made her grateful to fuss over someone. Her husband had abandoned her, and her sons were in America. She had a call from them every Christmas on a terrible line, but she couldn't afford to visit them, nor could they afford to come home. As she commented to Maeve one morning, 'Aren't the Green children all dotes? And the parents are so innocent, they needed someone to ensure they didn't fall into bother.'

Mrs O'Reilly liked a mission, and she would defend them all to the death if required.

Chapter 7 – The Slurry Pit, September 1969

As the days shortened again, Sean and Michael ventured further afield, exploring the fields and ancient hedgerows, and spying on neighbouring farms. Tom read them the Adventures of Sherlock Holmes, which he picked up in a second-hand bookshop, and the boys found the tales addictive.

'Does your Da always read books to you?' said Sean. 'My Da says books are stupid. We only have school books at home.'

Michael tried to imagine how it felt to have Brian O'Connor as a father and failed. Tom could be reticent with his children, but his love for them leaked through every pore. Sean did not complain about his father, but he spent most of his time avoiding him.

'Did Sherlock Holmes exist?' said Sean

'They say the author based him on a real policeman,' said Tom.

'Wow, I wish I could be a detective.'

Their imaginations fired up, the boys decided to scour the surrounding countryside for signs of murder and robbery in the traces left by man and beast.

'Can I be Sherlock?' said Sean, his eyes shining with excitement.

'If I can be Holmes,' said Michael, earning a nod of approval from his father.

'Great, let's go tomorrow.'

The detectives set out the next morning. They included Blue in their game, but she disappointed them in her role as bloodhound, wagging her tail and sprinting around the fields when she should have been sniffing for clues. Then she burrowed into a hedgerow and retrieved a lethargic rabbit with red eyes.

'Oh, it's a rabbit. Give it to me, Blue,' said Michael, removing it from her jaws. 'What's wrong with it?'

'That's a myxy rabbit,' said Sean, shaking his head.

'Myxy? What's that?'

'My Da calls it rabbit plague. They catch it off each other and die. We must kill this one and bury it.'

'Kill it? But what if we take it home? Can't we save it?'

'No, it'll die anyway, and if we leave it out here, it will infect other rabbits.'

Michael hesitated. The rabbit's pulse thundered in its chest under his thumb and its fear crept up his arm. Sean put a hand on his shoulder.

'There's nothing you can do. The creature is suffering, and we need to help it. Put it down and hold on to Blue's collar.'

Michael placed the rabbit on its side in the grass. The animal did not move, wheezing with its eyes oozing. Blue tried to pick it up again, but Michael held her back, wrapping his arms around her chest. *Don't cry, don't cry. You'll look like a wuss.*

Sean searched the ditch under the hedge and found a limestone block, which he strained to loosen from the earth. He staggered over to the rabbit, both grimy hands locked under the stone.

'I need to drop this rock on the rabbit's head, so look away,' he said.

Michael buried his face in Blue's neck, and Sean dropped the stone, which extinguished the rabbit's life in an instant. He stood wiping his hands on his shorts, unconcerned.

'Right,' he said. 'Let's get it buried.'

Michael lifted his head. The rabbit's body had deflated as if Sean had let the air out. *How could Sean be so blasé about killing it?* The death of the rabbit shocked him to the core. He had seen dead animals before. He vividly remembered the sparrow brought in by Granny Ellen's cat. The feel of its soft feathers on its still warm body had made him miserable.

He released Blue, who sniffed at the body but sneezed and walked away.

The boys dug a small hole using their penknives to loosen the ground and pulled up the damp sods of earth with their fingers. Blue, who had been watching them, dug at the earth with her claws, deepening the excavation, and enjoying the game. They soon had a deep enough hole for the rabbit and deposited the body inside, covering it with earth and putting the stone on top to prevent foxes digging it up again. Michael stared at the tiny grave.

'Right,' said Sean, shaking him out of his reverie. 'Let's go.'

'Where to, Sherlock?' said Michael, switching into character.

'We must spy on the dolomite mine.'

'Isn't that dangerous?'

'They don't work at weekends. We're only going on a recce.'

Michael's heart skipped a beat, as it always did, when Sean proposed something of which his parents might disapprove. *What if he got into trouble?* His father did not tolerate rule-breaking. He didn't bother to question Sean, who followed no rules. Sean's parents did not care if he had been out all day. He never admitted to being punished, but sometimes he had bruises on his arms and legs. And once, a black eye.

Had Brian O'Connor beaten his son? Maeve sometimes had a bruise on her face, and he had heard Mrs O'Reilly tell his mother stuff about Brian.

'You should've seen the other fella,' Sean said, when Michael mentioned it.

Bea had given up trying to persuade Michael to come home for lunch and instead made sandwiches for them both after Michael had begged.

'Please mummy, Mrs O'Connor never makes him anything.'

'I'm sure she's got better things to do. Like me.'

He carried two fat ham and chutney sandwiches wrapped in wax paper in his old satchel, along with a couple of plums from the garden. Anticipation made him salivate. At the border of the next field, the land dropped away into a quarry with white walls reflecting the sunlight and creating a bowl of light.

'Don't go too near the edge,' said Michael.

But Sean ignored him, lying on his stomach, and peering into the excavation with its steep sides.

'You can see the drill holes on that one,' he said, pointing downwards.

'Let's have our lunch,' said Michael. 'I'm starving.'

Sean rolled away from the edge and stuck out his hand. Michael handed him a sandwich, which Sean eyed with suspicion.

'Are ye poor?' he said, poking at the bread. 'My Da says only poor people eat brown bread.'

'I don't know,' said Michael. 'Maybe, but my father told me brown bread has fibre in it. It's good for…' He hesitated, blushing, and fished out a phrase of his mother's. 'making you regular.'

Sean sniggered. 'Oh, in that case,' he said, taking a large bite.

Michael ate his sandwich with relish, his appetite sharpened by the morning's ramble. To his surprise, Sean only ate half of his. Usually, he scoffed his food in a minute flat. This time he wrapped the rest in the greaseproof paper.

'We might need this later,' he said, handing it to Michael.

Mystified, Michael put it back into his satchel.

'Let's go,' said Sean.

'Are you sure we're allowed?'

'We'll skirt the quarry and drop down to the lane. It's loads shorter if we walk home along it.'

Before Michael could react, Sean started down the hillside parallel to the quarry, arms held out for balance, whooping with fear and exhilaration as he skittered down the hill followed by an excited Blue. *I'm not doing that.* They disappeared for a moment, but as Michael crested the hill, he saw them outside a small wooden hut. He skittered down to join them. Sean had a broad grin on his face.

Blue whimpered and scratched at the door which opened to reveal a slim youth who looked like a stretched version of Sean minus the freckles. Sean turned to Michael, a proud smile on his face, 'This is my brother Liam,' he said. 'He's run away from home to join the Lads. Liam, this is Michael. He's English, but he's one of us.'

Michael did not understand this statement. *Who were the Lads?* Not wanting to appear ignorant, he smiled and nodded.

Liam scowled at Michael.

'How can he be one of us if he's English?' he said, but he relented and shook Michael's hand, squeezing it hard.

Michael pretended not to notice, but he returned Liam's stare and squeezed back, determined not to seem intimidated.

'Have you got that sandwich?' said Sean, oblivious to the contest.

Michael handed it over. Sean unwrapped it and gave it to Liam, who sneered.

'I already ate thanks,' he said. 'But here's someone who'd like it.'

He tore the sandwich into pieces and fed it to Blue, who responded with adoration.

Sean's face fell, and Michael almost laughed at his crestfallen expression. Liam did not notice, ruffling Blue's ears and getting a lick for his troubles.

'Are you living here?' said Michael.

Liam snorted.

'No, it's just a pickup point.'

'A secret rendezvous,' said Sean. 'Like in Sherlock Holmes.'

Michael's eyes opened wide.

'You'd better not stay,' said Liam. 'Someone might see you. They wouldn't like an Englishman hanging around.'

'Will you be okay?' said Sean.

'Don't you worry about me. I'm being picked up today.'

He winked and slapped Sean on the back, shutting himself back into the hut. *Who would bother to pick Liam up at the abandoned quarry at night?*

Sean and Michael set off towards the mine's entrance, a five-bar gate with flaky paint which was chained shut with a hefty padlock. It creaked and rattled as they clambered over it and jumped to the ground. They started down the lane for home. Blue burst out of the hedge in front of them, wagging her tail in triumph.

'Doesn't your brother like English people?' said Michael.

'Don't mind him,' said Sean. 'He's IRA.'

Tall banks on the sides of the roads hid the surrounding countryside from the boys with a bright green windbreak of birch and hazel hedges. The canopy of oak and chestnut rustled in the afternoon breeze, a wave of sound broken by the knocking caused by a woodpecker digging for grubs. The boys walked for about five minutes before they got to a crossroads. Sean looked around and swore under his breath.

'We've been walking the wrong way,' he said.

'Seriously?' said Michael. Weariness hit him like a sledgehammer. His legs ached and his stomach rumbled. Trust Sean to get lost. Some Sherlock.

'No problem. We can cut across Gogan's farm to take us back to the right road.'

Sean's total lack of concern made Michael's blood boil, but he had no choice except to follow him. Sean ran ahead, as full of energy as he had been at the start of the day despite his half rations. He ducked into a field and ran across it towards a whitewashed farmhouse skirting the yard. Michael cupped his hands to his mouth to ask him to slow down, and in that instant Sean vanished from view as if the ground had opened up and swallowed him. Michael rubbed his eyes, but Sean had disappeared.

'Sherlock,' he shouted. 'Where are you?'

A faint cry rose from where Blue stood beside a red shrub. Michael quickened his pace as the realisation hit him that it was Sean's head. Breathless, he stopped at what appeared to be a bright green square of grass just as Sean's chin sank below the surface.

'Shut your eyes and hold your breath,' said Michael as Sean disappeared. 'I'll pull you out.'

He dropped to his stomach and shoved his hands into the grass, which parted. A foul stench rose as he disturbed the surface, and a slimy liquid invaded the gaps between his fingers. Michael shuddered with disgust, but he shoved his hands under Sean's armpits and hauled him upwards. Sean's head rose above the surface, covered in liquid cow dung. As his mouth lifted clear, he coughed and spluttered and drew in a huge breath which made him retch.

'Jaysus, thank god,' he said. 'I thought I was a goner.'

'What is this?' said Michael. 'Is it quicksand?'

'No, it's a slurry pit. Help me, please. I'll drown in here if you don't haul me out.'

Michael heaved with all his might, but he only pulled Sean closer to the edge of the pit. The slurry held Sean in its grip like a ghastly vacuum, sucking him under. Michael struggled to keep Sean's head above it.

'I'm sorry, I can't lift you.'

'Don't be such a sissy. Pull me out.'

'I can't.'

'I'll die if you don't.'

'No, you won't. I'm not leaving you. Would Holmes abandon Watson? Someone will come.'

'But what if they don't?'

Sean could not keep the panic from his eyes. Michael's anxiety rose as he felt his body slide nearer the edge of the pit on the slippery grass. He lay panting with the effort. *I can't hold on much longer.* Then he felt a cold nose in his ear. *Blue, she could get help.*

'Go home, Blue,' he shouted.

'It's not her fault,' said Sean.

'She's our only hope. If she arrives without us, they'll know something is wrong and come to look for us,' said Michael. 'Go home, Blue.'

Sean coughed and spluttered as some slurry crept into his mouth. Michael pulled him closer.

'Put your arms around my neck and keep your mouth above the pit,' said Michael.

Normally, Sean would have called him a poufter for even suggesting it, but now he clung like a limpet. Michael could feel his breath on his face.

'Don't you ever wash your teeth?' he said, causing Sean to snort. 'Right, one, two, three, Blue go home.'

Blue moved back a few yards, wagging her tail uncertainly.

'Go home now!'

Her tail dropped between her legs. Tom often shouted this at her. She knew what it meant. Suddenly, she turned and sprinted off. Sean groaned.

'She's going the wrong way,' he said. 'I can't do this much longer.'

'No, she isn't,' said Michael. 'Don't you dare let go.'

The boys remained in silence for a few minutes, straining to maintain their hold on each other. The sun had sunk low in the sky and the light faded with their hope of rescue. Michael felt himself move again and start slipping towards the pit. He shut his eyes and prayed. *Please God, do something.*

'Let go,' said Sean.

'No, I'd rather die too.'

'You're an eejit.'

Footsteps thudded up behind Michael and sturdy hands reached down over his head and grabbed Sean's arms, hauling him out of the slurry over the top of Michael.

'Hey, watch out,' said Michael as Sean's feet kicked his head, splattering his face in slurry.

'What happened?' said Liam, dropping Sean on the grass. 'Did you push him in?'

Michael rolled over to face him, but before he could reply, Sean interjected.

'Don't be stupid. He saved my life. I'm the one who fell in.'

'Jaysus, you're some fecking eejit. Everyone knows about the slurry pit at Gogan's farm. What possessed you?'

'I forgot,' said Sean, who sat bedraggled on the grass spitting and retching, trying to rid his mouth of the foul liquid.

Liam stood over them with his hands on his hips.

'You're lucky I gave Blue that sandwich,' he said. 'Who knows what germs are hiding in that filth? Get up and go home straight away.'

Sean and Michael stood shivering in the cooling evening breeze. Blue sniffed them and barked. Liam led them to the hedge and through onto the road. A milk cart pulled by a donkey rumbled into view and the farmer let the boys sit at the back 'where I can't smell them'. Liam waved them off and set off running back to the quarry.

The cart dropped the boys off in the road beside the O'Connors' farmhouse. They staggered around the back of the house, dropping with fatigue. Despite Michael's entreaties, Blue sprinted off towards Mrs O'Reilly's farm. Maeve O'Connor almost dropped her skillet when they entered.

'Saints preserve us. What happened?'

'I fell into the slurry pit at Gogan's farm. Mick saved my life.'

'No, I didn't,' said Michael. 'It was Liam.'

'They both did,' said Sean.

'Where is Liam now?' said Maeve.

'He's getting picked up from the quarry.'

'By whom?'

'It's a secret,' said Sean. 'I can't tell you.'

Maeve rolled her eyes and shook her head. She made up a disgusting potion of warm water and salt and made the boys drink it so they would vomit up any remaining slurry. Michael had not swallowed any, but she wouldn't take no for an answer. She shoved them out into the yard and used a hose to wash the slurry off them while they retched and coughed.

Afterwards they sat beside the Aga, wrapped in some old towels, and sipping hot tea. Michael glanced at the electric clock on the wall, stained yellow with nicotine, and slapped his forehead.

'Is that the time?' he said. 'I'd better go, Mrs O'Connor. My parents will be worried about me.'

'Thanks, pet, for saving my son. I'll never be able to repay you.'

'Liam pulled him out,' said Michael. 'I just held him above the slurry.'

'He saved me,' said Sean.

'I'd hug you if you didn't smell so bad,' said Maeve. 'You can bring me back the towels later.'

Michael stood up, carrying his stinking clothes in a cloth bag, and shuffled to the door. It swung open, almost knocking him off his feet, and a thickset man with black hair stumbled inside. Brian O'Connor screwed his eyes up as if trying to understand the scene in the kitchen. He focussed on Michael, who stood ready to leave. His face coloured with fury and he bellowed at Maeve.

'It's bad enough you let your bastard Liam into my house when I'm not here, but now we have the little English fecker as well. How dare you defy me like this? I'll whip the five bells out of all of ye.'

Bright spots of colour appeared on Maeve's cheeks. She pulled Michael behind her.

'You'll do no such thing. Sean almost drowned in Gogan's slurry pit, and if it weren't for Liam and Michael, he'd be dead.'

'Don't you dare talk back to me,' her husband said, raising his hand to strike her.

The kitchen door banged again and Tom Green, his hair wild, stood in the doorway breathing heavily. At his side, Blue barked and wagged her tail.

'Oh, they're here. Thank God. We were crazy with worry,' he said, wiping his brow.

Brian O'Connor dropped his hand to his side. Tom Green's physique intimidated most bullies, and Brian was no different. He puffed his chest out with false bravado.

'Well, take him out of my house. He's not welcome,' he said, swaying.

Tom looked as if he might say something, but one glance at Maeve's pleading face convinced him to withdraw. Michael ran into his father's arms, feeling him shake with emotion.

'Let's go home, Daddy,' he said. 'I'm tired.'

Tom's shoulders sank.

'Alright, son,' he said.

'See you soon,' said Sean.

Michael managed a timid wave.

'Get out of my house,' said Brian.

Tom walked down the path away from the farmhouse, shutting the metal gate behind them with a clang. He held Michael tight in his arms, despite the stench of slurry that rose from his now warming body. Michael drank in the rare sensation, saving it in the place reserved for his dearest memories. Tom did not do hugs.

'So, those were the O'Connors?' said Tom. 'I think you chose the best one.'

***

The Ford Anglia sat outside the gates of the quarry, its engine idling. Cigarette smoke leaked out of the partially opened window on the driver's side door. Colm McClusky, a middle-aged, stocky man with a red beard and dark brown hair, sat in the driver's seat. His eyes narrowed as he saw Liam approaching at a run and blow out his cheeks in relief as he spotted the car. He made signs to the man about getting his bag from the hut, but the man shook his head, indicating the passenger seat. Liam opened the door of the car and slid in.

'And where the feck were you?' said Colm. 'Do you think I have all day? The guards are looking for me.'

His hacking cough stopped his tirade. Liam blanched. *Not a brilliant start.*

'Sorry, it wasn't my fault. My stupid brother fell into a slurry pit. I had to rescue the eejit.'

Colm choked and laughed.

'No wonder you smell like that. I thought it was a new cologne.'

'Are we going north?' said Liam. 'I have my things in the shed.'

'No, we want you to stay here and spy on the English family.'

Liam's face fell.

'But they're just a normal family down on their luck. My mother says the father got made bankrupt, and they had to leave the country.'

'All the same. It's funny timing. We're not comfortable with them turning up out of the blue in our territory. They could be spying for the Brits.'

'Their son doesn't even know who the Lads are,' said Liam.

'You're a bit young for action in the brigades yet. You'll get training meanwhile. There's a shack in the pine woods near your brother's house that we use for meetings.'

'But how will I know when to start my training?'

'We'll deal with that. By the way, is your little brother receptive to our ideas? Maybe you could start working on him?'

'I'll have a go. He's a thick as a short plank, so he believes everything I say.'

'And do you?'

Liam felt the hairs stand up on his arms.

'Of course. What sort of question is that?'

'Just making sure. Get out. I've got to go.'

'Can I have a cigarette?'

'Feck off.'

Chapter 8 – Blood Brothers, September 1969

Over the next few weeks, Sean insisted on telling anyone who would listen that Michael had saved his life. The story embarrassed Michael, but it made the local boys less suspicious of him. They had aired their grievances when the British army had deployed to Northern Ireland in August. He didn't understand why they blamed him, and their hostility wounded him after the fine times they had enjoyed together. Only Sean stayed resolute by his side.

'Why are there British soldiers in Ireland?' Michael asked his father.

'Northern Ireland,' said Tom. 'It's not the same country. It's part of Britain.'

'Why?'

'Because many residents are British and don't want to be part of Ireland.'

This made zero sense to Michael, but he ploughed on.

'But what are the soldiers doing there?'

'They're keeping the peace. The local police couldn't control the rioting in the Bogside, so the government sent the soldiers to help.'

Why would anyone riot in a bog? These people are nuts. He grunted. Tom ruffled his hair.

'Don't worry. It's nothing to do with us in the south.'

But it was. At least that's what Liam said, and Michael held Liam in high regard despite Liam's obvious dislike for him. After years of playing with dolls and tea parties to please Liz and Isabella, Michael found both the O'Connor boys to be a breath of fresh air. He had always dreamed of having a brother, and now he had two.

Liam had set about indoctrinating Michael with Republican ideas. He found a willing audience in Michael, who had little understanding of Liam's political diatribes and agreed with everything Liam said as he did not wish to alienate him. Sean, whose understanding of the politics was even more limited, encouraged Michael to change sides. Sean's new enthusiasm swayed him despite his doubts.

'So, you're with us then?' said Sean.

'Um, of course,' said Michael.

'Well, we can't do anything about you being English, but I'm sure the lads will understand you've changed sides.'

'Which lads?' said Michael.

'The Lads? You mean you don't know?' said Sean, who couldn't keep the disbelief off his face.

Michael looked at the floor, scuffing his shoes on the concrete floor of the silage shed. The pungent aroma made him feel sick.

'Not really,' he said.

'The IRA. They're fighting for a united Ireland,' said Sean, thumping his chest. 'Liam says they're heroes.'

Michael could not make sense of the differing versions of Irish history Tom and Sean had given him. His father did not lie, and Sean could be prone to exaggeration and hyperbole, but he kept his doubts to himself and nodded.

'We need to ensure your loyalty,' said Sean. 'I'll meet you after dinner tomorrow behind the barn at our house.'

This sounded like a bad idea. *What is Sean planning?* He did not share Sean's relish for dangerous situations.

'What for?'

'You'll see.'

Tom rubbed his chin and examined his son's face for signs of irony or teasing.

'The IRA? They believe in using violence to get a united Ireland,' he said. 'Where did you hear that word?'

Michael blanched. *I can't rat on Liam.*

'Oh, I'm not sure. Maybe on the news.'

'The news? You're rather young to be worrying about stuff like that.'

'I was waiting for I Love Lucy to start.'

His father laughed.

'If you want to know the facts, I'll give you a book I have on Irish history. I picked it up in a second-hand bookshop. That should answer most of your questions, but you can ask me if it still confuses you. Don't listen to the O'Connor brothers. Their grasp of history is hazy, and young Liam is a bit of a hothead.'

Michael wondered if his father had understood the fanaticism behind Liam's diatribes. No middle way existed for Liam. He only accepted two options, good or bad. The Greens were English, so they were bad by default.

The next morning heavy black clouds loomed over the countryside, dropping their liquid cargo on the sodden fields so it sat in pools on the clay-rich soil. Blue picked her way through the puddles on the driveway, wagging her tail, anticipating an adventure. Michael dawdled, the gravel scrunching under his reluctant footsteps, unsure of what awaited him behind the O'Connors' barn. Large drops fell from the sodden leaves, making him jump as they landed on his skin and wended their chilly way into his clothes.

Above him, families of rooks fought and shouted, dislodging twigs from their nests in their frantic efforts for supremacy. He avoided one large twig which landed with a splash in front of him. A yell broke through the rooks' chorus, and he turned to see Liz running after him, cutting through the puddles, and throwing waves of muddy water up onto her dress. *What's she doing here?*

'Hey, wait for me,' she said, arriving breathless at his side.

'You can't come with me,' said Michael.

'But I want to. You never let me play with you any more,' said Liz, furrowing her brow. 'Please.'

'But this is top secret. Sean will kill me.'

'I won't tell anyone. Anyway, I'm bigger than Sean. He's afraid of me.'

Michael smirked.

'Don't tell him that.'

She tugged his arm.

'Please.'

He hesitated. Liz had not exaggerated. She had grown taller, and this had intimidated Sean, who had stopped teasing her. Also, he couldn't imagine what Sean had planned for him. *What if I need her help?*

'Okay,' he said. 'But don't blame me when he sends you away again.'

'I'd like to see him try,' said Liz, adopting a boxer's stance.

Michael shook his head, trying not to laugh.

'Hurry then,' he said. 'Sean will be waiting.'

They raced into the farmyard and around the back of the shabby barn with its year-old hay bales, musty in the damp. Sean sat on one of them, his scarred knees poking over the top of oversized wellington boots. His eyes widened when he saw Liz.

'What are you doing here?' he said. 'This is a secret ceremony. Girls can't take part.'

Colour rose to Liz's cheeks, but she didn't move.

'I'm not going,' she said. 'You can't make me.'

'But this is only for boys,' said Sean.

'Says who?' said Liz.

Sean looked around for support, and Liam stepped out of the shadows. He walked up close to Liz and looked her in the eye.

'Me,' he said, staring her down.

Liz did not look away.

'Who made you king of the world?' she said.

Liam laughed.

'How brave are you?' he said. 'I guess we'll find out.'

She forced a smile. Michael, who had not moved during this exchange, found his voice.

'What do we do?' he said.

'We will make you our blood brother. And sister.'

He winked at Liz, who looked at Michael for support, but he had gone white. *The O'Connors were a liability. Why couldn't he just go home to England and resume his old life?* Sean took out a penknife and pulled out a blade which he rubbed on his shirt.

'Did you sterilise it?' said Liz.

'It's clean enough. Come over here and hold out your thumbs,' said Liam.

Liz stuck hers out with bravado and Liam grabbed the knuckle between his thumb and forefinger, squeezing the plump pad upwards.

She looked away as he drew the blade across it. A sharp pain made her whip her eyes back to her thumb where a thin red crescent had appeared. Behind her, Michael swallowed, but he too held out his hand. *No turning back now.* Liam drew the blade across Michael's thumb, which peeled open. Blood spurted out and Michael gasped in pain.

'Feck,' said Liam. 'Too deep.'

But he didn't seem sorry. He pulled a dirty handkerchief out of his pocket and tightened it around the base of Michael's thumb. *I'll probably get gangrene.*

'Look what you've done,' said Liz. 'He will need stitches.'

'No, he won't. You can't tell anyone.'

He cut his own thumb and handed the knife to Sean, who did the same without flinching.

Liam put out his hand, palm upwards.

'Drop some blood in here,' he said.

Michael looked at Liz in disbelief, his face still white with shock. She shrugged and squeezed a drop into Liam's waiting hand. He did the same, wincing in pain. Liam mixed the four drops of blood with the end of a piece of hay. He looked up.

'Now put your right forefinger into the blood and hold it up.'

The four children dipped their fingers in the blood and stood in a circle. Michael wobbled and Liz put her free arm around his shoulders. He had never felt so glad of her comforting presence.

'Lick the blood off your finger and swallow it,' said Liam.

'That's disgusting,' said Liz.

'That's why girls aren't invited,' said Sean. 'It's not disgusting, it's a sacred ritual.'

Liz shook her head and pushed her finger into the blood. She licked it and grimaced. The three boys did the same. The metallic taste invaded Michael's mouth, making him feel sick. Sean wrinkled his nose, but he did not complain. Liam smiled.

'We are now blood brothers.' He caught Liz's eye. 'And sister. You must never betray the brotherhood or the consequences will be fatal. Do you understand?'

Liz and Michael both nodded.

'Go home now. And put cream on the cuts to stop them going septic,' said Liam.

'I'll see yous later,' said Sean.

The Greens walked halfway home before Liz guffawed.

'Oh my God,' she said. 'Can you believe it? Blood brothers?'

It was ridiculous, but he wasn't about to admit it.

'Don't mock,' said Michael. 'It's important. You won't tell, will you?'

Liz sighed. 'No, I won't tell. Let's go upstairs and find some plasters in the medicine cabinet.'

'You promise?'

'I promise.'

Chapter 9 – Starting School, September 1969

Nervous tension rose amongst the local boys as the date for the start of the school term approached. They talked in hushed tones about the sadistic punishments dished out to the unruly by the Brothers at the CBS. Michael did not speculate, as he had no intention of getting into trouble. He enjoyed learning, and he looked forward to attending a boys' school after being surrounded by girls at home. He excelled at sport and dreamed of being chosen for one of the rugby or football teams.

Oblivious to the fact that they played only Gaelic sports in Irish state schools, he practised football with Sean on most days in the yard behind the house, co-opting Mickey as the goalkeeper. Mickey wasn't much of a goalie. He leaned against the posts chatting as the balls flew past him and ricocheted off the wall into the wet sheets hanging on the line behind the mangle. He also needed constant refuelling with cups of tea from the kitchen.

Michael tried to recruit Liz and Isabella to play, but they were both occupied helping Mrs O'Reilly make a patchwork quilt for Bea and Tom's bed. He would have loved to play with his father, but Tom did not show any interest in his children's activities. Despite his good intentions of being a hands-on father, Tom had inherited the remoteness of his parents, and he did not play with his children, except for reading to them, which he considered educational. He spent his time at home hidden behind the newspaper, emerging to talk to Bea about politics and his plans for the shop.

The night before term began, Liz crept into Michael's room and slipped into bed beside him, pushing a reluctant Blue off the mattress and onto the rug.

'Your feet are freezing,' she said. 'Are you nervous about school tomorrow?'

'A bit. I'm glad I have friends who are going.'

'Sean will keep you safe. I'm not looking forward to the convent. We must put up with the nuns and all that nonsense about God.'

'Do you believe in God?' said Michael.

'I don't know. Sometimes I do, and sometimes I don't.'

'If there's a God, Sean's father is going to hell.'

They giggled.

'Did you see Liam again?' said Liz.

'No, he's disappeared. Mr O'Connor doesn't let him in the house.'

'That must be awful for him. I'm glad our parents aren't like that.'

'Me too.'

Liz cuddled him.

'Eu, get off,' said Michael, wiggling.

'I'm off to bed. Good luck tomorrow and tell me all about it,' said Liz.

'Okay, night, night.'

The next morning, the Green children got dressed in their new uniforms. Liz rolled up her sleeves and hitched up the waistband of her tunic, which Bea told her to lower again. Michael had to put on a belt to stop his shorts falling around his ankles. Isabella drifted around singing and twirling in her ill-fitting uniform. Bea made sandwiches for the children's lunch with slabs of cheddar and pickle and packed them into their satchels.

With Mrs O'Reilly in the passenger seat for reassurance, Bea drove north through Kilkenny to the grounds of the Loreto Convent. The junior school perched on the side of a hockey pitch, where the clumps of longer grass were being mown by a herd of cows. The children stood uncertain outside the front door while Mrs O'Reilly recruited some nuns to help direct them to the correct classrooms. A smiling nun proffered Isabella a hand.

'Are you in third class, pet?' she said. 'I'm Sister Bernadette, your form teacher.'

Isabella nodded her head.

'Ah, the strong, silent type,' said Sister Bernadette. 'Come with me.'

Isabella skipped into the front door of the school before Bea could give her any advice for her first day at junior school. Liz glanced backwards and mouthed 'good luck' at Michael who hung back, intimidated by the tide of women and girls all talking at once in their high voices. Bea glanced back as she walked to the car, but the pebble-dashed front of the school gave no clue to the whereabouts of the crowds of children who had entered.

'They'll be fine,' said Mrs O'Reilly. 'The Loreto has high educational standards.'

After their mother had gone, the girls faced their new classmates with varying degrees of trepidation. Isabella didn't have to work hard for attention. Blonde hair was a novelty in Ireland, and she found herself surrounded by the other girls who touched her curls and examined her from every angle.

'Girls, this is Isabella. Be kind to her if you want to go to heaven,' said Sister Bernadette.

A sea of smiles, some fake, turned on at this exhortation. Isabella blushed and looked down at the desktop where a past pupil had excavated a crude heart. MR loves SD. It made her smile and as she raised her head; she caught Sister Bernadette nodding her approval.

'You look like Shirley Temple,' said one girl. 'Do you want to sit beside me?'

'You get away now, Sheila Burns. Isabella's sitting beside me.'

This outburst came from Nuala O Connor, a small bossy dark-haired girl.

'She lives down the road from me,' said Nuala. 'We're best friends, aren't we?'

Isabella nodded, curls bouncing. Sheila Burns pursed her lips and crossed her arms.

'I'd be a better friend. The O'Connors are poor.'

'So are we,' said Isabella, slipping in beside Nuala and giving her arm a squeeze.

'Do you like Irish dancing?' said Nuala.

'I don't know,' said Isabella.

'You will,' said Nuala.

Meanwhile, Liz loitered at the back of her classroom, tugging at her loose tunic, self-conscious of its ill-fitting shape. Then she took the only free seat in her classroom beside a skinny girl with a shabby uniform with a mended tear on the skirt. She smelled of wood smoke and had dirty fingernails.

'Hello,' said Liz. 'I'm Liz. What's your name?'

The girl turned to look at her, her eyes wide.

'Oh, don't bother talking to her,' said one of the other girls. 'She's a traveller. The nuns let them come to classes out of charity. She'll leave when they move on.'

'Eileen,' whispered the girl, hiding her hands under the desk.

'No talking in class.'

A tall, thin nun with a pinched face had entered the classroom and stared at them in fury.

'You girl, you shouldn't be sitting there.'

Liz stammered in confusion. 'But there were no other seats. Nobody told me--'

'You should know. Traveller girl, stand up, go next door to Sister Ursula's class.'

Eileen slid off the bench and slunk past the rows of desks. Liz stood up, her mouth open, wanting to protest.

'Don't mind her. She won't be here next week. I'm Mother Rosalie and you are?'

'Liz Green.'

'Oh yes.'

She drew out the last syllable and rolled her eyes to heaven. 'The Sassenach,' she said. 'I should have guessed.'

Her parents had forced Mother Rosalie into the convent as a young girl. Her bitterness over the incarceration had stretched her out and eaten all her plump flesh away until she was as long and thin as a twig used for poking the fire. Her burning sense of resentment and injustice increased when the awful English pagans arrived in her convent. They would never have to suffer a life shut away. And they were evil, especially the new girl in her class who was pretending to be quiet and innocent, but harboured the devil inside her like all Protestants. She picked up a ruler and rapped it hard on the table in front of her.

'Okay, class, we start with Irish. Open your books at the first page.'

She looked up and saw Liz hesitating.

'Anne. Sit beside the new girl and share your book.'

A small red-headed child left her seat and sat beside Liz, opening the book between them with a sigh.

'Read it,' said Mother Rosalie.

Liz looked at the page in front of her. Irish. The alien words swam into view as she forced herself to focus.

'I can't,' she said. 'I don't know how.'

'You can't read? What sort of eejit are you? No wonder you sat beside the Traveller girl.'

Liz blanched.

'I can read,' she said. 'But I can't read that.'

'That, you nasty insignificant insect, is our language. You must study Irish to pass your exams in Ireland. I suggest you learn.'

She turned her laser stare at another child cowering at their desk. A hot flush spread up Liz's back and she tightened her fists. The girl beside her shook her head.

'She'll whip you,' she said. 'She's just looking for an excuse. Sister Rosalie hates the English.'

The Green sisters sat together at lunchtime to eat their sandwiches and compare notes.

'My nun is great,' said Isabella. 'She likes my hair. Can I have some milk?'

Liz sniffed the contents of the bottle. The milk had curdled in the warm classroom and the sharp odour made her wrinkle her nose.

'It's gone off,' she said. 'I'll pour it away.'

'How's your teacher?' said Isabella.

'I'm sure she hates me,' said Liz.

'Already?' said Isabella. 'It took me ages.'

Giggles rang out across the playground as Liz tried to pull her hair and chased her around the concrete square. Other children joined in the game of tag, and soon the Green children had melted into the crowd.

Chapter 10 – The Christian Brothers, September 1969

When Bea and Mrs O'Reilly arrived at the Christian Brothers, the scrum at the school gate almost swept Bea off her feet. There were hundreds of boys pushing and shoving and larking about. Bea tried to give Michael some last-minute encouragement and advice, but the size and sound of the milling schoolboys overwhelmed her soft voice and he couldn't hear it. He soon lost sight of her, as a crowd of eager students swept him away. Bea sighed and got into the car.

'All right, dear?' said Mrs O'Reilly.

'Let's go shopping.'

Michael watched his mother's car pull out and drive away, leaving him marooned on the pavement. He walked through the gates and a tide of boys swept him into the school. He didn't know where they were taking him, and panic spread throughout his chest. Someone grabbed his arm and Sean appeared at his side, his freckled face with its carrot top grinning in a sea of milling boys.

'Come on, you eejit, we mustn't be late for assembly,' said Sean.

'Where's Liam?'

'He left school at the end of last year. He's supposed to do an apprenticeship, but he's got other plans.'

They scampered into the assembly hall and pushed their way onto the hard, wooden bench near the front, which had been designated for their class. A Brother as plump as a pork sausage stood at the end. He had wiry hair, beady eyes, and ears that stuck out at right angles. He glared at the boys, inducing instant silence, and perched at the end of the bench, wheezing like the boiler in the farmhouse. Michael stared hard at the floor, hoping to avoid trouble.

'That's Brother Eamonn,' said Sean. 'He's our form teacher.'

The bell rang, and an expectant silence hung over the hall. An old priest, with his head thrust out in front of his chest like a vulture, shuffled onto the stage in front of the boys.

'Welcome back, lads. To new boys, I extend a blessing. I'm Father Patrick, the headmaster. We're proud of the CBS, and I expect you to work hard. If you have a problem, I will listen, but avoid being sent to me for poor behaviour. I hate to punish boys unless I have to.'

He produced a thin cane from behind his back and slapped it into his palm, causing the audience to shiver in anticipation. The assembly continued with the usual instructions, and some prayers and hymns that Michael did not recognise. He attempted to mouth them. Determined not to find out what sort of punishment awaited any boy sent to see Father Patrick, he tried to curb the butterflies in his stomach.

After the assembly, the boys swarmed out into the corridors, leaving the hall smelling of feet and hormones. Michael followed his classmates into their schoolroom and loitered at the door, wondering where to sit. Sean patted the seat beside him and gesticulated.

'I saved you a seat,' he mouthed.

Michael let out the breath he had been holding and slid onto the hard, wooden bench, shiny from hundreds of bony bottoms over decades of use.

'What's Father Eamonn like?' said Michael.

'You haven't heard about him? Seriously?' said Sean.

Michael shook his head, and Sean sighed.

'He's a monster. Keep your head down if you know what's good for you.'

The first morning at the CBS etched itself into Michael's memory as one of the longest he had ever experienced. The scourge of class six, Father Eamonn entered to an echoing silence, his black eyes searching for a victim to be the butt of his jokes. They lit upon Michael, who coloured under his scrutiny.

'So, boy, stand up so we can all see you. What's your name?' asked Father Eamonn.

'Michael Green, sir.'

'Mick Green, eh? Where did you get that posh accent?'

'I don't have a posh accent. I'm English.'

Father Eamonn glared at him.

'How dare you answer me back! Will I send you to the headmaster on your first day?'

Michael coloured.

'No sir, I'm sorry, I wasn't...'

But Father Eamonn cut him off.

'And I suppose you're a proddy too?'

'I'm sorry, I don't understand. What's a proddy?'

'Oh, so we have a joker, a nasty English Protestant joker, in our class this term. That's all I need. Sit down, you nasty boy.'

Michael embodied the perfect fall guy; quiet to the point of being withdrawn, with obvious failings like his nationality, religion, and shyness. He was an easy target for the vicious sadist harboured in the sausage-like body. Michael went bright red with shame and shock, and stumbled backwards against his bench, almost falling. All the other boys laughed at him, glad that someone else would be the victim of Father Eamonn's jibes.

Michael's head spun. He had imagined his first day at his school many times, and none of the scenarios resembled this. Sean, who was sharing a double desk with him, poked him in sympathy, but Michael kept his eyes down, terrified of attracting any more unwanted attention from his teacher. His heart was thundering in his ribcage with fright and fury. The slurry pit didn't seem so bad in comparison.

'Now, where were we, class? Fergus, will you hand out the grammar books please? I need these books covered tonight, boys. Brown paper only. Put your name on the cover. If you lose it, you must replace it. Everyone, turn to page one.'

By the time the bell rung for the end of lessons, the class had learned what to expect under Father Eamonn. The year stretched out before them like an assault course littered with mines. They had known it was coming - a year with the dreaded Father Eamonn – but the reality was even worse than the myth. Michael's dreams of being one of the boys evaporated in one day. The priest specialised in inventing cruel nicknames by which the boys were known for the rest for the rest of the year, and if they were unlucky, for the rest of their lives. Michael had acquired one after lunch when he failed to pronounce, despite prompting from Sean, an Irish word.

'So, Master Green. I think you need a name befitting your lowly status. Let me see. Hmm. You're stupid, that's pretty obvious, English, ditto, and a proddy.'

He wrote the letters S, E, and P on the blackboard.

'You're small too, like a flea or a tick. I have it!'

He spun around and continued to write T I C K on the board beside the other letters. Grabbing the duster, he erased the K.

'Septic Green, perfect.'

He beamed in self-congratulation, and all the boys roared with laughter and relief that it wasn't them. Michael looked down at his desk, concentrating hard on the ancient graffiti and trying not to lose his temper. The board duster flew through the air and hit him hard just above the ear.

'Wake up there, Septic, it's time to go home.'

Michael gasped in shock and rubbed his head. He turned pink with fury, but he swallowed his urge to throw it back. The priest mistook his colour for embarrassment and sneered at him. The other boys filtered out, minus their usual exuberance.

'Don't worry,' said Sean, once they were outside, 'it won't be you every day. Some other lad will get it tomorrow.'

But he was wrong.

Chapter 11 – Isabella, November 1969

Living in Ireland left its mark on the three children, who got into the car after school every day sounding as if they had been born in Kilkenny. Their Irish accents disappeared during the journey home, and by the time they walked into the farmhouse had become English again.

'Do you see how fast they're adapting?' said Tom. 'It's frightening.'

'Isabella has morphed into an Irish colleen,' said Bea. 'Are you sure she's ours?'

Isabella felt at home in Ireland from the start. Her mop of blonde curls gave her a resemblance to Shirley Temple, whose films monopolised children's television, being shown on a loop most weekends before the horse racing. This blonde mop gave her a novelty value which guaranteed she would be the centre of attention whenever they took her to Kilkenny.

'Oh well now, isn't she a little angel?'

'What a precious-looking child.'

Bea avoided the attention, but Mrs O'Reilly would preen herself, taking on the role of adoptive grandmother and shielding the child from people who tried to touch her.

'Isn't she a little dote?'

'Don't touch her. She's shy.'

There was nothing shy about Isabella Green. She understood the power of a glance from under her blonde lashes early in life and milked it for all she was worth. Mrs O'Reilly liked to welcome Isabella into her neat sitting room with a glass of milk 'straight from the cow' and some home-made biscuits still warm from the oven. Isabella could rely on Mrs O'Reilly to take her side against Liz and Michael, no matter the evidence.

In the convent, Isabella thrived under the tender care of Sister Bernadette, a cheerful and tolerant soul the shape of a butter ball, who could have come straight from the Sound of Music. Isabella absorbed the fresh information imparted to her like a sponge, especially regarding Catechism and the saints who had died for Jesus in horrible ways. She loved fairy tales and fantasy and treated the Catholic religion like an exciting saga.

I wish I was a saint. They all died for Jesus and won eternal life.

'Wasn't Jesus wonderful?' Sister Bernadette asked, after reading parables from the New Testament.

'Yes, Sister Bernadette,' chorused the girls.

Nuala O'Connor elbowed Isabella and rolled her eyes, but Isabella gazed at the plump nun with devotion. *She's so kind and holy. Unlike Sister Rosalie, who hates us.*

Sister Bernadette was a devotee of the Virgin Mary, whom she idolised like a rock star.

'You should aspire to be as pure and holy as the Virgin,' she said to the class.

Isabella found the idea thrilling.

'I want to be a virgin when I grow up,' she said to Bea.

'That's nice, darling,' said Bea, pretending to be busy with the Aga and avoiding Tom's glance. She stifled a laugh with the dish cloth.

The girls in Isabella's class were discussing their first Holy Communion dresses and Isabella joined in, unaware that as a Protestant she would not be taking part in this ceremony. She took to swotting her catechism with the passion of a new convert.

Who knows what all this stuff means? Maybe I'll get some communion money from Mrs O'Reilly.

'We can't let her take part. Perhaps we shouldn't let her do catechism at all,' said Bea.

'Don't fret, pumpkin. She possesses the attention span of a goldfish. It'll blow over; like the need for a pony, and her ambition to be an Olympic gymnast,' said Tom.

They didn't have to wait long. The two sisters attended compulsory Irish dancing classes on Saturday mornings. Bea dropped Liz and Isabella at the convent on their first Saturday while she did the weekly shop.

'Have fun, girls.'

Irish dancing took place in the cold, unheated gym, which had one wall covered in mirrors. The gymnastics bar and vaulting horse sat at the back of the room, and the rolled-up mats had been piled against the climbing bars. An acrid smell of sweat and hormones hung in the air. Liz and Isabella stripped down to their gym uniform of black leotards and plimsols. A sea of blotchy legs milled around in the cold room. Some girls wore black dancing shoes with ribbons braided up their calves. Isabella found her plimsols wanting in comparison and stared longingly at them.

'I'd love a pair of those,' she said, but Liz ignored her.

Their teacher, Mrs Talbot, bustled into the room wearing an enormous pair of sunglasses. Her outfit comprised pink slacks and a black shirt with her hair scraped back into a face-lifting bun and tied with a Hermes scarf. She reviewed the room with something approaching distaste but set her face into a fake smile which showed the lipstick on her teeth.

'Right, girls, let's get started. This will be great craic.'

Liz had no intention of enjoying herself, but Isabella couldn't wait to get started. She pushed through the girls and stood in the front row, flicking her curls, and doing twirls in front of the mirror, while Liz stood in the back row, sulking. Isabella noticed Liz's reflection in the mirror and pulled the corners of her lips up at her, receiving a roll of the eyes in return.

Liz is no fun any more. I love dancing.

She had seen the dresses for Irish dancing competitions in the display window of the Monster House, and she did the classes with the gusto and enthusiasm of someone who wanted a Ceilidh dress and a sparkly headband. *Daddy will buy one of those for me, whether or not he wants to.*

Michael and Liz left her out of their elaborate story games and late-night excursions to each other's beds for the secret whispering of confidences. She had learned to use the situation to her advantage, whining to her parents about how unfair it was and getting special treats to placate her. Somehow, when faced with Isabella's big golden brown eyes, Tom could not repeat his mantra about the unfairness of life. He would sweep her up into his arms and sit her on his lap instead, singing songs in her ear.

Mrs Talbot observed Isabella with her hands on her hips.

'Are you sure you haven't tried this before?' she said. 'You've got a natural ability.'

Isabella smirked. 'Thank you, Miss.' I'm good at everything.

When she got home, she sat on her father's lap and snuggled up to him while he read the newspaper in the sitting room.

'You're the best Daddy in the whole wide world.' she said.

'Only when you want something,' her father said. 'And what is it this time, sausage?'

'I really, really need a dress for the Irish dancing competitions. All the other girls in my class own one.'

'Oh, do they now? And where would we find one of those? I thought you really, really wanted a dress for Holy Communion?'

Hoist by her own petard, Isabella made a lightning decision.

'Holy Communion is for Catholics. We're Protestants, but anyone can do dancing.'

'I see. Well, I'll think about it. Isn't there a competition coming up?'

'Yes, Daddy.'

'Well, if you get on the team, I'll buy you a dress.'

Isabella took to practising her steps all over the house. Liz banished her from the bedroom, and Bea from the kitchen, but her enthusiasm remained high. Mrs O'Reilly let her practise in her sitting room before the Angelus and sat for hours giving her tips on how to keep her knees up, and chocolates from her tin of Quality Street.

'You must have Irish ancestry,' said Mrs O'Reilly. 'You've taken to this like a fish to water.'

Isabella started out in the beginners' class, but Mrs Talbot promoted her after a few lessons to the more advanced sessions, where she joined her new best friend, Nuala O'Connor. Her prowess caused some jealousy among the other girls of her age who resented an English girl taking the spotlight. Nuala did not dance as well as Isabella, but she didn't have a jealous bone in her body and revelled in her elevated position as Isabella's friend.

Isabella and Nuala gave demonstrations to the captive audience of the Green parents, Mrs O'Reilly, and Mickey, but they had no idea if she had talent or not. Isabella overcame their usual resistance to showing off by telling them she wanted to fit in.

'Sorry about this, Jacinta,' said Bea, as they waited for yet another private dance show, 'they're obsessed right now. You don't have to watch, you know.'

'Nonsense. I don't mind at all. It's not like there's anything on RTE, unless you like nuns singing.'

Mrs Talbot approached Bea when she collected the girls after class one Saturday.

'She's going to need proper shoes and a dress if she wants to compete in An Fheis Mhór,' she said.

'An Fheis Mhór?'

'The County dancing championships. They're in a few months' time. In May. Do you want me to enter her?'

'I don't know. I'll ask my husband.'

'You do that. Isabella's going to dance those other girls right off the stage.'

Isabella's small chest swelled with pride at hearing this, but her mother did not look as pleased as she expected. In the car on the way home, Isabella caught her mother glancing at her in the rear-view mirror. She tried to hide the smug expression on her face.

'I can't wait to dance in An Fheis Mhór,' she said. 'Mrs Talbot thinks I'll win easily.'

Liz blew out her cheeks.

'I'm not sure she said that,' said Bea. 'Anyway, it's not until May and we haven't decided you are going yet.'

'But Mummy, Daddy said he would buy me a dress and shoes, if I was good.'

'Daddy doesn't have money right now. We need a washing machine. You may need to wait until next year.'

'A stupid washing machine instead of my dress? You're so cruel.'

Isabella let her lip quiver and her tear-filled eyes accused Bea in the reflection.

'If you help me with the washing, we can buy you a dress,' said Bea.

'Me?' said Isabella. 'I'm not a maid.'

'Neither am I,' said Bea, and fixed her eyes on the road before she lost her temper. Liz elbowed Isabella hard in the ribs and hissed in her ear.

'What is wrong with you? I told you we don't have any money now.'

Isabella wondered if she had gone too far. She found her mother more resistant to her plans than her father, who always capitulated. She bided her time until they got home and then flung herself into her father's arms.

'I got on the team,' she said.

'Well done, darling. That's amazing.'

Isabella looked up at him from under her eyelashes, doing her best puppy impression.

'So, will you buy me the dress and shoes now?'

Tom hesitated and Bea shook her head.

'You promised,' said Isabella.

'I did,' said Tom. 'You've got me there.'

Isabella ran up the stairs screaming with excitement and burst into the bedroom where Liz had gone to shelter.

'I hope you're pleased with yourself,' said Liz. 'You made Mummy sad.'

In the kitchen, Tom shrugged at his wife.

'A promise is a promise,' he said to Bea. 'I never expected her to do so well. It distracts her from being left out by the other two.'

'This Fheis Mhór thing takes place in Wexford,' said Bea. 'It's a long drive on these roads.'

'I don't mind taking them,' said Tom.

'No, I'll go. Maeve will want to come too. Nuala is also dancing, but she hasn't organised a lift for her yet. We can share a girls' day out.'

'That's settled then. I'm sure it will be fun.'

Chapter 12 – Changes, November 1969

The move to Ireland had been a nightmare for Liz. As a Protestant English girl in a class of Catholic Irish girls, she stuck out like a sore thumb, and unlike Isabella, she had no intention of going native. She missed her friends and her school, and she hated Irish and Catechism, but there was no alternative to keeping her head down, with her father's mantra ringing in her head. *Life's not fair, and the sooner you get used to it the better.*

The convent had saddled Liz with Mother Rosalie as her class teacher, a wizened resentful sadist who punished her for the slightest misdemeanour, real or imagined.

'Nasty girl. I don't know why we have to tolerate Protestants.'

Liz's resentment at being removed from England without being consulted almost rivalled Mother Rosalie's rage at being forced to teach her. She picked up on the nun's obvious dislike of her and refused to adapt to the school regime or make any effort to catch up on her lessons. She sat at the back of the classroom with her arms folded, radiating rebellion. *You won't get the better of me. I'll never learn any catechism.*

Her resentment raised hackles among her classmates who considered her to be a snob. They steered clear of her prickly exterior, reinforcing the mutual distrust. Worse still, she couldn't hide her hatred of Irish dancing, which she considered a waste of time, only marginally better than sitting at home on a Saturday morning with the danger of being asked to help with the laundry or the cleaning. Her opinions grated on the other girls who loved their Saturday mornings with Mrs Talbot.

All that ridiculous bouncing up and down with our hands pinned to our sides. We look like pogo sticks. And that Mrs Talbot. Who does she think she is? Grace Kelly? She's far too fat for that.

Liz had an ally in Michael, who was having a tough time in the CBS. He found going to school in Ireland an ordeal. A slow learner, he had enjoyed the small class size in their local school in England. Irish class sizes were much bigger. Father Eamonn called him an eejit and hounded him all the time because he was not used to having to learn everything by heart as they did in Ireland.

'He's always giving out to me, mummy, even when I get all my answers right,' complained Michael.

'Giving out what dear?' said Bea, distracted as she tried to get the Aga going for supper.

'Giving out, you know, being cross with me.'

He did not tell his parents about his nickname, and the constant physical punishments meted out by the sadist who taught his class. Michael had become Father Eamonn's victim and fall guy, and the abuse ground him down. He became withdrawn and only cheered up when he played with Sean and Blue.

'Let's run away,' said Liz, as they sat on the steps in the small garden at the front of the farmhouse.

'But where would we run too?' said Michael. 'They'd only find us and bring us back.'

He threw several stones over the fence with a grunt.

'Maybe Liam could help us. He knows about running away,' said Liz.

'Liam's got somewhere to run to. And he's much older than us.'

'He's only fifteen. I'm twelve,' said Liz.

'But he's disappeared again and, anyway, he hates the English.'

'He likes us, though. We should ask him when he comes back. Until then, we'll just have to put up with it.'

'You don't know how tough it is in the CBS.'

'Well, I would if you told me.'

Michael fiddled with his shoelaces. He opened his mouth to tell her, but at that moment, Isabella appeared in the doorway.

'Suppertime,' she said. 'Mummy says to come straight away.'

Michael rolled his eyes.

'Come on,' said Liz. 'You can tell me later.'

But he never got the chance.

Half way through supper, Liz let out a cry and rubbed her stomach. *What's wrong now? It's probably some Irish germ. I hate this place.* Bea did not approve of antics at the table, but Liz's pale face and wide eyes spoke volumes.

'Are you okay, darling?' said Bea.

'I have a funny pain,' said Liz. 'Down here.'

She pointed to her pelvic region. Tom looked up from his plate and drew his eyebrows together in concern.

'Appendicitis?' he said to Bea. 'She's the right age for it.'

'It may be something else she's the right age for,' said Bea.

'What's that?' said Isabella.

'Eat your supper. It's going cold,' said Bea. 'Is it any better, Liz?'

'Yes, I think so,' said Liz, looking down at her lap. But it wasn't. Sharp pains stabbed at her ovaries. She bent double, which relieved the pain a little.

Michael elbowed her and mouthed, 'What's up?' but she ignored him.

'Finish your food, Liz, and I'll make you a hot water bottle,' said Bea.

One of the family staples for illness. A cup of tea, a hot water bottle or an aspirin, or all three.

When they got up to leave the table, Isabella squeaked and pointed at Liz.

'Look, is that blood? What's wrong with her?'

Liz looked around in panic, pulling at the hem of her dress so she could see the red stain which had seeped into the material. Before anyone else could react, Bea took her daughter's hand and led her upstairs to the bathroom. Liz sobbed in fright as she sat on the toilet while her mother sponged the stain from her dress.

'Am I dying?' said Liz.

'Of course not. This happens to girls at your age.'

'But what is it?'

'It's called a period, and it's part of being a woman. From now on, this will happen every month. It lasts for a few days. I'll buy you some sanitary towels to use. Meanwhile, here's one of mine.'

She pressed the bulky towel into the gusset of some clean knickers. Liz poked it with a grimace.

'Every month?' she said. 'But it hurts.'

'There's nothing we can do about that.'

'Do boys get this?'

'No, only girls. It means you're growing up.'

'I don't want to grow up if I have to have periods.'

Liz stood in front of Bea with her hands on her hips. She looked far too young to have periods. Bea's heart contracted with pity, but she ploughed on.

'You might as well get used to it. Your breasts will grow soon.'

'Breasts? Like yours?'

Surely she was joking? But her mother nodded.

'Yes, just like mine. And hair down there and under your arms.'

'But it's not fair. I don't want them.'

For once, her mother did not recite the family mantra about fairness.

'No, it isn't. But there's nothing you can do to stop it. Come here and give me a cuddle. You're my big girl now.'

***

Outside the door, Michael slid down and sat on the hall carpet, his mouth open as he struggled to take in this information. He had seen his parents naked many times, so he knew they had hair in funny places, but they were grown-ups. Liz wasn't a grown-up. He had never considered the transition to adulthood, or when it might take place. *Am I going to look like Daddy soon, with bristles and hair in funny places?* His head whirled with this strange revelation.

His father appeared on the landing and took in his shocked expression.

'Don't worry. It's not dangerous.' He paused. 'Well, not much anyway. Women get moody when they have their period.'

'But Liz isn't a woman.'

'Girls grow up much quicker than boys. She'll leave you behind soon. You will catch up in a few years' time, but meanwhile you must be patient and accept things the way they are.'

'I don't believe you. You're lying.'

Michael stomped past his father and into his room, slamming the door theatrically. He sat on the edge of his bed, misery seeping from his pores. Something radical had happened. A change he could not fathom. *Would he lose Liz forever?*

Later, he ignored a gentle knock on his bedroom door, but Liz came in, anyway, clasping a hot water bottle to her tummy.

'Why are you shut in here?' she said

'I know about your period,' he said. 'I heard Mummy talking to you.'

He poked the water bottle. 'Does it hurt much?'

'It's like a cramp, but the bottle helps.'

Michael sighed.

'I don't want you to be a woman,' he said.

'I'd much rather be a boy,' said Liz, shrugging. 'You're so lucky. Being a girl is stupid.'

'I'm sorry,' said Michael.

'Me too,' said Liz. 'Don't worry, nothing will change. You're still my favourite brother.'

She gave him a cheeky grin.

'Do you promise?' he said.

'I promise.'

But Liz stopped coming to cuddle him at night after that. Try as she might, her hormones made her grumpy and difficult to be with. She had more homework than him, and she studied constantly in order to catch up with her class. As his sister distanced herself from him, Michael came to depend on his friendship with Sean, the odd visit from Liam, and Blue's unconditional love. Unable to confide in Liz, he weathered the storm at school for the most part, but the better his work, the more Father Eamonn despised him, picking on him most days, and clattering him with a ruler.

Demoralised, Michael begged his father for permission to watch the Apollo 12 moon landing. The family had not seen the more famous Apollo 11 expedition because of the upheaval caused by the bankruptcy of Tom's business. Space travel held the world in its thrall for several years after that, and Michael could recite the names of all the astronauts by heart.

The Apollo 12 module touched down on the lunar surface in November 1969. The entire family stayed up to watch on Mrs O'Reilly's television, even though the broadcast went on until the small hours of the morning. Tom had to wake the children up for the astronauts' first steps on the moon as they had long fallen asleep wrapped around Blue on the sofa. The hazy pictures of men in large white suits with what looked like goldfish bowls on their heads caused great excitement in the O'Reilly household.

'Saints preserve us,' said Mrs O'Reilly. 'Do ye think they'll ever get back to earth at all?'

'It's a queer long way right enough,' said Mickey shyly standing at the door of the sitting room. He had accepted the invitation to watch, but couldn't quite sit down too.

'I want to be an astronaut when I grow up,' said Michael.

'And me,' squeaked Isabella. 'I want to be a 'stronaut too.'

'Astronaut,' said Liz. 'And you can't. Only boys can be astronauts.'

As usual.

'Is that true, Daddy?' asked Isabella. 'Why can't girls do anything boys can? It's not fair.'

'My girls can be anything they want,' said Tom.

Isabella smiled at Liz as if to say 'now, didn't I tell you'. Michael rolled his eyes. It was tough being the only boy between two bossy sisters.

'Off to bed with you all now,' said Bea, 'and you,' she said to Tom poking him in the stomach. Mickey had already slipped away. They left Mrs O'Reilly pooped out on her sofa, still muttering about rockets.

Chapter 13 – Rebellions, Easter 1970

At Easter 1970, following a march to commemorate the 1916 Rising, the violence in Northern Ireland got worse. The British Army established a cordon around parts of the Catholic Bogside to protect the people living there. Rioting followed in the Springfield road in Belfast after Catholic youths confronted an Orange Parade.

The violence did not fit in with Tom's idea of Ireland as a rural idyll. When the Greens had planned their move to Kilkenny, they were aware of the civil rights marches and sporadic violence in the North, but they were going to the other end of the country and believed it would blow over. The passions aroused by historical events were incomprehensible to the taciturn Tom.

'But why do they march at all?' he said. 'King William's been dead for hundreds of years. They're only inciting people.'

'Weren't the Bogsiders doing the same?' said Bea. 'Why are things that happened so long ago so important?'

'Maybe it's young unemployed lads letting off steam,' said Tom.

'I hope it doesn't spread down here,' said Bea.

Mrs O'Reilly would not comment, and most people ignored the Troubles, as they became known, but

Michael's school contained many hotheads, who reacted badly to the news, and overt expressions of support for the IRA increased.

Michael did not understand the passionate interest of the boys in Irish history. They had never mentioned Ireland in his history class in England. He read well from an early age and devoured books like some children consumed cartoons and westerns on television. At his prompting, Tom bought him a tattered Irish history book from the second-hand bookshop. He curled up on the battered sofa in the sitting room and read until his eyes ached. *Could this be true?*

The history of England's intervention, or the lack of it, in Ireland made him ashamed to be English. His horror at the consequences of the potato famine gave him an insight into the burning sense of injustice driving Liam into the arms of the IRA. He would have liked to talk to his father about it, but Britain could do no wrong in Tom's eyes, and platitudes could not assuage Michael's mood. Michael's patriotism evaporated, replaced by a guilt he could not throw off.

Some boys at school had taken to re-enacting the 1916 Rising in the playground at break time, with the rebels and the hated British army fighting it out. A dividing wall in the playground acted as the post office building and the 'rebels' pelted the imaginary soldiers with sticks and stones while shouting nationalistic slogans about free Ireland. Sean and Michael joined the rebels and fought side by side against the hated soldiers until one of the older boys picked up on Michael's accent.

'Why's this English bastard fighting for the rebels?' he said.

'Michael's one of us,' said Sean. 'He saved my life.'

'I don't care who he saved,' said the boy. 'He can't fight on our side. He's the enemy.'

Some older boys surrounded Michael and started jeering and pushing him out of their half of the playground. He fell over and one of them kicked him in the back.

'Get out of here. You don't belong with the proper men. We Irish are the winners.'

Michael had no comeback. He had always been proud of being English, but he understood why the boys picked on him. He refused to be a soldier and spent break in the classroom. Sean didn't comment when he joined him after the break, but he couldn't look Michael in the eye.

Tom laughed when Michael told him about this game (without mentioning the bullying).

'The rebels didn't win in 1916. The British army defeated them and executed their leaders.'

'But the boys told me the rebels fought to free Ireland from British rule.'

'They had already got Home Rule,' said Tom.

'What's that?'

'Like Australia or New Zealand. The final agreement got postponed by the start of World War I. Two hundred thousand Irish men joined the British army in the fight against tyranny. They hoped to secure an Independent State by goodwill rather than revolution, but a small band of hot heads, who couldn't wait for the end of the war, incited the rebellion in Dublin.'

'If the rebels didn't win, how come Ireland is free now?' said Michael

'The execution of the leaders of the rebellion turned the Irish public against the British government, and people flooded to the rebel cause.'

'But why did they execute them? Couldn't they have put them in prison?'

'The British government believed the rebels had collaborated with the Germans to get arms. That made them traitors,' said Tom.

'But the rebels won.'

'Yes, I suppose they did. But not in 1916. Ignore those boys. Just walk away and avoid getting into fights. There's no point arguing with people who ignore the facts, and you're outnumbered.'

Michael returned to school buoyed by his knowledge of history and determined to follow his father's advice. He tried to stay in the classroom at break-time, but Father Eamonn turfed him out. He avoided contact with the boys doing re-enactments, but they came looking for him and subjected him to the usual abuse, pelting him with small stones and spitting at him.

'Why do we have to put up with a foreigner like you?' said a boy with bad acne.

'Ireland won. Ye lot are scum,' said another stocky lad, looking around at his friends for approval. 'Septic is the right name for you.'

The hateful nickname made him see red. Michael felt his blood boil, and he turned to face his tormentor.

'You're telling lies,' he said. 'The British defeated the rebels in 1916 and executed the leaders of the rising. The rebels were traitors. Two hundred thousand Irishmen fought in the first World War alongside Britain. It says so in my history book.'

'It's you who are lying. The men who fought in the trenches should have been fighting for Ireland. They were the traitors.'

'Why were the rebels executed then, if they weren't German collaborators?' said Michael.

He noticed Sean at his side, staring at him in horror.

'You're the feckin traitor,' said Sean. 'What about Liam risking his life fighting for our freedom?'

He ran off, leaving Michael surrounded by furious boys who tightened the surrounding circle. The stocky boy who had been arguing with him pushed his way into the ring and put up his fists. Michael's stomach knotted as he reciprocated. The boy looked twice his size.

At that moment the bell rang, eliciting a groan from the crowd who had been anticipating watching Michael get beaten up. The fear of being caned by the Brothers overcame their bloodlust and they all filtered back to the classrooms, leaving Michael trailing in their wake. The adrenaline coursing around his body made him feel sick. He took a few deep breaths and waited for his heart rate to normalise. Then he entered the school building and headed for his classroom.

When he got there, the door hung open and Father Eamon sat behind his desk, slapping a cane into his hand. Sean stood at his side; his hands clenched; their knuckles white.

'Go raibh maith agat, Sean. You can go now,' said Father Eamonn.

Michael considered running, *but where to?* He waited, rubbing the scar on his thumb under his forefinger. The rebels weren't the only traitors.

'Sean is after informing me about your outburst in the playground. Do you want to give me your version?' said Father Eamonn.

'I told the truth,' said Michael. 'The rebels did not win independence from Britain in 1916. I have a history book and it says that Ireland won independence in December 1922.'

'I don't care what your English book says,' said Father Eamonn, sneering.

Dislike for the sausage-like tyrant made Michael's usual reticence evaporate.

'It's an Irish book. My father bought it in Kilkenny. You can't change history just because you don't like the facts,' he said, white hot with rage and indignation.

Sean looked as if he might vomit.

'Mick, leave it now. Apologise,' he said.

'Why should I?' said Michael. 'It's the truth.'

Father Eamonn grabbed Michael by the collar and half-slammed-half-lifted him onto the raised teachers' desk. He held Michael face down with his left hand and grabbed the cane in his right.

'Did you hear what Septic said about our heroes?' he asked the class. 'We'll thrash the lie out of him right now. Sean, hold him down.'

But Sean had disappeared.

'Where is that boy? Oh, never mind. Kieran, hold Septic's shoulders for me.'

The stocky boy strode up and pushed Michael's head into the desk.

'English bastard, he'll show you,' he hissed.

Father Eamonn pulled Michael's shirt up around his head, and then he brought the cane down several times with all his force on Michael's back. The first few stokes elicited cheering and clapping from the jeering boys. But when blood appeared on the wall behind the priest's cane arm, the boys went quiet. Michael, who had not released a sound, fainted with pain and his eyes rolled back in his head. Kieran let go of his shoulders.

'Don't you think that's enough, sir. I think he's learnt his lesson.'

'Ha! Enough? I'll kill the little fecker.'

Father Eamonn raised his arm for another blow as the class winced in harmony.

'What is going on here?' said Father Patrick, who had come in unannounced, accompanied by Sean, whose face shone with snot and tears. He stared at Michael's back in horror.

'For God's sake, Eamonn. He's just a confused little boy. The punishment should fit the crime. I'll talk to you later.'

Father Patrick rolled Michael, who moaned with pain, into his arms and carried him out of the classroom, followed by a chastened Sean. He proceeded to the infirmary, where he laid Michael face down on a trolley.

'Nurse, put some arnica and iodine on this boy's back,' he said.

While she attended to Michael's wounds, he opened his eyes and fixed them on Sean. The pain made him lucid. *The traitorous dog. So much for pacts and blood brothers*. Sean avoided his stare. Father Patrick put a hand on his shoulder.

'You were right to come and get me,' he said. 'But tell your friend not to goad Father Eamonn again. Next time I might not be around to help.' He looked at his watch. 'The bell's about to ring for the end of the day. Get your schoolbags from the classroom and meet Michael at the gate.'

The nurse helped Michael into his shirt and gave him a tin of arnica 'for later'.

'Go home, son. And let that be a lesson to you. You're not in England now.'

Sean waited at the gate with his bag, panting with exertion. He held it out and Michael snatched it and snarled at him.

'Don't you dare talk to me. You are no longer my friend.'

'I didn't know what to do.' said Sean. 'We're blood brothers, but you were betraying the cause.'

'What cause? I'm English. You're Irish. Why don't you feck off?'

The expletive sounded hollow, even to him, but Sean flinched and tears appeared in his eyes.

'I'm sorry,' he said. 'You knew how important it was to me, to Liam. I should've known I couldn't trust you.'

'Trust me? You're the one who betrayed me to Father Eamonn.'

Sean's face fell.

'But—'

'Here's my mother. Don't you dare tell her what happened or I'll never forgive you.'

The journey home in the car went on forever. Somehow Michael managed not to cry out. He bit his lip so hard it bled, but not a whimper escaped. He stared out of the window, willing the trip to be over as he tried to put his weight onto his thighs and avoid touching his back on the seat. Liz raised her eyebrows at his weird pose as he balanced on the edge.

'Why on earth are you sitting like that?' she said.

'I'm practising,' said Michael without turning to look at her.

Tears threatened to pool in his eyes, and he jumped out of his door the second the car stopped, almost falling over on the gravel.

Once in his room, he stood and sobbed into his pillow, hiccuping with the effort of smothering the noise. A knock on the door startled him, and he threw the pillow away, hovering in the middle of the room. Liz came in and scrutinised him.

'You're behaving oddly,' she said. 'What's up?'

'I can't tell you,' said Michael. 'You'll tell Mummy and Daddy.'

'Not if you don't want me to.'

'Do you cross your heart and hope to die?'

Mystified, Liz complied.

Michael unbuttoned his shirt and shook it off, turning around so Liz could see his back.

Her hand flew to her mouth to stifle a gasp.

'Bloody hell. What happened?' she said.

'Father Eamonn beat me in front of the class for saying that the rebels lost in 1916.'

'Is that all? He beat you for telling the truth. What a monster! Why didn't Sean defend you?'

'He's the one who told on me.'

Michael sobbed. She tried to touch his back, but he shrank from her touch.

'Don't,' he said. 'It hurts.'

'Is this the first time they beat you?' said Liz.

'Father Eamonn hasn't beat me with the cane before, but he hits me and calls me Septic and Stupid.'

'But why didn't you tell me?' said Liz.

'You haven't talked to me for weeks. I thought you didn't care any more after what Daddy said.'

'What on earth did he tell you?'

'Daddy said you were growing up faster than me, and wouldn't be interested in me.'

'Since when?'

'Since you got your period.'

'Oh. That,' said Liz, deflated. 'It not true, you know. I still love you. But I have to tell.'

Michael's eyes widened.

'Please don't.'

'But I have to.'

'They'll go to the school and complain. The bullying will get worse.'

'But--'

'If I take my punishment, they might accept me.'

'But what if they don't?'

'The holidays start on Friday. I'll be safe for a few weeks. Maybe they'll forget what I said.'

Liz sighed.

'I wish I hadn't sworn. Can you at least pretend to be ill until the holidays? Mum will believe you after your strange behaviour in the car. You shouldn't go back until your back is better.'

Michael sniffed.

'Okay. Can you please put some arnica on the bruises?'

'I'll get it from the bathroom. You have cuts too.'

She fought back tears.

'How could he do this to you? He's an animal. Please let me tell Mummy.'

'No, you mustn't.'

Liz sighed and shrugged her shoulders. Trying to force Michael only made him more stubborn. She would work on changing his mind.

'I'll get the cream,' she said.

Chapter 14 – Revelation, Easter 1970

George Kennedy smacked his lips in appreciation as he swallowed the last of his apple crumble.

'That's why I came here from England,' he said. 'Bea's cooking.'

Bea blushed and wiped her hands on the apron sitting in her lap.

'Thank you, George. You need spoiling, and Jacinta has half a tray of stored apples left over from last year waiting to be stewed.'

'I'm delighted you're using them. So many of them go to waste,' said Mrs O'Reilly. 'But I shouldn't eat any more pudding or my skirt will need an extra button.'

The children giggled as she stuck her finger in her cheek and flicked it out, making a popping sound.

'Who wants to visit the beach tomorrow?' said Tom. 'The weather's meant to be sunny for once.'

Everybody, except Michael, cheered and stuck their hands up. He couldn't imagine anything worse. His glum expression did not change.

'I'm not well enough,' he said.

'Don't be silly,' said Tom. 'You've just scoffed two helpings of lunch. The sea air is bracing. It'll do you good.'

'Do I have to go?' said Michael, making sheep's eyes at his mother.

'Yes, you do. Mrs O is joining us for a picnic. She would have to stay at home to look after you if you don't come.'

'It's compulsory fun,' said George, rolling his eyes, but Michael didn't smile.

George's visit had been much anticipated, especially by Michael, but now he lived in fear of someone discovering his secret. Instead of fading, his bruises had acquired multicoloured hues, making his back appear like an expressionist painting of a ploughed field with black and purple lines interspersed with yellow.

Liz gazed at it in admiration. 'It's beautiful,' she said. 'I wish I had a camera.'

'Don't be ridiculous. It needs to fade before someone spots it.'

'It's still amazing. Does it hurt?'

'Not any more. How will I hide my bruises at the beach?'

'Just keep your t-shirt on. You can say you're cold,' said Liz.

'It'll probably rain, anyway.'

'That's the spirit.'

The next morning, they piled into the old green jalopy and Mrs O'Reilly's Hillman Hunter car. They had filled two of her picnic baskets to the brim with sandwiches, iced buns, and flasks of tea and coffee. A bottle of Robinsons squash nestled in a tartan blanket beside a flagon of icy water. An enormous bunch of bananas and some less-bruised windfalls made up the feast.

Michael made a last-minute bid for sympathy, but Tom bundled him into the car.

'For God's sake, stop whingeing. What will George think?' he said, under his breath. 'You don't seem ill to me.'

The convoy set off through the boreens that wandered through the luxuriant countryside to the beach. The light rain and intermittent sunshine had combined to cause an explosion of growth amongst the hedgerows which invaded the already narrow roadways, scratching against the sides of the cars that navigated past each other in them. Inside the car, anticipation rose as the thin blue line appeared on the horizon of an almost cloudless sky. Michael's feeling of dread increased.

'Drive quickly, Daddy, before it rains,' said Isabella, who had already undressed and pulled at the straps of her swimming costume, which no longer fitted her after a year of accelerated growth.

'It's not just the grass that's growing this spring,' said Bea, when Isabella had tried on her summer clothes, all of which were tight. 'These won't do another season.'

They pulled into an almost empty car park and rolled up to the sand dunes which had spilled onto the tarmac. Stiff sea grasses sprung from them in exuberant clumps. The odour of seaweed drifted into the windows, making everyone take a deeper breath. Liz and Isabella made a break for the beach.

'Not so fast,' said Bea. 'Carry something with you.'

Tom opened the boot and handed over buckets and spades to Isabella, who jumped about in impatience. He handed the flagon of water to Liz, who frowned.

'This is too heavy,' she said, and gave it back.

'Take the bottle of squash then. Don't run though.'

Liz cradled the bottle and set off down the path, being swallowed by the dunes in an instant. Michael resigned himself to his fate and took Mrs O'Reilly's deck chair with as much goodwill as he could muster.

'Good lad. I've no intention of getting sand in my clothes,' she said. 'I'll be sweeping it out of my house for weeks.'

They staggered through the dunes and arrived at the long sandy strand which stretched for miles on either side. The tide was retreating and the wet sand shimmered a welcome. Two or three other families had set their camp a little further down the strand. Isabella had already dug in the sand near the entrance to the beach.

'We might as well sit here,' said Tom. 'It'll be easier later.'

Tom and George set about erecting the wind shelter and unfolding the deckchair for Mrs O'Reilly. Bea spread out the big tartan rug and pinned down the corners with rounded stones still chilled from the night air. The children ran shrieking through the wet sand to the sea, sending showers of water into the air. They cheered with glee as Blue took off at top speed, sprinting in large circles and playing chicken with them as she whizzed past, her ears flying behind her head.

'Wow, she's so fast,' said Michael, lost in admiration.

'She's probably bred from racing dogs,' said Tom, who had joined them, lanky and white in his tight polyester swimming trunks. 'Are you coming for a swim?'

'No, I'm too cold. Maybe later.'

Tom rolled his eyes. He grabbed Isabella and ran towards the sea. Her squeals of enjoyment pierced the air. Liz ran after them with Blue, who stopped dead when the sea water wet her legs. She dropped her muzzle and licked the water, shaking her head in disgust at the salt. Relieved at his narrow escape, Michael walked back up the beach and sat beside George, who had burrowed his feet into the warming sand. George half turned and ruffled his hair.

'You feeling better?' he said. 'It's not like you to be down in the dumps.'

'Just cold,' said Michael. 'I stayed at home last week with a germ of some sort.'

They sat in companionable silence watching the seagulls swoop over one family who had taken out their sandwiches and were lobbing crusts to them. The gulls emitted sharp cries of excitement as they followed the victor with his booty. Isabella came running up the beach and planted herself in front of Michael.

'Daddy says you're to come now. We can't go swimming for ages after lunch.'

Michael frowned.

'I don't want to.'

Isabella knitted her eyebrows. Then she puffed out her breath in frustration and walked behind him. Before he could react, she had grabbed his t-shirt from the back and tried to pull it over his head. She let out a gasp.

'What's wrong with your back?' she said. 'Mummy, look at Michael's back. It's rotten, like the meat in the pantry.'

Michael pulled down his t-shirt, white as a sheet. Isabella stared at him; her mouth open. Bea, who had been trying to get a tan from the gentle sunshine, jumped up from the rug.

'Michael?' she said.

'Don't touch me,' said Michael, standing and stumbling backwards. 'There's nothing wrong. I just fell.'

'You must show me, sweetheart,' said Bea, kneeling in front of him. 'Turn around so I can see.'

She put her hands on his hips and forced him to swivel. Then she lifted his t-shirt again, examining his back in shocked silence.

'What happened, darling,' she said. 'Who did this to you?'

Michael tried to speak, but his voice caught on a sob, and he turned into his mother's arms, gulping with misery. Her cries alerted Tom who came running up to them holding Isabella's hand, concern written on his face. Liz observed the kerfuffle and, guessing its reason, pretended not to hear at first, continuing to pick up shells at the sea edge. Bea lifted Michael's t-shirt and Tom examined Michael's back, his jaw muscles working in his face. Mrs O'Reilly, who had been asleep, almost fell out of her chair with fright.

'Saints preserve us, child. Who did this to you?' she said.

Michael shook his head. 'I can't tell you,' he said. 'It was my fault.'

'Your fault? Who could punish a boy so severely?' said Tom, fury sparking in his eyes.

George lifted Michael's chin up and looked into his face.

'You poor little bugger. Those priests beat the shit out of you, didn't they?'

Michael nodded and lowered his head in shame.

'The evil sods,' said George. 'Some things never change.'

Tom reached out to Michael, and he sat on Tom's lap where he cried his eyes out, sobbing with a combination of relief, misery, and fury.

'Why didn't you tell us about it? It isn't correct for a grown man to beat a small boy like this,' said Tom.

'You told me life isn't fair, and we aren't to make a fuss,' said Michael, sniffing.

Tom sighed and hugged him.

'You're not making a fuss. I didn't mean something like this,' he said.

'I didn't want you worry about me.'

'Worry? Good God, Michael, it's a parent's job to decide what to worry about.'

'You're not cross with me?'

'No. How could you think that?'

Bea stroked Michael's cheek.

'You poor thing, since when has this been going on?'

'Since the first day at CBS.'

'What's the name of the evil bastard responsible for this?' said Tom.

'Father Eamonn.'

'Father Eamonn, eh? Some man of the cloth,' said George.

Tom shook his head.

'What cloth?' said Michael.

'Nothing. Don't worry, son. I won't let that man touch you ever again.'

'Promise?'

'Oh, I promise all right. Father Eamonn will get a taste of his own medicine.'

A tiny smile crept onto Michael's face. This reaction surpassed anything he had expected. Maybe things would be alright after all.

Liz and Isabella peered at their brother as he recovered his composure.

'Are you all right?' said Liz.

Michael nodded and looked embarrassed.

'He is now,' said George. 'The seagulls are getting restless. I think it's time we started our picnic.'

Michael enjoyed the rest of the day at the beach more than anyone. The burden of his awful secret had lifted, and he felt young and free again. The knowledge that Father Eamonn could no longer torment him filled him with hope. He chased Blue around the strand until they were both exhausted and fell sound asleep on the back seat of Mrs O'Reilly's car.

'My poor baby,' said Bea, gazing in at him. 'I can't believe he kept this from us.'

'It's my fault,' said Tom. 'I thought I was preparing him for life, but I turned him into a martyr.'

That evening, Liz let herself into Michael's room and sat on his bed beside him. She looked into his eyes, trying to read his expression.

'What happened on the beach?' she said.

'Isabella tried to take off my t-shirt and everyone saw my bruises. She showed them to Daddy.'

'What did he say?'

'He wants to give Father Eamonn some medicine.'

'What does that mean?'

'I don't know. His face went white, and he said some rude words I've never heard before.'

'How do you feel now?'

'I don't know. Lighter, I think. Why don't you come and talk to me after bedtime any more? Have I done something wrong?'

'Wrong?' said Liz. 'Oh no, nothing like that. It's just girl's stuff. I need to talk to mummy about women's secrets.'

'Why can't you tell me? Is it such a big deal?'

'Well, it's only for girls, but I suppose you'll find out about them. It's my periods.'

'I know. I heard Mummy talking about it. Why were you bleeding?'

'Well, blood comes out of girls once a month, down there,' she said gesticulating, 'something to do with eggs and babies.'

'Does it hurt?'

'It's uncomfortable, and it puts me in a terrible mood. That's why I don't come and cuddle you any more. I feel different.'

'Every month? But for how long?'

'I don't know. Forever, I think. I've got to go to bed. Sleep well and don't worry. George will fix this. He fixes everything.'

***

Liz crept out of Michael's room along the stuffy landing towards her bedroom. She could hear faint voices from the garden. She lifted a sash window open a crack and listened. George had brought a bottle of Jameson whiskey down from his room, and he sat in the garden with Bea and Tom. He poured whiskey into each of three glasses and handed them out. Bea poured some water into hers.

They sat under the starry sky, sipping the golden liquid, each lost in his or her own thoughts. George moved his chair closer to the wrought-iron table, almost knocking over the bottle as he bumped into the table leg.

'We need to report that bastard to the CBS,' said Tom.

'You're on a hiding to nothing if you go that route,' said George.

'How can you say that? They beat my little boy to a pulp,' said Bea, her fists tight in her lap. 'If we were in England, I'd go to the police.'

Tom noticed her white hands and reached across, gently pulling her fingers apart. She gazed into his eyes in entreaty.

'There's no point,' said George. 'The Catholic church has an iron grip in Ireland. They're the real government in this place.'

'But we have to do something. They can't get away with it,' said Tom.

'They can and they will,' said George. 'No one here will challenge their authority.'

'But we can't send him back there,' said Bea.

'Now that I can agree with. We need to get him away from Father Eamonn and his cohort. I mentioned Whittingham as a possibility to Bea when I discovered Michael would go to the CBS. I still think it's an excellent choice for him.'

'But he's too young to go to boarding school,' said Bea.

'I understand you're worried, but he could live with me and attend the prep school as a day boy, before going on to the boarding school next year. That way he will make friends before he attends the senior school. Whittingham is a lesser public school, so it's smaller and friendlier than some others.'

'I don't know. It's awfully far away,' said Bea.

'Don't decide now,' said George. 'We can talk about it over the next part of my holiday and make a plan.'

'The only plan I have is to beat the crap out of Father Eamonn,' said Tom. 'Refill my drink before I drive over there and drag him out on the street.'

Upstairs, Liz shut the window. She stayed on the sill for a while, hidden by the curtain which she wrapped around her for warmth. The thought of Michael going to school in England made her miserable, but it was Hobson's choice. George's croaky tone rose to the window, soothing and sensible. She sighed and went back to bed.

Chapter 15 – Back to England, April 1970

The railway station sat on the eastern side of Kilkenny, on the line between Dublin and Waterford; solid dark grey blocks of limestone topped with a slate roof. The bright green gloss on the door and window frames matched the benches on the platforms. Tom, George, and Michael stood outside on the pavement searching for things to say. Michael tried to appear nonchalant, but his heart tightened in his chest. He couldn't decide if he wanted to leave more than he wished he could stay.

Things had happened fast after the trip to the beach. For the first time in months, Michael and Liz revelled in each other's company. Isabella had been gently persuaded to leave them alone, and for once she understood. Michael had forgotten how much he had in common with his sister. While the shock of Sean's betrayal lurked in his unconscious mind, he still gave himself over to their old games and jokes with no regrets. But things had changed. Liz looked more and more like their mother, and her figure had changed out of all recognition. He mourned the end of their childhood as he faced the reality of growing up far from her unconditional love.

A wild excitement grabbed him when Tom and Bea told him he would return to England with George, but this evaporated as reality ssnk in. He longed to take Blue with him, but the rabies regulations made this impossible. Six months in quarantine didn't sound like much fun for anyone. *I can't leave her in a cage for that long.* This morning he had buried his face in her neck, sniffing her doggy odour and rubbing her silky ears. It was the closest he came to tears. Liz had hugged him a little too long and parted from him with red eyes, and his mother stayed stoic, her arm around Mrs O'Reilly's waist for comfort as she waved goodbye.

'I'm sorry I can't take you to the ferry,' said Tom, breaking his reverie. 'The new consignment of electrical goods should arrive today and I need to check the manifest.'

'We'll get a taxi from the station at Dun Laoghaire,' said George. 'We've got loads of time. Maybe we'll get something to eat in a café near the docks. How long does the train take to reach Dublin?' said George.

'About two hours,' said Tom, although he had heard it could be closer to three. 'They've got new diesel engines on the lines to replace the steam trains. I wanted to tour the country in one before they disappeared, but CIE, the state railway company, beat me to it. I'll get the tickets.'

Before George could protest, Tom disappeared into the ticket office. Michael stood beside his suitcase, scuffing his shoe along the pavement to dislodge a piece of chewing gum stuck on the surface. His satchel swung back and forwards from his shoulder, hitting his legs. George put up a hand to stop him, but thought the better of it and lowered it again.

Tom emerged from the station and handed George their tickets for the trip to Dublin, which he folded with exaggerated care and placed in the top pocket of his tweed jacket. Time stood still as Tom and George watched Michael's dogged fight with the chewing gum. Michael gave the piece of gum one last vicious kick. It flew into the air and bounced on the grating in the gutter before falling between the rusty grilling and disappearing.

'All that work,' said George. 'Now, you'll never get to chew it.'

The joke fell into the space between them.

'Are you ready?' said Tom.

Michael nodded. His eyes threatened to fill with tears, but he rubbed them away.

'George will take good care of you.'

'I'll treat him like my own. I promise,' said George.

'Spoil him rotten, like Ben.' said Tom, checking his watch. 'Okay, the train's due, better get to the platform.'

Michael launched himself at Tom's waist, hiding his face in Tom's shirt. Tom ruffled Michael's hair and freed himself from the fierce hug. He handed Michael the suitcase.

'Can you manage?' he said.

The phrase hung in the air for a moment while Michael grappled with its meaning.

'Yes,' he said.

Michael grabbed the handle with two hands and staggered towards the platform, trying not to look backwards at his father. By the time he turned around, Tom had reached their car. He opened the door and glanced up, catching Michael's pleading look. He mouthed goodbye and gave Michael a shy wave before getting into the vehicle. A piercing whistle made Michael jump as the train pulled into the station. He hauled the suitcase to the nearest door and heaved it up into the carriage, followed by George.

They left the bags in the luggage rack by the exit and sat facing each other with a sticky table between them. The material of the seats bore the marks of lit cigarettes on its surface, already made shiny by hundreds of impatient backsides. Michael wrinkled his nose at the smell of cigarettes that permeated the fixtures and the nicotine that yellowed the ceiling.

'Filthy habit,' said George.

The train shuddered into action, squeaking and groaning as it picked up speed and left Kilkenny behind. Michael pressed his nose up against the filthy window, trying to gaze between the thick hedges. The glass tickled his eyelashes, and he blinked and moved back into his seat.

'Not much of a view. I expect you can see more in the wintertime,' said George.

'Probably,' said Michael.

His stomach contracted as the distance back to Blue and Liz and his family increased. He hadn't expected to regret leaving Ireland. Since arriving in Ireland, he had spent almost every waking minute resenting their move there. *Except for Blue. And Sean.* He sighed.

'I'll bring you home, if you hate it,' said George. 'You're not going to prison.'

Michael squirmed and blushed. He pulled a comic out of his satchel and tried to immerse himself in the world of the Bash Street Kids and Dennis the Menace. But Dennis and Gnasher reminded him of Sean and Blue, and a tear leaked out and slid down his cheek. George passed him a handkerchief and waited while Michael recovered his composure.

'Why don't you tell me what happened with Sean?' said George. 'I thought you boys were close but he didn't come to say goodbye.'

Michael sniffed.

'He did, but I wouldn't see him. It's too late now.'

He opened his comic again. George didn't pry. There would be later opportunities to sort this out. He hid behind his newspaper.

Once his excitement at the journey and his new surroundings dissipated, Michael missed his extended family, including, to his surprise, Mrs O'Reilly, and Mickey. Even Sean. Regrets about leaving without making up with him swamped his quiet moments. Michael could still visualise the hurt and anger in Sean's eyes over the betrayal he had committed. Father Eamonn was the real villain of the piece, his delight in thrashing Michael all too obvious. No doubt he revelled in his victory over the proddy bastard. *Had they bullied Sean on his return to school?*

Since Michael had arrived in England, George had tried to make him feel at home in the creeper-covered cottage, but his domestic skills left a lot to be desired. The phantom smells of his mother's cooking haunted Michael's memory, making his mouth water and his stomach mourn. George tried hard, but meals were a plain affair, often over- or undercooked. And then there were the chores. At home Michael made his own bed and kept his room tidy, most of the time, but nothing else. His move to George's house heralded a sea change in his responsibilities.

'Do you prefer to wash up or dry?' said George, on their first evening.

Michael swallowed his intuitive response of neither and muttered, 'Dry, I s'pose.'

But washing up was only the beginning. There were carpets to be vacuumed, rubbish to be taken out, bathrooms and kitchens to be scrubbed with Jif. Michael found it hard to contain his resentment at the new regime. Father Eamonn had a lot to answer for, but he blamed Isabella for tearing off his t-shirt. He could have managed in the CBS if they had let him return. The golden days he spent with Sean and Blue, roaming the fields, mocked him as he shoved the ancient lawnmower across the uneven grass in the back garden.

At least he made a new friend. Dennis Graham, a plump boy with a thatch of blond hair and a face that lit up like a red traffic light at the least embarrassment or exertion, became Michael's friend at the prep school. They met on Michael's first day before the creases fell out of his brand-new uniform.

George took Michael to the headmaster's office from where he had been collected by his form master, an ex-military man with a limp and a handlebar moustache. On being informed Michael would be added to his set, Major Tufton muttered 'Most irregular' and 'Follow me, quick march' before setting off at speed down the corridor, listing like a holed ship.

'Keep up, boy,' he said. 'No dawdling.'

But the eyes giving the orders were kind and his moustache creased upwards as Michael struggled to keep up with him.

'Graham shift up and let Green sit beside you,' bellowed Major Tufton. 'Stop staring at the new boy and open your history books at page fifty-one. Roberts, you start reading.'

Michael slid onto the bench beside Dennis, who offered his damp hand for a limp shake.

'Don't worry,' he said. 'We've all been new once. I'll show you the ropes.'

'No talking back there. Don't teach the new boy bad habits on his first day.'

Again, the twinkle in his eye belied the stern tone of his voice. Michael's shoulders relaxed for the first time in weeks as he recognised the era and events being described in the lesson. A feeling of coming home enveloped him. Soon his hand shot up to answer a question and even to ask one. Major Tufton thawed even faster when he realised his lukewarm set had acquired a history buff.

Soon Michael settled into the class where he found himself ahead in Maths and English and behind in French and Sciences. Major Tufton offered to tutor him to get him up to snuff, but George decided to let Michael ride out the term before getting extra summer teaching if necessary.

As promised, Dennis took Michael under his sturdy wing. Dennis did not suffer from an overdose of charisma, and had an appalling case of halitosis, but his large bulk made him impossible to exclude from most scenarios, being almost twice the size of the smaller boys in the year.

'I'm big for my age,' said Dennis, nudging Michael, and winking.

Relieved by Dennis's willingness to protect him, Michael slowly let down his guard. Major Tufton did not possess a cane and only used his walking stick as a badge of honour. Soon Michael blended in with the other boys as his uniform took the brunt of their rough games. The fact they beckoned him to join them behind the shed, where most of their nefarious schemes were hatched, spoke volumes about his levels of acceptance.

He also blossomed under the tutelage of Major Tufton, who always had time for his questions and had a natural affinity for lost boys.

'To what event do we owe the pleasure of your company?' said the Major, one day after class. 'How were the planets aligned? I understand from the headmaster that your parents live in Ireland. Why don't you attend a school over there?'

Michael hesitated.

'I had problems fitting in,' he said finally, looking at his shoes.

Major Tufton waited. Michael took a deep breath.

'How come the Irish make such a fuss about Independence?' said Michael. 'The British were invaded loads of times. The Vikings, the Romans, the Normans. We don't go on and on about it. The Protestants in Northern Ireland are still marching about some king from four hundred years ago too. I don't understand.'

'Because it's not history for some of them. It's their present. Until Ireland is united, they will feel the same way about the British. It's like the Second World War for me. I fought in the African campaigns. It feels like yesterday and my souvenir reminds me every day.'

He rapped his lower leg with his cane, producing a clonking sound. Michael's eyes opened wide.

'You lost your leg?' he said.

'Well, I didn't exactly lose it. It got blown off. Although, come to think of it, they couldn't have found it or they would have sewn it on again.'

Michael giggled, unable to help himself.

'History is in the eye of the beholder,' said Major Tufton. 'And don't forget, it is also written by the victor. That's why there are troubles in Ireland. Nobody wants to admit they lost.'

***

Raucous laughter attracted Michael to the shed at the end of the playground. He sneaked behind it and peered into the gap between the blackened fence slats and the tarred shed. A group of boys ogled a foldout pin-up, creased by the grasping of many small sweaty hands. In it a young bottle blonde woman lay on the bonnet of a car, her hand covering her genitals and large purple erect nipples dominating her petite breasts.

'Oy. Green, come and get a load of this,' said Dennis Graham, his face flushed with excitement.

'It's only a naked woman,' said Michael. 'What's the big deal?'

'Oh, and you've seen lots of them?' said another boy.

'Mostly my mother.'

'Your mother? What a pervert.'

They all guffawed.

'Come and see a real woman. Here, move over you lot.'

A branch of the old apple tree in the garden tapped the glass in the window of Michael's bedroom, penetrating his brain and disturbing his odd dream. He groaned and pulled the pillow over his head, trying to block out the bright June sunshine which streamed through the thin curtains in his room. An odd sensation in his pyjamas made the back of his neck prickle in shame. He rolled onto his back and examined a wet sticky patch in his groin area.

Hot waves of shame engulfed him. *Had he peed in the bed? Maybe the trauma of moving to England caused him to revert to childhood.* He threw off the blankets, exposing a small damp patch on the lower sheet. Aghast, he sniffed the patch and recoiled. It didn't smell like pee, but something had happened.

Whatever would George say? How would he explain something he didn't understand himself?

He ripped the sheet off the bed and bundled it up, throwing it in the bottom of the wardrobe. His bed looked as it always did once he had remade it. George would never know. He would wash the sheet when he got back from school. Another domestic chore to add to his list. He sighed.

When Michael got home from school, George looked up from his newspaper and patted the cushion beside him on the sofa.

'About that sheet,' he said.

The colour rose in Michael's cheeks, darkening as his shame mounted under George's scrutiny. He fought for something to say, flapping his hands about, but failed to find anything which covered the situation.

'It's called a wet dream,' said George, taking pity on him. 'It's part of growing up. All boys get them. Why don't you tell me about it?'

Michael swallowed.

'Someone brought a rude magazine to school, and I had a weird dream last night.'

'What do you mean by rude?'

'There were naked women in it.'

'Did you look at it?'

'Not much. I've seen Mummy naked lots of times. She and Daddy never hide their bodies from us. Daddy says it's natural to be naked and we shouldn't be ashamed.'

'Have you heard about puberty?'

'Oh yes, Liz has periods every month now. She told me all about them. We tell each other everything.'

'And what about boys? Do you know what happens to boys when you grow up?'

'Not really. I suppose I'm going to look like Daddy when I'm older, but he didn't talk to me about it yet.'

George cleared his throat.

'I guess I'm in loco parentis for the time being, so if you'd like me to explain…'

'Yes, please, if you're not embarrassed.'

'I am a bit, but I've done this before with Ben. Hold on to your hat, it's quite strange the first time you hear it.'

'I have heard some versions from other boys, so I'm not worried, just confused.'

George laughed.

'I can imagine,' he said.

Chapter 16 – Two Mothers, May 1970

Bea nearly missed the soft knock on the back door as she bashed the stewing steak with a tenderiser, hitting the meat with resentful venom as she tried to rationalise the events of the last few weeks. Michael's departure had ripped the family apart. No amount of rationalisation about him being happier in England could make the chasm narrow. Her lips set into a tight line as she tried not to think of Michael so far away.

She raised her head to brush the stray hairs away from her face and picked up the faint sound of someone knocking. A faint apologetic knock, as if they didn't want anyone to hear it and ask them in. *Maeve, who else?*

'Come in,' she said.

Maeve O'Connor pushed the door open and hovered in the entrance as if unsure of her welcome.

'It's me,' she said. 'Am I disturbing you?'

Bea smiled.

'No, but you saved the meat from being pulverised into mince. Come in and sit down. I'll put on the kettle.'

'I'm so sorry about Michael,' said Maeve. 'Sean's racked with guilt. He keeps saying it's his fault Michael has gone away. I can't get him to tell me anything.'

'I'm not sure I can explain,' said Bea. 'It's a delicate matter. Political. I don't understand it myself.'

'Look, I know we're not close friends, but we could be. Michael saved Sean's life and I'm forever indebted to you for that, but if I don't find out what happened, I can't help Sean.'

The kettle whistled on the Aga. Bea scalded the teapot with some boiling water before adding two heaped teaspoons of black tea into it. She picked up the kettle and poured it on top of the tea before giving it a good stir and putting the lid on. Maeve pulled at the loose threads hanging from her dress hem, unwilling to disturb the ritual.

Bea put the teapot, milk, sugar and two mugs on the table and sat down facing Maeve. She poured out two cups and offered the milk and sugar to Maeve, who spooned in two large teaspoons of sugar and added a dollop of milk.

'Father Eamonn thrashed Michael because Sean told him Michael lied about Irish Independence,' said Bea.

Maeve, who was taking a cautious sip of the scalding liquid, spluttered into her cup. She lowered it, furrowing her brow.

'What? Is that all? Not the thrashing, I mean, the reason.'

'A row broke out in the playground when Michael claimed Ireland became Independent in nineteen-twenty-two and not nineteen-sixteen,' said Bea.

'That makes sense. Liam has filled Sean's head with Republican nonsense and Sean won't tolerate any deviation from his heroic stories, even by Michael. They're blood brothers, you know.'

'Blood brothers? Oh, the cut on his thumb,' said Bea, her mystified expression dissolving. 'Liz said they were playing with a penknife.'

'Anyway, Father Eamonn had been looking for an excuse to punish Michael, and Sean gave it to him,' said Maeve.

Bea's hand flew to her mouth.

'The bastard,' she said. 'That priest is a sadist.'

She sipped her tea, rubbing her forehead.

'So, Sean thinks Michael is a traitor and vice versa. I'm embarrassed to say I don't know enough about Irish history to understand why this is so important, but Michael told us Father Eamonn has been bullying him and calling him names all year, so we took him out of the CBS. It will only get worse next year with bigger boys, and the troubles getting worse in Northern Ireland,' said Bea.

Maeve sighed.

'It's Liam's fault. He's been telling both boys all about the injustices of the past and the wonders of the IRA. He's my firstborn, and he's running wild living with my sister. She encourages him.'

'At least you kept him, if only at arm's length. What would have happened if you'd gone to St Joseph's?' said Bea.

Maeve's eyes opened wide.

'Who told you about St Joseph's?' she said.

Bea flushed.

'Old Mother Reilly just can't keep her mouth shut, can she?' said Maeve.

She snorted and sipped her tea.

'She didn't tell me anything. Just that by marrying Brian you escaped from St Joseph's. Is it an orphanage?' said Bea.

Maeve sighed. 'No. It's a mother and baby home.'

'That doesn't sound so bad.'

Maeve cackled. 'It's a Magdalene Laundry,' she said. 'They're institutions for fallen women. Getting pregnant in Ireland when you're unmarried is a mortal sin. The priests take girls from their families if they find out they are pregnant and unmarried, and put them into these places.'

She paused, staring into the distance. Bea stood up to put some more water in the teapot. Maeve shook her head as if trying to dislodge a memory.

'Families don't need priests to do it,' she said. 'Most times they do it themselves. Most women never come out again, and those that do are broken. They're used as slave labour by the nuns.'

A bluebottle flew into the kitchen, buzzing around in circles as it sought the source of the smell of carrion. Bea could hear her own heart beating as she asked the next question.

'But what happens to the babies?'

'They give them away to childless couples. There's a rumour they're selling them to America. I got lucky.' A faint smile ghosted across her face. 'If you could call marrying Brian O'Connor lucky.'

'Where's Liam's father? Is he still around?'

'He left. I haven't seen him since I found out about the pregnancy.'

'I'm not sure what to say,' said Bea. 'I'm sorry for prying but I'm sad you got a life sentence for one slight error of judgement.'

'I shouldn't have told you, but it's so nice to speak to someone who doesn't judge you. This country is infested with Catholic busybodies who are only dying to rat on you to the local priest and win their place in heaven.'

'You're safe enough in here,' said Bea, glancing around the room in jest. 'There isn't a vicar for miles.'

Maeve relaxed.

'So how did you meet Tom?' she said. 'He seems like a good man.'

Bea smiled.

'In a coffee shop. I popped in one lunchtime to have a coffee and read my book. I picked my usual table in the corner where I didn't get bothered so much, and made myself at home. After a while I got that feeling, like someone's watching you?'

Maeve nodded.

'So, I looked up and saw a tall, well-built man with sad eyes staring at me. I felt so drawn to him, I can't explain it, as if two spaceships had docked together after wandering alone for years in outer space. I'm a bit shy so I kept reading my book, but I could feel him looking. Before I could react, he had come over to my table and asked if he might join me. Normally, I'd have said no, but I couldn't speak.'

'Jesus, Mary and Joseph,' said Maeve. 'How romantic. And what did he say?'

'Like a rich jewel in an Ethiope's ear,' said Bea, hesitating.

'Beauty too rich for use, for earth too dear,' said Maeve, smiling. 'I did that book in the Inter Cert before I left school at sixteen. What happened next?'

'We just clicked. I reminded him of his friend Lee Kennedy, who had died of cancer. Mrs O'Reilly knew Lee. That's the connection with Dunbell.'

'Oh, I wondered how you found us.'

'Well, both Tom and I came from rather cold families, not nasty or violent, just lacking in affection, and we found the love that was missing in each other. After a few months, we announced our intention to get married and had a small ceremony in a registry office. Our parents were lukewarm about the whole thing, but we didn't care. That's the entire story.'

'And you lived happily ever after.'

Bea sighed.

'Well, not quite, but we are trying.'

'I heard about your troubles from Mrs O'Reilly. How devastating for you after ten years of hard work. You must have been crushed. I admire your guts in coming to live here, where you don't know anyone. It must be hard.'

Bea laughed.

'Thanks. She's the bush telegraph around here. What would we do without her?'

'She has a heart of gold. You've fallen on your feet having her as your surrogate family.'

Bea put her arm across the table and squeezed Maeve's hand.

'She's not the only one. I hope you and I can be as close as our children are.'

'That would be nice. I don't have any close friends around here. I'm sorry about Sean and Michael. It's broken his wee heart, poor little fella.'

'They'll work it out. Michael is miserable too. Perhaps Sean and Liz can be friends?'

'Give them time,' said Maeve. 'I'm looking forward to An Fheis Mhór next week. I hardly ever leave home these days. Brian's always got the car and...'

'Next week? Time flies. I'll pick you up at first light on Saturday.'

'The things we do for our children.'

Chapter 17 – An Fheis Mhór, May 1970

Bea and Maeve set out for the festival at dawn. The two girls compared dresses and chattered in the back seat while Bea and Maeve put the world to rights in the front. Bea noticed people staring at them.

'Why are they looking at us like that? I feel like I'm in a cage at the zoo,' she said.

Maeve laughed.

'It's the novelty of seeing a woman at the wheel. Few women learn to drive in Ireland. Their families won't pay for lessons when they are young, and their husbands like them to stay home doing the housework, not be gallivanting around the countryside going to dancing competitions,' said Maeve, her voice lowering in a bad imitation of her husband's.

'Will you get in trouble?' said Bea.

'I expect so,' said Maeve. 'But you only live once.'

They pulled into the outskirts of Wexford with time for a quick breakfast in a café, and to get directions to the town hall.

'It's going to be a long day,' said Bea. 'Shall we have a fry?'

Maeve avoided her eyes, and the penny dropped.

'My treat. Tom's had a profitable month in the shop.'

'Are you sure,' said Maeve. 'I wouldn't like to impose.'

'I'm the one who dragged you out of your house into the wilds of Wexford. It would be my pleasure.'

'Can I have beans, Mammy?' said Nuala.

'Not if you want to dance quietly,' said Maeve, making her giggle.

Where did the Maeve who made jokes hide when Brian came home? A wave of sadness hit Bea, but she forced out a laugh.

'It's called Irish dancing, not Irish farting,' said Isabella.

When the food arrived, Bea watched Isabella wolf down her breakfast as if she hadn't eaten all week. Isabella treated food as she lived her life, greedy for new experiences and possessions, but never slowing down to enjoy them. Desperately desired presents put aside after one day, rare visits to a restaurant going almost unnoticed in her acquisitive fever. Instead of life passing her by, Isabella was passing life by.

'Try to chew your food, darling,' said Bea. 'You don't want it reappearing on the stage.'

Isabella frowned. She rolled her eyes at Maeve.

'But I'm excited.'

'You've got hours to wait. You should pace yourself.'

The town hall's pillared entrance hinted at grandeur within, but the interior had light green paint on the walls making it look like a hospital, and the parquet floor had buckled because of water damage. Maeve and Bea found two chairs near the stage and settled down to enjoy the competition. The girls had been scheduled to dance at midday, but to Bea's annoyance, their performance had been postponed until late afternoon.

'Some local dignitary needed to get away early, and they swapped the age-groups,' said Maeve, sitting down beside her.

They watched an endless succession of girls mount the stage and dance their hearts out, only to be disappointed and to do their best to congratulate their smug colleagues without crying. The stage creaked and groaned under the stomping of feet and tap dancing of the more agile girls. Bea bought a newspaper and shared half of the pages with Maeve. Nuala and Isabella lined up at the edge of the stage, waiting for their turn.

'We could have got up hours later,' said Bea.

'A day out, is a day out,' said Maeve. 'I want my full value.'

'How are the toilets?' said Bea.

'Bedlam, but there's still toilet paper if you go now.'

Bea returned to her seat to watch Nuala and Isabella go through their paces with a dozen other girls on the stage. The grim expressions on the girls' faces, and the odd combination of their arms glued to their sides, and their bottom halves kicking and twirling like demented mechanical dolls, made Bea cover her mouth to stop herself laughing.

'They're all great,' she said to Maeve. 'How will the judges pick a winner? Who's that girl on the end?'

'Sheila Burns. She's a right bossy little miss in the same year as the girls at Loreto. She has had it in for them since Isabella chose to sit beside Nuala in class and not her. Her father's a politician, Fianna Fail I think.'

'Girls can be quite competitive,' said Bea.

The judges formed a huddle to discuss their scoring, cackling like chickens and prodding their fingers at their clipboards. The head judge, a tiny woman with her hair scraped back into a severe bun, held up her hand for silence.

'Can all the competitors please line up on the stage behind me?'

The girls stood in single file, still pink and sweating from effort. Isabella and Nuala stood side by side, holding hands. Bea waved at her daughter and mouthed well done at her. In her head, she prepared platitudes to soothe the wounded pride she expected if Isabella did not win. *Mrs Talbot had predicted victory, but you never knew.*

The head judge shuffled her papers and balanced her reading glasses on the end of her nose. She cleared her throat.

'In third place, we have Maureen Duggan of New Ross. Come forward and get your medal.'

The child stepped out of the line, crimson in the face with effort and embarrassment. The judge hung the bronze medal around her neck. The medal sat on her tummy, which heaved in and out.

'And in second place, Fiona Hurley of Enniscorthy.'

Fiona separated herself from the line, panting with anticipation as the judge hung her medal around her neck. She kissed it and waved to the crowded hall. The tension had risen and fingers were crossed as the judge paused, enjoying the drama.

'And the winner is…'

Bea found herself on the edge of her seat, holding Maeve's hand in an iron grip.

'Isabella Green, from Kilkenny. Congratulations.'

Isabella smirked and skipped over to the judge, her blonde curls bouncing to receive her medal. A skinny woman in an expensive suit stood up at the front of the audience and approached the stage.

'Excuse me,' she said, stretching out and tapping the judge's ankle. 'You can't give that child the gold medal. It isn't right.'

Paralysed with surprise, Bea stayed rooted to the spot, but Maeve dropped her hand and reached the stage in a couple of quick steps.

'Don't start, Denise Burns,' said Maeve. 'There's no room for sour grapes here.'

'I don't understand,' said the judge. 'Is the child too old for this category?'

'She's too English,' said Mrs Burns.

Bea had finally moved nearer the stage, and the nasty comment took her aback. Isabella's face turned white with shock as she hovered behind the judge.

'But I'm the best,' she whispered.

'Is there any rule that says you have to be Irish to win?' said Maeve. 'This protest is a disgrace. You're upsetting the child.'

'And what about my child? You can't give the medal to a foreigner.'

The judge drew herself up to her full height, turned on her heel, and planted the medal around Isabella's neck, before turning back to hiss at Denise Burns.

'It's a dancing competition. She won fair and square, and I don't care if she's from Mars.'

Isabella's smile had reappeared as quickly as it had faded, and Nuala gave her a big hug. Bea held out her arms for Isabella to run into.

'Well done, darling, I'm proud of you.'

She gave Maeve a grateful smile over Isabella's shoulder.

'Let's return to that café and have some chips and ice cream to celebrate before we drive home again. Tom won't mind if we spend all his money on a good cause.'

Bea drove home into a night illuminated by an intermittent moon which hid behind small clouds driven across the sky by a stiff breeze. They could also see Venus shining bright and barren under her cloak of vapours like an aging childless hippy. Beside her, Maeve tapped her feet and sang along to the Beatles on the radio.

'Aren't they only great?' she said. 'I love that John Lennon. I'm sure he's Irish.'

A rebel without a cause, thought Bea, but she smiled.

'Are you all right back there?' she said, but Isabella and Nuala had conked out either side of the massive trophy with green ribbons dangling from the handles.

'I thought they weren't going to give it to her,' said Bea. 'It would have been so mean. She's practised every God given minute for months. Anyway, it's a dancing competition. What's nationality got to do with it anyway?'

'I'm sure you're right,' said Maeve.

'You've no idea how much I appreciate you sticking up for Isabella,' said Bea. 'I'm grateful to have such a good friend.'

They continued on in silence, only broken by the screech of an owl that ghosted across the road, its wingtips almost touching the windscreen. Then, the full moon popped out from behind a cloud, lighting up the road into New Ross and bringing a roadblock into sharp relief. Behind it, two men stood guard dressed in black, their faces hidden by balaclavas.

'Oh, what's this now?' said Bea. 'Why would the police have a road block here?'

'Maybe they are looking for drunks?' said Maeve.

'Why are they wearing balaclavas then?'

The wind blew the smoke from the men's cigarettes along the road, scattering the clouds of midges hovering over its glistening surface. They approached the car and one of them did a strange double take, grabbing the other man by the arm and whispering in his ear.

'Isn't that—?' said Bea.

'Oh God,' said Maeve.

The two men withdrew again and had an animated conversation out of earshot. Nuala woke up and rubbed her eyes.

'Why have we stopped? Are we nearly home?'

She peered through the windscreen.

'Liam?' she said, shaking Maeve's arm. 'Mammy, that's Liam.'

'Shush, you're dreaming. Go back to sleep.'

'But Mammy—'

'I mean it.'

Nuala sat back again, pouting.

'What do they want?' said Bea.

'I don't know,' said Maeve. 'Don't worry, they won't hurt us.'

The older man came forward again and lifted the barrier. He beckoned the car forward and Bea wound down the window.

'Is there some sort of problem?' she said.

'No bother, madam, we're just doing a customs spot check for smugglers. Carry on.'

Bea edged through the gap. Nuala yelled 'Goodbye Liam' as they passed through.

'No supper for you, my girl,' said Maeve.

Chapter 18 – Reconciliations, July 1970

Liz stood at the door of Michael's room, staring at the pristine bed, covered in a thin wool blanket, pushed up against the wall to make the room seem larger. Michael's absence made the small room seem cavernous. She wondered how a quiet boy like him could fill so much space with his mere presence.

Her heart ached with missing him, as if part of her had been amputated. She could picture his soulful brown eyes with their flecks of grey under his floppy brown fringe. Tom did not "want him to look like a beatnik" and had forced him to cut it before he left for school, despite Michael's protests. *How was Michael coping at Whittingham? Were the larger boys bullying him?* She tried to read his thoughts, but he remained distant, hidden across the Irish sea.

Bea hurried past her with a pile of sheets and towels bound for the airing cupboard, still warm from the drying rack in front of the Aga. She opened the door and shoved them into its hot interior without stopping to wrap a towel around the copper boiler to insulate the precious hot water.

'The only warm place in the house,' she muttered to herself, shutting the door.

She came back up the corridor and leaned over her daughter, crossing her arms over her thin chest. She didn't have to lean far. Liz had sprouted several inches over the summer, and her budding breasts now pushed against her tight tank top.

'Are you okay, darling?' said Bea.

'How would I be okay?' said Liz. 'My only friend has gone back to England and abandoned me to the nuns and stupid Irish dancing. Why can't I go back too? I hate it here.'

Bea turned Liz around to face her.

'I'm sorry. I know it's hard, but we couldn't ask George to pay two school fees. We had to rescue Michael from the CBS. You saw his back. He wouldn't have survived the senior school.'

'And I will? Have you any idea what the nuns are like? They talk about the Virgin Mary all bloody day. I don't even believe in God.'

'Don't be dramatic. And don't say bloody. It's not ladylike.'

'Well, that's good because I hate being a girl. It's pointless. I can't do anything I want to.'

Bea sighed.

'It's not that bad, darling. I have everything I ever wanted right here.'

'You're worse than they are. When I grow up, I don't want to clean and cook all day. I want a proper job.'

The look of disappointment and hurt on Bea's face told Liz she had gone too far.

'I'm sorry, Mummy. I didn't mean to insult you. Times are changing, and Ireland is being left behind. I don't want to stay here and miss out.'

Bea sighed and stroked Liz's rebellious black curls.

'That's okay, darling. Michael has escaped to England and Isabella has morphed into an Irish colleen. I know you feel left out. Not everyone wants to get married straight out of school, or ever. But if you want to triumph in this modern world, you must compete at a high level. Women will find it difficult to get established in a man's world without the tools to succeed.'

'What tools?'

'You must be twice as qualified as a man if you want to get noticed and overcome prejudices and preconceptions. Education is the best escape tunnel. Your father is right. You can achieve anything you want, but no one is going to help you. Why don't you get your head down and study like mad? Your future is in your hands, no one else's.'

'But what about the nuns? Mother Rosalie hates me.'

'The exam results from Loreto are fantastic. Even if you don't like the teachers, their results speak for themselves. Ignore her and find your own way to succeed.'

At first, Liz found Bea's advice annoying. *Easy for her to say.* But Bea had planted a seed. The voice in her head became louder, urging her to grab the lifeline and haul herself out of the doldrums. She went back to school with a new resolve and to her surprise discovered a steel streak and single-minded determination lurked in her hormone-befuddled brain. Mother Rosalie must have noticed the change in attitude, but she kept pushing Liz anyway, picking up every fault, real or imagined. This had the effect of spurring Liz on and at the end of term, Liz came top of the class in everything except Gaelic and Catechism.

'Miracles are in short supply,' said Mother Rosalie, with grudging respect. 'But this is close.'

Liz took a deep satisfaction from her progress towards the top of the class. It didn't increase her popularity much as some girls took to calling her swot and teacher's pet. She found it hard to plough on alone, and she lived for Michael's letters. Not that they were eloquent, consisting of snippets about the weather and sport, and inquiries about health. She made a crude calendar of the summer term and crossed off the days remaining until Michael's return to Ireland.

An unspoken truce came into being between the two families. Sean visited the Greens' house to inquire about Michael, and he and Liam took Blue for long walks. Liam enjoyed taking her into the local pine forest, a copse on the slope at the foot of the local mountain, too small for a name but responsible for the constant cloud cover over Dunbell. He ignored Sean's entreaties and would let no one accompany him, except for Blue.

To everyone's surprise, Liam had become a frequent visitor to the Green household. His discussions with Tom Green about the politics of the Troubles and the latest atrocities were often heated as each fought to convince the other of his point of view. Liam did not bother with other members of the household, but despite his remoteness, Liz looked forward to his visits to the house. Liam's slim frame had filled out as he reached adulthood, and his narrow face with its sad green eyes appealed to her romantic core. His presence made her blush and her dreams were full of confusing chasing and catching scenarios.

Bea noticed how Liam reduced Liz to a stammering wreck, but she didn't comment to her husband. Tom could be over-protective of his girls and schoolgirl crushes were harmless. Anyway, Liam did not seem to register her presence, galling for Liz, who always brushed her hair before coming down to the kitchen to moon over him, but reassuring for her mother.

'Why do you think he comes here?' said Bea.

'Oh, I don't know. Perhaps he needs a father figure.'

'But he hates the English.'

'No, he doesn't, he's just miserable, and he needs someone to blame.'

'Just be careful he doesn't blame you.'

**

After what seemed an eternity, Michael returned home at the end of the school year. He had travelled by ferry with a friend of the family who gave him a lift to the train station. Tom shut the shop early and waited outside the station for the train to arrive. It had only been ten weeks, but he scarcely recognised the confident boy who stepped from the train looking around the platform for his family.

Michael waved at Tom and came over to him with eager steps, but stopped short of hugging him, appearing unsure. Tom did not notice, or ignored, his reticence. He swept his son off his feet in a warm hug. Michael stiffened, but then relaxed.

'Did you have a pleasant trip?' said Tom, releasing him.

'Yes, thank you,' said Michael.

His accent had changed again to a public-school one, which rang out in the station car park. People turned to stare at them, making Tom shuffle his feet.

'Come on then,' he said. 'I won't ask you about George and school and so on. Everyone is waiting at home, and you can tell us all together.'

Michael smiled.

'There is someone who refused to wait though,' said Tom, opening the car door.

Blue leaped out, wagging her tail, and barking in excitement. She jumped up, putting her paws against

Michael's chest, knocking him down as she tried to lick his face.

'Get off, you great big silly,' said Michael, but his voice broke. He buried his face in her neck, scratching her ears and grabbing her massive chest closer to him. Tom stood back, respecting their reunion until Michael could stagger to his feet.

'Let's go home then,' he said. 'By the way, how do you feel about seeing Sean? He hasn't been the same since you left, you know. He feels responsible for what happened.'

'That's because he is.'

Michael looked out of the window, avoiding his father's scrutiny. Tom pulled out of the station and started for home down the narrow roads and boreens to Dunbell farm. The leaf canopy almost blocked out the sun, and the car drove in and out of shadow, making it hard to see oncoming traffic. Blue put her head over the back of Michael's seat and rested her chin on his shoulder. The smell of boiled lamb rose from her whiskery mouth and he wrinkled his nose in disgust.

'They should invent dog toothpaste,' he said.

'Eau de Chien. It's a doggone exclusive,' said Tom.

'Well, I wish she wouldn't share it with me,' said Michael, but he reached up a hand and caressed Blue's head. 'She's looking great.'

'She's been well cared for. Sean and Liam have walked her most days.'

'Liam?'

'Yes, he pops in often. I guess he doesn't have anywhere else to go.'

The car drew up to the farmhouses at Dunbell. Michael peered out of the window and noticed Sean loitering in the farmyard, pretending to talk to Mickey. He got out of the car, intending to ignore him. Liz and

Isabella flew out of the house and hugged Michael before he could protest. Tom noticed Sean too.

'Okay, everyone back inside and help Mummy get the tea ready,' he said.

'But it's so ready the cake's going stale,' said Liz.

Tom flicked his head towards Sean, and Liz got the hint. She grabbed Isabella's arm and dragged her to the house. Tom picked up Michael's bag.

'I think someone's waiting for you,' he said.

Michael sat on the wall beside the cattle trough, unwilling to make the first move. Blue had no such qualms. She bounded over to Sean and back to Michael and stood between them, refusing to take sides. Sean used her as an excuse to move closer and he gave her a vigorous rub.

'Who's my best girl?' he said.

'So you still don't have a girlfriend,' said Michael, jumping off the wall and approaching them. 'That figures.'

Sean raised his eyebrows.

'That's rich coming from you. Where did you get that posh accent?'

Michael grinned.

'It's better than sounding like a culchie,' he said, flashing a beseeching glance at Sean. 'Did you miss me?'

Sean gulped and tears swam in his eyes.

'I'm so sorry,' he said, his head on his chest.

Michael lurched forward.

'Christ, eejit, don't cry. You'll have me at it too.'

The boys had an awkward hug with Blue squashed between them. Sean wiped his nose on his sleeve, refusing the cotton handkerchief offered by Michael.

'Yuck. It's used.'

'Come in for tea. Knowing my mother, there'll be enough to feed the five thousand,' said Michael.

'You think I came here to see you?' said Sean. 'Ouch my arm, there's no need for violence.'

'That's what you think.'

Chapter 19 – The Pact, August 1970

The six children congregated in the hay barn. The Greens, breathless after their dash from Dunbell, held torches which played on the bales stacked around them, throwing sinister shadows.

'What's it about?' said Sean. 'This summit. Shouldn't we have met in the kitchen?'

'And have the adults interfering? No way,' said Liz. 'It's too important.'

'What could you discuss that would concern me?' said Liam.

'Don't be rude,' said Liz. 'You can leave now if you like. No one's stopping you.'

Liam raised an eyebrow. He pulled out a packet of cigarettes and lit one, throwing the match on the floor. Isabella stamped on it, muttering.

Sean sat on one bale, joined by Michael. Isabella and Nuala stood, restless, beside them.

'It's this Irish thing,' said Liz.

'Irish thing?' said Liam. 'That's rich.'

'Shut up,' said Sean. 'Let her speak.'

'It's the Troubles,' said Liz. 'People are upset with the English, with us. We don't understand everything, but we're your friends and that won't change.'

She paused, picking up a piece of straw and knotting it.

'What I mean is, Nuala and Mrs O' Connor stuck up for Isabella at the dancing competition, even though they're not English. And Michael saved Sean from the slurry pit—'

'That was me,' said Liam. 'They would have both died without me.'

'Exactly, and Mrs O Reilly has been kind to our parents. She helped Daddy set up his new shop.'

'And your mother is my mother's best friend,' said Nuala. 'She never had a friend before.'

'No, she isn't,' said Liam.

'Actually, she is,' said Isabella. 'They talk all the time, and drink tea and laugh together.'

'And Isabella is my best friend,' said Nuala, reaching out to hold Isabella's hand.

'And Michael is mine,' said Sean. 'Even if he has a poncy accent.'

Michael blushed and punched him in the shoulder. Liam gave Sean a dirty look, which he ignored. Liz held up her hand for silence.

'So, I thought we should make a pact,' she said.

'A pact?' said Liam. 'With you?'

'We're blood brothers, don't forget,' said Liz. 'That's a sacred bond.'

'Broken by Michael,' retorted Liam, scowling.

'Not on purpose,' said Michael. 'I didn't understand how important nineteen-sixteen is, but now I do. And it's not like I didn't pay the price for it.'

He lifted his shirt and Isabella illuminated the thin white scar across the rib cage.

'We forgave each other,' said Sean. 'It's in the past.'

'What kind of pact should we make?' said Michael.

'I thought we should stand in a circle and hold hands, one Green, then one O'Connor like a necklace. Then make a promise to each other, to always stay friends, and never let the Troubles come between us,' said Liz.

'You must be codding,' said Liam. 'Make a pact with English bastards? Never.'

'Please, Liam. These are our friends. We don't have many. Mammy didn't have one, 'til Bea came along. Do it for me,' said Sean.

Liam took a deep drag on his cigarette. He rolled his eyes to heaven.

'Saints preserve us from the soft-hearted and soft-headed,' he said. 'On one condition.'

'And what's that?' said Sean.

'You swear an oath, never to tell anyone about the pact. If the Lads ever discovered, I'd be a goner.'

He brought his forefinger up to his temple and made a clicking sound with his tongue.

'Okay,' said Liz. 'Everyone, get into a circle and hold hands. Remember Greens, you should be holding hands on both sides with an O'Connor and vice versa.'

The children organised themselves into a circle. Liam made sure he got to stand beside Liz, who tried not to tremble at his closeness, but smelling the mixture of sweat and cigarettes on his skin made her dizzy. The callouses on Liam's hand felt rough against Liz's soft palms. Then he scratched her palm with his middle finger. She gasped, and he smirked.

'Please repeat after me,' she said, recovering her poise. 'We swear to defend and support each other, whatever happens, and never to let the Troubles come between us.'

The incantation echoed around the barn as the children repeated it.

'Now, spit,' said Sean. 'That's what the travellers do to seal a deal.'

'Eu, what if I don't have any spit?' said Isabella.

'Just do your best,' said Liz.

Giggling, Isabella ejected a small gob which landed on Sean's shoe.

'For feck's sake,' said Liam. 'Can I go now? I've more important things to do.'

'What's more important than friendship?' said Isabella.

'Don't mind him,' said Nuala. 'He hates everyone and everything.'

Liam turned to go, but first he pressed something into Liz's palm.

'For your aching heart,' he said, and exited into the black night.

Liz opened her fist with care, her excitement extreme, to find a Band-Aid lying there, soiled, and curled up in a ball.

'What did he give you?' said Michael.

'Nothing. He's not the giving type.'

'Will he keep to the pact?'

'I doubt it, but at least we tried.'

The Greens headed for the iron gate out onto the road, torch beams waking startled sparrows in the hedgerows. Behind them, Sean appeared. He tugged Liz by the arm.

'Can I talk to you, please?' he said.

'Sure,' said Liz. 'But make it quick, we said we'd only be five minutes.'

'Alone,' said Sean, as Michael hovered.

Michael handed Liz his torch and followed Isabella, looking over his shoulder at the pair huddled at the gate.

'What's this about?' said Liz.

'It's a bit embarrassing,' said Sean. 'Perhaps another day.'

'No, tell me now.'

'Um, I'm behind at school, especially at maths, and the priests have it in for me. My Mammy told me you are top of your class.'

'Second,' said Liz. 'So?'

'I thought perhaps, well, you know.'

Liz sighed.

'Spit it out, Sean.'

'Can you help me with my studies, please? I don't want to end up like my Da. He didn't finish school and he can't get a job. I want to be better than him. It's the drinking too, I—'

He choked up, and Liz couldn't look at him. His desperation sounded like hers. *Maybe they could both escape their destinies. Hadn't they just sworn to support each other no matter what?*

'Did the pact mean nothing to you?' she said. 'You're a pain in the arse, but if you promise to study hard and stop messing, I'll help you.'

Sean sniffed.

'You will? Oh.' He hesitated. 'You won't regret it.'

'I'm sure I will, but anyway, I've got to go now.'

Before she could stop him, Sean kissed her on the cheek.

'Thanks,' he said. 'You've saved my life. No one believes in me, but I've got plans. I'll show them all.'

And he ran back into his house before she could react. Stunned, Liz made her way back to the farmhouse.

'Ah, there you are, sweetheart. I was about to send out a search party,' said Tom. 'Is everything okay?'

'I think so,' said Liz. 'I'm a little confused.'

After she had gone, Tom turned to Bea.

'What were they plotting over there? Liz looked shell-shocked.'

'I don't know. At least they are all friends again.'

'But for how long?' said Tom.

Chapter 20 – Whittingham, October 1970

The long driveway up to Whittingham public school gave Michael butterflies despite the spring in his step after his summer holidays. His adored older sister had grown into a young woman, which he found hard to accept, but he was no longer alienated from his blood brother, Sean, a huge plus. A brighter future loomed after the trauma of the past year.

'Would you prefer to board weekly?' said George. 'You could come home for weekends and take refuge at the cottage until you find your feet.'

'I'd like to try full-time boarding at first. I don't want to miss out on the extra sport and larking about with the boys in my class. That might label me as different,' said Michael. 'Dennis will be there, so I'm not starting from scratch.'

The Senior school had a similar daily routine to the Junior School, so he found it easy to adapt. Every day started with a service of hymns and prayers, followed by announcements. The sound of five hundred boys booming out 'Jerusalem' made Michael's hair stand on end, and, even though he had little interest in his religion, he revelled in the familiar drone of the incantations and blessings. He would have liked to sing in the choir, but his voice had broken and he could not control his pitch any more.

His mornings were composed of four classes, split by a fifteen-minute break. Typical boarding school food was served for lunch in the refectory: over-stewed vegetables, gristly meat, and potatoes, and a dessert of stewed apples, rhubarb crumble or Eve's pudding accompanied by inevitable vats of custard. If Michael couldn't face the offering, he bought something in the tuckshop, a fixture in every boarding school, selling sweets and crisps and bottles of pop to the boys. George gave him pocket money to buy treats and other essentials like toiletries.

Three more classes completed the afternoon's education, except for Wednesdays on which they did compulsory physical exercise. More sport filled the gap to supper, after which they required all pupils to complete their prep. The younger boys filed back into their classrooms, and the top two years chose where they preferred to study. Michael's term at junior school had levelled him up in most subjects, but he still found the amount of work hard going.

More lessons filled Saturday mornings, and they devoted the afternoons to sport. To Michael's relief, all his favourite sports were on the menu and he soon found himself on the rugby and hockey teams for his age group. His enthusiasm and dedication soon made him a valued member of both teams. Dennis spent a lot of time avoiding sport by any means possible. Michael found his lack of interest disappointing but predictable. Despite Dennis's lukewarm reaction to team sports, they stuck together like limpets in the autumn term as they learned their place in the hierarchy.

'I can't believe we have to fag for the older pupils. It's like something out of Tom Brown's schooldays,' said Michael, making a pot of tea for the senior common room.

'Most of the prefects are good eggs. Making beds and waking people up in the morning is a pain, but it's not onerous, is it?' said Dennis.

'At least there aren't too many sadists in the top form. Tarzan isn't exactly vigilant.'

'It's not surprising. He's retiring as housemaster after twenty-five years at the end of the year. He can't be bothered with controlling the older boys most of the time. Anyway, fagging is traditional.'

'Traditions are a mixed blessing,' said Michael.

'Everyone goes through it. Just remember, you'll get your revenge in your final year,' said Dennis.

'If I'm a prefect.'

'If you are? You're nailed on. You work hard and keep your nose clean. And you don't even smoke.'

'I can't afford to smoke,' said Michael. 'George doesn't give me enough pocket money. I can barely afford a Mars Bar at the tuck shop.'

'I'll bring more tuck next time. My mother likes to feed me up. She can't bear to think of me starving.'

Michael tried not to laugh. Dennis had got even fatter this term, and his podgy tummy spread over his knees as he struggled to buff a pair of Cadet Corps boots to a military shine.

'I don't mind the other stuff, but I don't see why we have to do this,' he said. 'It's not on the list.'

'There's no point sneaking to Tarzan. He has no interest. And that Hugo Longford is a nasty piece of work,' said Michael. 'He kicked me yesterday for no reason.'

'He's a sadist,' said Dennis. 'Best to keep on his good side, if you ask me.'

But it was easier said than done. From assembly in the morning until prep at night, Hugo's eyes bored into him. Michael could find no explanation for this apparent obsession. Some boys had strange interests in other boys that he didn't understand. He caught Smedley Major staring at him in the shower once. The intensity of his gaze had caused Michael to blush a deep beetroot red.

'Everyone knows that Smedley Major is a poufter, I think Smedley Minor may be batting for the other side as well,' said Dennis, by way of explanation.

It didn't enlighten him, but Michael avoided undressing in Smedley Major's vicinity from then on. Rumours of physical relationships did the rounds on occasion, but for Michael, poufters and their habits remained a mystery.

Nobody called Hugo Longford a poufter unless they wanted a bloody nose. He revelled in his reputation as a complete bastard, and it didn't take much to set him off as Michael soon found out. One day as he inched his way through the senior common room with a pot of fresh-brewed tea, Hugo Longford crooked his finger at him. Michael placed the tray on the table, alert for trouble. The odour of smelly feet made his stomach heave as Hugo and his companions warmed their sweaty feet near to the fire.

'Come here, boy,' said Hugo.

Michael shuffled closer to the armchair in which he sat, checking over his shoulder for the nearest exit.

'Can I get you something else?' said Michael.

'Where are you from?' said Hugo.

'From? I'm from England.'

'No, you're not. I can hear an accent.'

'I was born in Surrey.'

'Where do you live now?'

Michael prevaricated, sensing a trap.

'I'm living with a friend of the family, in Brookham.'

'And where are your parents?'

Later, on reflection, Michael realised that he should have said 'dead' and won the day, and the sympathy of the older boys. But he didn't have the guile of Dennis.

'They live in Ireland,' he said.

'The North?'

'No, the south. Kilkenny.'

Hugo stood up. He poked his face into Michael's and grabbed him by the ear.

'Ouch, feck off,' said Michael, moving backwards.

'Ha! We've got a Paddy in our midst, chaps, a filthy Mick.'

'I'm not a Paddy,' said Michael 'I was born in England and my parents are English.'

'Prove it.'

'Yeah, prove it,' said another boy.

One of the other boys started chanting 'Paddy, Paddy, Paddy' and the rest joined in. Michael felt his blood boil with rage and shame, and he turned to leave, but Hugo grabbed his arm.

'We haven't finished with you yet, Mick.'

Michael swung his fist with all his might and caught Longford flush on the nose, causing him to let go again with a shout.

'You dirty Irish bastard. How dare you punch me?'

'Don't call me Irish then.' said Michael. 'I'm not Irish. I'm English.'

All the boys were standing now, chanting 'fight, fight, fight'. Michael hyperventilated from fear as Hugo clenched his fists. Suddenly, the boys sat down again and feigned indifference.

'What's all this then?' said George Clayton, or Tarzan as they knew him, pushing his way through the melee, his breath heavy with brandy. 'Are you boys bullying a fag? That's not cricket, is it?'

'He punched me, sir,' said Hugo.

'Did he, by Jove? Stroppy little bugger, is he? Get lost, Green. I'll deal with this.'

Wheezing with relief, Michael ran out of the room and took refuge in his dormitory, shaking with shock. To his surprise, George Clayton walked in a few minutes later and sat on the bed opposite him.

'I'm not one to take much interest in the individual boys in my house,' he said. 'But I've made an exception in your case.'

'Why?' said Michael.

'Because I don't like jingoistic bully boys much. And I don't need any hassle in my last year. So, are you Irish or not?'

Michael shrugged.

'It depends who you ask,' he said.

'I'm asking you.'

Michael took a deep breath.

'Well, if you asked the priest in Ireland who beat me senseless, I'm a stupid English Protestant. And if you ask Hugo Longford and his pals, I'm a filthy Mick. I can't win. It's like a horrible nightmare. I came to school here to escape the Christian Brothers bullying me because I'm English, and now I'm being bullied by English thugs who think I'm Irish just because I live there. I hate Ireland, and I hate my parents for dragging me there. I never asked for this. I'm...'

Michael's words stuck in his throat and he couldn't go on. He stared at the floor in misery, unable to look his housemaster in the eye.

'Ah, now that is a conundrum.'

Clayton sighed and a cloud of brandy fumes enveloped Michael.

'I don't expect you to sympathise,' he said. 'But Hugo Longford's older brother is a lieutenant in the army. He got posted to Northern Ireland, to Belfast. Hugo doesn't like to show it, but he's worried sick. I imagine you're an easy target for his frustrations.'

Michael looked up.

'Belfast? Oh, I see.' He rubbed his forehead.

'I can't do much, but I'll make sure you don't fag for him any more. And I'll have a word with him. Just stay out of his way and keep your head down. You should join the Combined Cadet Force too. Being a member of the armed forces should deflect most of the criticism, and don't forget, there are still a few Irish regiments full of ferocious fighting men in the British Army.'

'But I'm not Irish.'

'I know, but you live there, and the boys need someone to blame for the IRA bombs. Any flaw gets punished around here. Why don't you play up to it? If anyone calls you Irish, say 'Just because I live in a stable doesn't make me a donkey'. That's Wellington, you know.'

'Okay, I'll try.'

'I recommend the army cadets. It's more popular. Don't give up. Hugo leaves at the end of this year, and he'll have his head down studying for A-levels. There will soon be a new intake of first years for the prefects to martyr.'

Clayton stood up, unsteady on his feet, and steadied himself on the bedpost.

'Thank you, sir,' said Michael.

'No need, part of the service,' said Clayton, without turning around.

Chapter 21 – Darlene – October 1971

Liz hurried down the corridor to the classroom, balling her hands up into fists as she fought her panic. *How will I weather another year under Sister Rosalie?* Her anxiety rose as she pictured the pinched face inches from hers, judging her, always finding her wanting. She hated this school and all it represented, losing her friends, the hateful obsession with all things religious, the stupid rules. She clenched her teeth, hoping for a headache, an easy out these days when she couldn't cope any more.

Her difficulties in bridging the gap with Michael had increased her feeling of loneliness and desperation. He had been odd when he came back on holiday, unwilling to share confidences like before. His public-school accent had become pronounced, and it didn't soften when he came home. He also had a military haircut which made him appear much older and increased the already startling effect of his deep voice.

He spent almost all his time at home with Sean, walking Blue and fixing up some second-hand bicycles a client had given Tom Green.

'Why did you give Sean a bicycle? What about me?' said Liz.

'Because Sean and Michael want to go exploring together and Sean's parents can't afford one. Anyway, you'll have Michael's bike all year while he's at school,' said Tom.

'I don't want a boy's bike,' said Liz.

'Fair enough. It's up to you.'

Her gripe at being left out again now extended to Sean too. Since his request for help, he did his homework on the kitchen table in the Greens' house, leaning on her for advice with it. Despite their differences, they shared a burning ambition and a similar sense of humour which evened out their quarrels. She even enjoyed his visits. Not counting Michael, Liz had never been friends with a boy before. Sean's obsession with football and lists confounded her almost as much as her mooning over the Osmonds annoyed him.

'But look at their teeth,' he said. 'They've got to be false. Nobody has real teeth like that.'

'You're just jealous,' she said. 'If you brushed yours more often, they might be white too.'

This stinging rebuke had the effect of making Sean brush his teeth with religious zeal, and Liz could often smell toothpaste on his breath when he came over after his supper to do homework. It surprised her more than she liked to admit. Her crush on Liam had only got worse, but after the humiliation of the Band-Aid she never talked to him again, and he ignored her. Boys were stupid.

A powerful Cockney accent penetrated the silence of the school passageway. Liz froze. Her heart rate increased. *Am I imagining things?* She slipped through the half-open door of the classroom with goose pimples on her arms. Her classmates were reacquainting themselves with squeaks of recognition and guffaws of laughter. Liz barely acknowledged their waves and smiles. Her gaze fixed on a plump, blonde girl standing in the centre of the room like a Lindor truffle in a box of Smarties. Her expensive school bag hung from her shoulder, advertising its newness. She had trapped her bottom lip between her teeth to stop it wobbling.

Liz tapped her on the shoulder, and the girl jumped, turning a pair of bright blue eyes, wide in fright, to focus on her. Liz smiled.

'Hello, I'm Liz,' she said.

The blonde girl's eyes opened even wider. She grabbed Liz's arm with her stubby fingers.

'Am I glad to see you,' she said, her loud cockney voice ringing. 'I thought they only had Paddies in this convent.'

Liz gave a startled glance around the room. Yes, everyone had heard. Not a brilliant start. She leaned closer and whispered.

'Um, best not to call them that.'

'Oh, that's alright, ducks. I'm a cockney barrow girl. Everyone's better than me. My name's Darlene, Darlene Edmunds. We moved here from the East End, in London.'

She fingered a chunky gold necklace as she examined Liz, who became acutely aware of her ill-fitting school uniform and baggy sweater. Darlene noticed her eyeing the necklace.

'It's Chanel,' she said. 'Do you like it? My Dad bought it for me.'

'It's gorgeous,' said Liz, who found it vulgar beyond belief, but knew what the correct answer should be. 'You ought to hide it under your jumper, though. The nuns won't let us wear jewellery.'

Darlene laughed, a rich fruity sound, but her eyes narrowed.

'Nobody tells an Edmunds what to do,' she said. 'So, are we going to be pals?'

Liz felt like a rabbit in the headlights under her laser-like scrutiny. Her gut told her Darlene represented trouble of a type yet undefined, but she had longed for a friend with whom she could reminisce about England, and talk disrespectfully about nuns and religion. If God existed, she blamed him for sending Darlene to her just when her loneliness had become unbearable. Karma could not be avoided according to Mrs O'Reilly, who had a side-line in every belief, creed, and superstition, as well as being a less than enthusiastic Catholic.

'Of course,' said Liz. 'Would you like to sit beside me this year?'

'Well, I'm not sitting beside a Paddy,' said Darlene.

Liz shrugged at the sea of resentful faces glaring at Darlene. Her bridges burned and crashed into the sea as she experienced a shudder of anticipation and ignored her misgivings. *We're fourteen years old. How much trouble can we get into?*

The first Saturday of term, Darlene didn't turn up for Irish dancing classes like everyone else.

'Maybe nobody told her about them,' Liz said to her mother.

When Darlene arrived for school the next Monday, Liz was waiting for her outside the gates. A large silver Jaguar ghosted down the street, driven by a burly man with a receding hairline, his black hair slicked back with Brylcreem. He stopped the car and walked around to Darlene's door to let her out of the car, wearing a camel-coloured cashmere coat. Darlene hopped out in a cloud of expensive perfume and he kissed her cheek.

'All right, love?' he said to Liz. 'I heard Darlene had a mate. Hope to see you at our house this week.'

Before Liz could answer, he waved as he drove off, leaving Liz and Darlene smiling at each other.

'Hi,' said Liz. 'I missed you on Saturday. Did they forget to tell you about the Irish dancing classes?'

'No, I didn't want to come.'

'I think it's compulsory. Why don't you have to dance?'

'You won't catch me up on the stage in a short skirt flashing my knickers at the world,' said Darlene. 'I've got asthma.'

'Really?'

'No, but the penguins don't know that. Anyway, my father has donated a ton for new school equipment so I doubt anyone will complain,' she said, flicking her hair back. 'When are you going stay the night at our place? My mother wants to meet you.'

The Green parents were thrilled Liz had made a friend and agreed to her staying the night as soon as she asked them for permission. Bill Edmunds swung by the farmhouse to collect Liz and shook hands with Tom and Bea, before ushering the girls into the back of the Jaguar.

'What a relief,' said Bea. 'I thought she'd never smile again. I don't think Sean and Blue are the sort of company a teenage girl needs.'

'Did you see his motor?' said Tom, as the car drove away. 'That's the latest model Jaguar. It costs a fortune, and the import taxes would have been eye watering.'

'If he paid them,' said Bea.

'Why do you say that?'

'Oh, I don't know. There's something dodgy about Mr Edmunds, isn't there?'

'He's a bit of a wide boy, but I think he's harmless. Too late now anyway.'

Liz stepped over the threshold of the massive new faux-Colonial carbuncle where the Edmunds lived into a new world lined in fluffy white carpets and shelves of fake books concealing stashes of illicit money and expensive whisky. The stench of cigar smoke infiltrated the room, overpowering her senses. The sitting room had gold and chrome fittings with smoked glass tables and leather chairs. Massive Dunhill lighters sat on several surfaces accompanied by chunky crystal ashtrays. In the corner, the biggest television Liz had ever seen sat framed in teak.

'Wow, what size is that?' said Liz.

'Twenty-one inches. And it's in colour,' said Darlene.

'Colour? Can I see?'

After doing their homework, the girls watched an episode of the Osmonds, and ate supper on trays, an unheard-of indulgence in the Green household. Liz sighed with pleasure.

'Donny's even more handsome in colour,' said Liz. 'Why don't Irish boys look like that?'

'English boys aren't much better,' said Darlene. 'My boyfriend is dead scruffy.'

'You have a boyfriend?' said Liz.

'Well, not any more. He's in London. How about you?'

Liz laughed.

'There are very few boys in the convent. But…' she hesitated. 'There's a boy I like. He just doesn't like me. And he's sixteen.'

'Mine was seventeen. Although you'd never guess it. I didn't tell Dad. He'd have had him shot.'

Something in her tone made Liz shiver, despite the yelp of laughter that followed.

Marion Edmunds, Darlene's mother, came in wearing a dowdy dress covered in a floral pinny. Her shy demeanour contrasted with the rest of the family. Liz helped her take the trays into the kitchen and almost tripped over a Siamese cat eating out of a golden bowl.

'She likes fillet steak best. Everyone says cats like fish but she won't eat it,' said Marion. 'I've tried salmon and plaice, but she just turns her nose up.'

Liz, who had tried none of those exotic foods, and lived on a diet of mince, stew, and game hunted from the fields by her father, struggled to keep her thoughts to herself. Marion poured some single cream into a silver dish and placed it beside the gold one.

'She's a champion, you know. Bill bought her for me.'

As they returned to the living room, Liz resisted the temptation to run her hands through the shag pile carpet.

'I think it's time you girls went up to bed, don't you?' said Marion. 'After all, it's a school night.'

She looked at her watch and then out of the front window.

'But, Mum, it's still early. Can't we stay up a little longer?' said Darlene.

The front door opened, and the sound of gruff male laughter boomed in the hall. Bill Edmunds and several other stocky men in matching coats with fat cigars strode into the living room, their cigar smoke mixed with the odour of Brut and Old Spice.

'What's all this then?' said Bill, turning to his wife. 'I thought I told you to 'ave the girls in bed by now?'

His tone grated and Liz jumped up.

'Oh, it's my fault, Mr Edmunds, I lost my purse, and it's taken ages to find.'

'All right, darlin'. Orf to bed wiv you both then.'

Darlene flashed her a grateful glance.

'We're off now, Dad. See you tomorrow.'

The girls ran upstairs and shut themselves in Darlene's room, a boudoir more suited to a brothel than a fourteen-year-old girl. They lay on the shiny, white, quilted bedcover under the canopy of the four-poster bed.

'Thanks,' said Darlene. 'Dad can be over gruff when the uncles are here.'

'The uncles?'

'Oh, lawks, they're not real uncles. They're business associates of my father.'

'Are they here on business?' said Liz.

'Oh no, I think they're cooling off. Whatever you do, don't tell anyone you saw them.'

'I won't.'

But she didn't promise. A knock on the door sent them scampering for their nightdresses.

'Go to sleep now, girls,' said Marion. 'No more talking.'

Liz lay awake for hours, buzzing with excitement and unanswered questions circling around in her head. Despite Darlene's admonishment, she would tell Sean about the uncles and swear him to secrecy. His interest in Sherlock Holmes had given him a love of mystery, and this smacked of intrigue. Things were looking up at last.

Chapter 22 – The Secret, November 1971

'What's the big secret?' said Liam, finding Liz and Sean whispering at the kitchen table.

Sean shut his notebook and put his forearm over it.

'We're investigating,' he said.

'With her?' said Liam, sneering at Liz. 'If it's important you need a man to do it. Let me see.'

'You?' said Liz, colouring. 'You're not a man, just a stupid boy who thinks he's great.'

'Please don't fight,' said Sean. 'This is a real-life mystery, Liam. Liz has discovered something amazing.'

Liam rolled his eyes. Sean had such a massive crush on Liz, it embarrassed him to watch them.

'Actually, I have,' said Liz. 'But it's a secret.'

'A secret? You two are so pathetic. You should grow up.' said Liam.

Sean bristled and blurted out.

'You don't know anything. Liz has discovered that a crime family from the East End of London is living near New Ross,' said Sean.

Liam froze. A crime family in New Ross? Holy crap.

'Have you now?' he said, leaning over Liz.

She pushed him back.

'You shouldn't have told him, Sean,' said Liz, pale. 'I promised Darlene I'd keep quiet.'

She hadn't promised, but she hadn't intended to say anything about the uncles. In her excitement, she couldn't resist the temptation to tell her parents more than she should have. Tom Green had raised an eyebrow when she described the uncles and the opulence.

'Fillet steak for a cat? I'd kill for a nice steak. Should I learn to miaow?'

'It's well for some,' said Bea.

Tom slapped his forehead.

'What an idiot,' he said. 'Bill Edmunds. Of course.'

'Of course, what, dear?' said Bea, looking around from the Aga where she was warming her hands.

'You were right about him being dodgy. He might be the brother of Steve Edmunds, the crime boss. Their gang pulled off that massive robbery in London last year.'

'I remember. They got away with almost a million pounds.'

'Didn't they shoot a policeman?' said Tom.

'No, they knocked him out,' said Bea. 'But that explains why the house is full of uncles,' said Bea.

'Darlene said they were cooling off. What does that mean?' said Liz.

Tom laughed.

'The UK police must want them. Maybe they've come here to escape the heat?'

'While everyone is excited about the robbery,' said Bea. 'I expect they'll go back when things calm down again.'

Liz's eyes were like saucers.

'Darlene's family are criminals?' said Liz.

'Hold your horses,' said Tom. 'We're only guessing. Just have fun with Darlene for now. She may not be here for long.'

'Are you sure Liz will be safe with them?' said Bea.

'Darlene's the apple of her father's eye. He's not interested in her friends. Liz won't come to any harm as long as she keeps quiet.'

'I won't tell anyone, I promise,' said Liz, but she had already told Sean, and now Liam knew too.

Liam's expression changed as his mind went into overdrive. Finally, something big to tell the Lads. They might take him seriously if this proved true.

'I'm sorry, that sounds incredible. You're a real detective, Liz.'

Liz blushed crimson as he touched her arm. Like shooting fish in a barrel.

'Please let me help you. I promise not to be mean,' said Liam, pulling up a chair. 'How did you find out?'

Liz and Sean looked at each other and nodded.

'Okay,' said Sean. 'But you can't tell anyone. This is top secret.'

Liz recounted the tale of Darlene's appearance at school, the visit to her opulent house, the sinister men with their cashmere coats and Cuban cigars. Liam listened intently, filing the information away for his meeting with Colm. He couldn't believe his luck. This might be his lucky break. The Provos had to accept him as a member after this.

Colm sat in a car full of cigarette smoke, tapping his finger on the dashboard in impatience. While he waited, he listened to a cassette of Taste blasting out a Rory Gallagher riff. The music blasted into the street as Liam let himself into the car.

'What the devil kept you? You're always late.'

'I had to walk. It's a long way,' said Liam.

'Why do we bother with you? You're useless,' said Colm.

Liam feigned embarrassment and then looked Colm straight in the eye.

'Oh? I guess you don't want me to tell you about the crime family who moved to New Ross then?'

He gripped the door handle to open it, but not before Colm seized his shoulder in a painful squeeze.

'And where do you think you're going?' he said.

'You called me useless. So, I'm going home,' said Liam.

'You're not going anywhere until you spill the beans on this family.'

'Give me a cigarette then.'

Colm scowled, but he shoved the packed along the dashboard.

'Talk,' he said.

Liam told him everything he could remember. Afterwards Colm didn't speak for a while. He turned up the music again and wound down the window to blow smoke rings. Liam sat beside him quivering with anticipation, his hand on his knee to stop himself bouncing his leg on the ball of his foot.

A minute passed. Colm drew in a deep breath and turned to face him.

'This is huge,' he said. 'You've done well, but I need you to do more.'

'Sure, anything,' said Liam.

'I want you to have a snoop around the house and draw me a layout. Also, if you can, count the adult males. If you can get their names, that would be even better.'

'But how—'

'Here we go. Use your imagination, amadan. They have a daughter your age, don't they? Well, I'm not asking you to reinvent the wheel, just use your charm.'

'I'll do my best.'

Colm gave him a shrewd glance.

'You must do better than that if you want to join a brigade.'

'A brigade?'

'Get the information we need and I guarantee it. Now get out.'

Liam jumped out of the car and floated down the road, humming a tune from the cassette that had been playing in the car. He had cadged another cigarette, and he tried to blow rings with the smoke, ending up bent double in a ditch, retching. Nothing could diminish his excitement though, not even the lack of a plan for seducing Darlene. *He should start with Liz and go from there. She would be a pushover.* He rubbed his hands together.

But Liz proved resistant to his overtures, turning her back on him when he tried to flirt with her.

'Who do you think you are, Liam O'Connor?' she said.

'I'm not an O'Connor. That alcoholic sod is not my father.'

'Who is then?' said Liz.

'My mother won't tell me.'

Liz relented.

'Oh, that must be hard,' she said. 'I'm sorry.'

'Me too, but not about that, about the plaster. I thought it would be funny. I didn't realise—'

'That I fancied you? Yes, I used to. Now, I prefer Sean. He's not a pig like you.'

'Sean? But he's younger than you, and he's an eejit.'

'And you aren't? Get out now, I'm busy.'

Liam persisted. He had stolen some money from his aunt's emergency kitty and bought her a cassette tape with music by the Osmond Family.

'It's not much use without a cassette player,' said Liz, tossing it aside and continuing her homework.

Liam couldn't understand why Liz didn't find his fresh interest in her thrilling. She had suffered from his studied indifference. He had watched her reaction with glee. She should have revelled in his awkward attempt at rapprochement. But she wouldn't budge. The curious timing of his renewed interest just after he heard about her discovery had alerted her to its fakery.

Liam didn't give up though, and his persistence gave him a shortcut. One day when he was hanging around waiting for a chance to waylay Liz again, the Edmunds's Jaguar glided up to the gate of the farm. Liam's heart jumped, and he waved, running to open the gate. Darlene looked him up and down from under her made-up eyes as they passed him. He gave her a grin and a cheeky wink. She raised an eyebrow.

Liz came running out of the house, holding her coat. She had a pair of flared jeans on and a striped tank top, Bea's idea of fashion. When she saw Liam, she glared and ignored him.

'Who's that?' said Darlene.

'Liam,' said Liz.

'You're Liz's…?'

'Friend. Well, she's friends with my little brother, Sean. They do homework together,' said Liam, raising his middle finger to Liz behind his back and leaning in through the open window.

'And where do you do yours?' said Darlene.

'I'm too busy for school. I left.'

Mr Edmunds guffawed and winked at Liam in the mirror. 'A man after my own heart,' he said. 'I left school at fifteen as soon as it was legal.'

'That's the last legal thing you did then,' said Darlene, cackling. Liz couldn't believe her ears.

'Are we going then?' she said.

'Yes, get in or we'll be late,' said Darlene. 'Do you want to come, Liam? We're going to the cinema.'

Liam smirked.

'Sure,' he said.

Darlene jumped out of the passenger door.

'Get in the front with my Dad. Us ladies will sit at the back,' she said.

Liz opened her mouth to protest, but she had nothing to say.

'Great, let's go,' she said instead.

Chapter 23 – Sex Education, May 1972

A buzz of anticipation rippled around the classroom, as one girl spotted the Mother Superior walking across the schoolyard from the cloister. Nuala elbowed Isabella, jogging her out of her daydream.

'Are you excited? The old bat is on her way,' she said.

'I don't know what the big deal is,' said Isabella.

'Sex,' said Nuala. 'Life is all about sex.'

'What's the point of getting someone who has never even had sex to tell us how it works?'

Nuala snorted. *Sometimes Isabella sounded like she had come from a different planet. Not a different country.*

'She won't be doing that.'

'What is this talk about then?'

'It's about morals and mortal sin.'

'What about the facts of life?'

'You can't get pregnant if you're not married. That's the only fact we get taught in Ireland.'

Before Isabella could comment, the Mother Superior of the convent, Sister Angela, came into the room. She glanced around at the eager faces and pursed her lips.

'Good morning, girls,' she said, interlacing her fingers around her rosary.

'Good morning, Mother Superior,' they chorused back.

'Today I'm going to talk to you about boys,' said the nun, clearing her throat. 'Well, boys and men.'

A frisson of excitement rippled through the class. Isabella rolled her eyes.

'My mother told me all about this not long after I got my period,' she said. 'The mechanics sounded revolting. And Liz has already told me some of Darlene's dirty stories. What can a nun tell me I don't already know?'

'You think Mother Superior is going to talk about the mechanics?' said Nuala. 'Don't be an eejit.'

Mother Superior drew herself up to her full height, all of five feet, and put a hand up for silence.

'First, our duty as good Catholics is to be as pure as the Virgin Mary,' she said.

Isabella tutted.

'The Virgin Mary was married,' she whispered. 'Wasn't she allowed to have sex either?'

'Shh,' said Nuala.

'Boys and men are the spawn of the devil,' said the Mother Superior. 'They have urges they can't control. You must avoid contact with them if you want to go to heaven. Now, I know that it isn't always possible to avoid boys at parties and dances and so on. You may even have to sit on a man's lap, getting a lift in a car, for instance. In that case, you will need to put a newspaper on his legs before you sit down.'

A thin girl with an earnest face put her hand up. The Mother Superior sighed.

'Well? What is it, girl?'

'Why do we need a newspaper, Mother Superior?'

The Mother Superior pursed her lips again and crossed herself.

185

'Because intercourse is a mortal sin. Isn't it obvious?'

'What's intercourse?' said the girl, missing the warning signs from her companions.

The nun's face blanched, and she swayed with shock for a second. A ripple of suppressed laughter swept through the ranks of girls. Mother Superior straightened her wimple and grabbed her rosary beads like a drowning man with a lifejacket.

'Intercourse is dirty,' she said, trembling with fury. 'Only married people can have intercourse, and only when they want a child. At all other times, they should abstain.'

'Abstain from what?' piped up the girl.

A silence which screeched followed the communal intake of breath. Nuala didn't know whether to laugh or cry. She sat on the edge of her seat, her mouth hanging open with anticipation of the answer. But the Mother Superior ignored the question.

'Just remember. Boys only want one thing. Don't let them take advantage of you. No kissing, no touching is allowed until they marry you in a church. If you let a boy touch you before then, you will go to hell.'

She stood up and swept out, shaken by the effort of talking about the hated subject. A disappointed sigh emanated from the girls, robbed of their only opportunity to learn about relationships by one girl's total ignorance.

'You silly girl, Siobhan,' said Sister Bernadette. 'You upset the Mother Superior. Say a rosary and ask for forgiveness.'

'But, Sister, I only asked her a question. I still don't know what intercourse is.'

'And you can come with me and wash your mouth out with soap for saying that word again.'

After Sister Bernadette had gone, dragging a confused Siobhan with her to the bathroom, Nuala turned to Isabella.

'See?' she said. 'Everything's a mortal sin, but nobody knows what everything is.'

'If you have sex before you are married, you'll go to Hell,' said Isabella. 'I'm glad I'm not a Catholic.'

'That's why my mother has no friends and they treat her like a leper,' said Nuala. 'Father Doherty, our parish priest, has forbidden them to speak to her because she got pregnant before she married.'

'What's the priest got to do with it?'

'Priests run this country. They can have you thrown out of the church with a word. People are terrified of them. They take unmarried girls away from their families if they get pregnant and put them in the laundries. Father Doherty tried to put my mother in one, but she escaped because she married my father.'

'But why doesn't Liam live with you?'

'My father calls him the bastard. He hates him. He made my mother give Liam away when he was born, but people still talk about her, about us. Father Doherty is always giving out to me, no matter how many rosaries I say. He says I'll end up like my mother if I don't go into a convent.'

She sniffed. Isabella put an arm around her shoulder.

'We don't care what your mother did. And you are my best friend. I wouldn't have won the dancing trophy without you. As for Father Doherty, there are enough nuns already and you're a hopeless case. By the way, if you want to know about sex, Liz's friend Darlene is an expert. We can ask her.'

They both giggled.

'I bet she's not a Catholic,' said Nuala. 'Hey, do you want to come to the hop with me tonight?'

'A dance? Where?'

'In Brannigan's Barn. It's a short walk from our houses.'

'That sounds like great craic. I must ask my parents, but I don't see why not.'

'Can you bring any drink?'

Isabella guffawed.

'We don't have drink in our house, unless you count Daddy's bottle of whisky and some old sherry for making trifles. I couldn't take either of those without causing a scandal.'

'Won't your parents let you drink?'

'I don't like whisky or sherry. Anyway, they wouldn't mind me trying some, it's the stealing they wouldn't like. I can bring a bottle of diluted Ribena?'

'For feck's sake, why are you such a goody two-shoes? I'm only nine months older than you and I drink whenever I can.'

'Who's stopping you? You can go by yourself if you don't like it.' said Isabella, but she relented. 'What time do you want me to meet you?'

'How about eight o'clock at our gate?'

'Grand.'

***

Isabella's outfit, a flowery mini skirt with a tank top, worried Bea more than the dance, until Liz asked if she could go too. Bea relaxed, but Isabella pouted.

'But Mummy, I don't want Liz spying on me.'

'I won't be spying, I promise. I just want to dance,' said Liz, twirling and pointing her finger in the air.

'I'd feel happier if Liz came too,' said Tom. 'Then you can walk home together.'

A blanket of stars held the full moon hostage as Liz and Isabella walked up the drive, gazing up at the sky.

'I still want to be an astronaut,' said Isabella. 'Perhaps I could go to see the Space Centre in Florida now Daddy's business is going well. After all, Mummy got her fridge and washing machine.'

'You're a space cadet, if that helps,' said Liz, dodging her swinging arm.

Nuala sat on the stone wall outside her house, wearing hot pants and a crop top. Liz looked her up and down, but she didn't comment. The sound of breaking crockery broke the spell spun by the quiet night. Brian O'Connor's drunken ranting followed Sean as he ducked out of the front door of the farmhouse. He approached the girls, rubbing his shoulder and wearing a sheepish grin.

'Is he drunk already?' said Nuala.

'Plastered. I think he's getting worse,' said Sean. 'I tried to stop him hitting Mammy, but he punched me.'

Isabella flashed an alarmed glance at Liz, who shook her head.

'Why don't you come to the dance with us?' said Liz. 'That should give him time to cool off.'

'I'm not much of a dancer,' said Sean. 'But if you girls don't mind.'

'It'll be fun,' said Isabella.

'As if I needed my brother supervising my fun,' said Nuala. 'You can come, but only if you dance with Liz and leave us alone.'

Sean shrugged. 'Okay,' he said.

'You didn't ask me if I want to dance with him,' said Liz, but she took his arm.

The dance took place in a large barn-like structure at the back of a bar full of middle-aged farmers in dirty corduroy trousers and flat caps, who followed the girls with hungry eyes.

'She's a fine healthy lass,' said one, gesturing at Nuala. 'Beef to the heels like a Mullingar heifer.'

'I bet she can toss a hay bale,' said another.

They sniggered into their pints of Guinness. Oblivious to their comments, Nuala and the others pushed their way through the swinging door to the dance. The walls of the barn were made of wooden planks covered with an eclectic selection of posters of popular bands of the day; Creedence Clearwater Revival, the Jackson Five and the Carpenters. A large glitter ball hanging from the ceiling reflected the illumination from spotlights surrounded by disorientated moths.

The barn walls were lined with young men and boys, leaning in various nonchalant poses, determined to appear cool to the heaving mass of girls dancing on the dirt floor. Sean hung back and seemed destined to join the other lads, but Isabella pulled him with them.

'Don't be shy,' she said. 'Girls love a boy who dances. We'll show you how.'

To everyone's surprise, including his own, Sean overcame his reluctance to dance and started enjoying himself. The other boys watched the usurper surrounded by girls, and showing off for all he was worth, and felt challenged by his presence. They moved away from the walls and plucked up courage to ask the girls for a dance. The couples joined the mass of heaving bodies under the glitter ball.

After a while Nuala found herself a stocky local boy with a foghorn voice, and Isabella danced with his shyer friend. The night slid by and the dancers grew more tactile. Just before the end of the dance, the sound track changed from 'American Woman' to 'We've only just begun' and all the couples came together for a slow dance.

Liz blushed to the roots of her hair as Sean moved towards her and held her close. The heat of his body made her reaction worse, but she couldn't refuse without embarrassing him. As they touched, a bolt of electricity shot up her spine and prickled the hairs on her neck. He had grown taller than her and her head rested on his shoulder. At first, he seemed unaware of the effect his nearness had on Liz, but then he lowered his head, and his cheek burned against hers as he caught his breath.

'Wow,' he said. 'You're so soft.'

He closed his eyes and shuffled around the floor with her, sealed in a warm cocoon of mutual discovery. After the slow dance, Liz pulled away, unable to look Sean in the eye.

'We should get the others,' she said, scanning the room.

Isabella came running up.

'Have you seen Nuala anywhere?' she said. 'She was dancing with this older man who bought her a drink, and then she disappeared.'

'Let's spread out. She must be here somewhere,' said Liz.

Sean had already left, searching among the couples snogging goodbye beside the walls. Liz went up one side of the barn, and Isabella up the other, but Nuala had gone.

'I told her not to accept the drink,' said Isabella, pale with worry. 'That man was far too old for her.'

'Maybe she's outside,' said Liz. 'Get Sean and we'll check.'

Despite their ever more frenetic efforts, they could not find Nuala.

'She could have gone home,' said Sean. 'She does that when she's annoyed.'

'We'll look for her along the road, and if we don't find her, Daddy can help us in his car,' said Liz. 'Don't worry. She'll turn up.'

Chapter 24 – Nuala, May 1972

Nuala flicked her hair back and sipped her Babycham, trying to appear sophisticated. It didn't taste as sweet as she expected; it burned her throat and made her cough. The drink sat hot in her stomach. Perhaps the one she had tried behind the bicycle shed at school was a different flavour? The young farmer who had bought it for her sat opposite, drinking a pint of Guinness. She couldn't believe he had picked her. Normally Isabella garnered all the attention. She batted her eyelashes at him across the top of her glass.

He sucked air through his teeth as he gazed at her legs.

'You're a fine-looking girl,' he said. 'And a wonderful dancer. How come I don't see you down the pub?'

Nuala laughed.

'I'm only thirteen,' she said. 'What would I be doing in a pub?'

'Thirteen? You seem much older.'

'Everyone says that. I'm nearly fourteen. I go to the pub sometimes, but only to drag my father home for lunch on a Sunday.'

'Who's he then?' said the farmer.

'Brian O Connor,' said Nuala. 'And what's your name?'

Shock ghosted across the man's face.

'It's Stephen Hegarty,' he said. 'Are you sure your father won't mind?'

'I'm hardly going to tell him, am I?' she said, rolling her eyes. A woozy sensation came over her as the adulterated Babycham got absorbed into her bloodstream.

His hand caressed her leg, and she brushed it off, ignoring the alien thrill which coursed through her body. To her annoyance she remembered the Mother Superior telling them about newspapers on laps. She looked around at the tables despite herself, but she couldn't see one. Her head felt funny, as if it didn't belong to her. She shut her eyes and opened them again as a wave of nausea hit her.

'I don't feel so good,' she said.

'Do you want to come out and get some air?' said Stephen.

'Okay.'

She slid out of the seat, the bottom of her thighs squeaking on the plastic cover. Tugging at her shorts, which now seemed an awful choice of outfit, she followed him across the floor of the bar and out of the side door. Moonlight threw shadows across the carpark as she leant on a wall, gulping in the fresh air. Stephen slid a hand around her chest and left it on her tiny breast.

'Hey, what are you doing?' said Nuala. 'That's not allowed.'

Stephen turned her around and shoved his face in hers. He reeked of stout and cigarettes. Nuala wrinkled her nose and tried to back away. Her heels pressed up against the kerb and an icy breeze gave her goose pimples. This wasn't fun any more.

'I've got to find my friends,' she said, trying to push past him.

'Give me a kiss first.'

He grabbed her and pressed his lips to hers and forced his tongue into her mouth. She pushed him away.

'No, stop. I don't like it.'

'But I bought you drink. You shouldn't have accepted if you didn't want to.'

New rules. *Was it true? Did you have to kiss a man if he bought you something?* Her friends hadn't mentioned this when they were giggling about boys. She let him kiss her without joining in. Then he put his hand between her legs and shoved it upwards.

'No, I don't want—'

But he pushed her backwards, and she stumbled over the kerb and found herself on a patch of long grass. He dropped beside her and inserted his knee between hers, holding her hands down when she tried to push him away. He had powerful arms and she couldn't stop him.

'I know all about your type,' said Stephen. 'You're a prick tease, aren't you?'

'A what? I don't know what that is. Let me go or I'll scream.'

'No, you won't. I'll tell everyone you're a slut and you were drinking. They won't believe you.'

Shocked, Nuala stopped wiggling and snivelled.

'I don't want to. It's a mortal sin.'

'It doesn't hurt. No one will know.'

He grabbed her shorts and undid the zip, pulling them roughly over her knees, slipping one foot out of them. Then he pushed his fingers into her. She gasped and tried to scream, but he put his hand over her mouth. He was much heavier than her and she was torn between yelling and what people would say if they saw her naked.

He thrust his penis into her before she could protest and pumped it in and out. Her shock at this violent and painful act stopped her reacting to it. *What was he doing? Was this sex? Jesus, Mary, and Joseph. Get him off me.* She bit his hand as he collapsed on her with a curse.

'Jaysus,' he said. 'Why did you do that? Didn't you like it?'

He jumped up and pulled his trousers back over his waist, buckling his belt. He looked down at her and shrugged.

'What are you doing down there? Get dressed before someone sees you,' he said.

Nuala struggled to her feet, hopping on the tarmac as she put her shorts back on. A dull pain throbbed between her legs. *Was that it? The thing everybody whispered about and no one had tried. The nuns said you couldn't have sex if you weren't married, but they had lied. Have I committed mortal sin, or did the fact I didn't want it lessen my guilt? How many Hail Marys will I have to say after confession? Hundreds?* She hobbled towards the road.

'Hey, don't you want another drink?' said Stephen.

She shook her head, vomiting into the hedge, and when she turned around, he had gone. Confused and mortified, she set off down the road to her house. Her head spun from the drink and the horrible thing that had just happened to her. She couldn't be sure she hadn't imagined the whole incident. It finished almost before it started. Her breath came in gasps as she tried not to cry, and when she slipped and fell into the ditch, she lay there unwilling to get back up. *I should just die here. My life is ruined.*

The moon had slipped below the horizon, but the stars still shone bright when she realised that the others were calling her with increasing desperation. She waved a limp arm and Liz spotted her cowering in the ditch beside the road.

'What happened? Are you all right?' said Isabella.

Nuala tried to speak, but only a whimpering sound came from her mouth. Liz got Sean to shine a torch while she slid down the bank to Nuala.

'What are you doing here?' said Liz, putting her arm around her.

'He hurt me,' whispered Nuala, weeping. 'I didn't want him to, but he did something dirty to me. I want my mammy.'

'Oh my God,' said Liz. 'You poor thing. Don't worry, we'll get her.'

'We can't risk running into Mr O'Connor,' said Isabella. 'Let's take her to our house. Mummy will know what to do.'

Sean's white face hovered above them. Nuala shrank back in shame. *What would he say if he knew what she had done?*

'Are you okay?' he said.

Nuala didn't answer.

'She will be. But she has to come with us,' said Liz.

'Can I come too?' said Sean

'Not now. Go home. I promise we'll take care of her.'

'But what happened?'

'I don't know yet. Trust me, please,' said Liz.

'If someone has hurt my sister, I'll kill them.'

'Go home, Sean. Bring your mother to our house. Don't frighten her, just tell her it's important,' said Liz.

Liz and Isabella helped Nuala out of the ditch and straightened her clothes. Then they took an arm each and helped her walk back to Dunbell. Nuala wanted to lie down and die, but their firm determination inspired her and she put one foot in front of the other until they got to the farm house. Bea opened the kitchen door with a big smile on her face, which faded as the girls stepped into the light and she saw Nuala. Her hand flew to her mouth.

'Oh dear,' she said. 'What on earth happened to you? Have you had a fall?'

A great wave of shame washed over Nuala, who turned puce and shook her head. Tears streamed down her cheeks. *How can I tell Bea about the filthy man who violated me?* Bea looked over Nuala's head at Liz, who bit her lip.

'A man hurt her,' said Isabella. 'She disappeared from the dance and we found her in the ditch. It's my fault. I shouldn't have let her go with him.'

Nuala looked up.

'No,' she said. 'I wouldn't listen to you. I thought having a drink would be fun. Grown up. I didn't realise—'

She broke down again. 'I want my Mammy. Where is she?'

Bea took Nuala's hand and led her into the little sitting room. She sat her down on the sofa.

'No one's going to hurt you in my house. You are safe now.'

Chapter 25 – No Justice, May 1972

Maeve turned up at the farmhouse not long afterwards. She knocked on the back door, harder than usual, and, without waiting for an answer, entered the kitchen where Tom had kept Liz and Isabella for a calming cup of tea. She stood deathly pale, misery hunching her shoulders, Sean beside her holding her hand.

'Where's my little girl?' she said.

Tom stood up, wordless with sympathy. He left Sean in the kitchen and took her through to the little sitting room. Nuala sat on the sofa, dishevelled, and bruised, with leaf debris in her hair and mud on her clothes. A rip in her t-shirt revealed a scratch across her chest. She did not notice her mother enter as she sat catatonic with shock, having her grazes wiped clean by Bea, who looked up with relief as Maeve came in.

'Is there anything I can do?' said Tom.

Bea shook her head. He backed out, shutting the door.

'Here's your mother,' she said to Nuala. 'Everything will be all right now.'

Nuala turned into Maeve's arms, her shoulders heaving. Her mother also cried silent tears; grief written over her face in deep lines. Bea waited, putting the cream and sticking plasters back into the first aid box.

'I'm so sorry, Mammy,' said Nuala.

'Sorry? You did nothing wrong.' said Maeve.

'Did you see his face? Can you identify him?' said Bea.

'He said his name was Stephen Hegarty. He bought me a drink, which made me feel funny. Then he asked me to come outside and see the stars. I thought he might kiss me, but he did something far worse.'

'What did he do, mo chroí?' said Maeve.

'He forced me down on the grass and did dirty things to me.'

'What do you mean dirty?' said her mother, her voice trembling.

'He put his thing in me,' said Nuala, her eyes wide with shock. 'It hurt me.'

'He raped her?' said Bea. 'Maeve, we have to call the police.'

Nuala rocked on the sofa, moaning. 'No, please, don't tell anyone.'

Maeve took Bea by the shoulders.

'We can't go to the police. You're not in England now. They won't take her seriously. They'll say she was asking for it, wearing those shorts and accepting a drink. He'll get off scot free.'

'But he'll get away with it. What about the next girl, and the next?' said Bea.

'I'll not have people talking about my daughter and saying she's easy like me. They'll take his side. The woman is always at fault, even if she's a little girl.'

Maeve folded her arms.

'Okay,' said Bea. 'You know best. Let me run a hot bath. We need to clean her up before Brian sees her.'

She left Maeve comforting Nuala and climbed upstairs. She turned the taps on and ferreted in her closet for a douche bag given to her by her well-meaning mother after the birth of Isabella. Her parents had always been matter-of-fact about contraception and sex because of her father's role as confidant to his men in the army. Given the depth of ignorance among most women her age, which seemed worse in Ireland, she doubted Maeve be familiar with a douche, but she shrank from explaining its use. The likelihood of Nuala being pregnant was so slim, anyway.

While Nuala and Maeve used the bathroom, Bea entered the kitchen where Tom and the girls were trying to calm Sean down.

'Is Nuala okay?' said Sean.

'Yes. She's just shocked and scared that man will tell people lies.'

'Does she know who attacked her?' said Sean.

Bea nodded.

'I'm going to kill him.'

'No, you can't do that. It won't help if you get arrested. Nuala's ordeal will be all over the papers.'

Tom stood up. He ran his fingers through his hair. The muscles in his cheeks stood out white against his face, ruddy from the hot tea.

'However, we can put the fear of God into him. What's his name?'

'Stephen Hegarty.'

Sean shoved his chair back, and it clattered onto the tiles.

'I can show you where his farm is. It's nearby. Let's go then.'

'Stay here girls,' said Tom. 'Don't tell Maeve where we've gone.'

'But, darling—' said Bea.

'We must do this,' said Tom. 'Before the bastard tells someone. He won't tell the truth. He'll say she asked for it, that she's a slut. We must stop him.'

He headed out of the door, followed by Sean. Bea sighed. Once Tom had made up his mind, she could not change it. She returned to the little sitting room where Maeve and Nuala were whispering together. Nuala's cheeks had recovered their normal pink colour, but Maeve looked dreadful. *You'd be forgiven for thinking Maeve was the one who got raped,* thought Bea. But, in a way, she had. Everyone would blame her for bringing up Nuala wrong, using Liam as proof.

What a country. England had its fair share of hypocrites, but Ireland was flooded with them. The Catholic religion had a lot to answer for. Men invented all religions to keep women in their place. How many rules were there for men? None that she could remember. But for women, a load of contradictory rules made to confuse and subjugate.

She pondered on this as she helped Maeve walk Nuala home. Then she returned to the farmhouse where Liz and Isabella lay squashed together in Liz's single bed, subdued and quiet, the air thick with unanswered questions.

'Are you all right, my darlings?' said Bea, trying to sound normal despite the lump in her throat.

'Not really,' said Isabella, her voice breaking.

Bea pulled up the Lloyd loom bedroom chair and sat beside them, caressing their hair to soothe them.

'Why did that man hurt Nuala?' said Liz.

'I don't know, sweetheart. Sometimes when people drink too much, they do horrible things.'

'But she's only a year older than me,' said Isabella. 'And she doesn't really understand what sex is yet.'

Bea shrugged.

'I realise that it's hard to appreciate, but her ignorance may help her. She doesn't seem to comprehend what happened to her. Perhaps it would be better, if we behaved like it hadn't.'

Liz grimaced.

'Knowing Nuala, she'll soon forget it, anyway.'

'I hope so,' said Isabella, sniffing. 'I'm never going to a dance again.'

'That would be sad,' said Bea. 'The moral of the story is not to avoid dancing. It's to stick together and never to accept drinks from a stranger. You had fun, didn't you?'

Isabella snorted.

'Liz snogged Sean.'

'I did not.'

'Sean?' said Bea. 'I thought you liked Liam?'

Liz rolled her eyes.

'I only had a slow dance with Sean. That's all. We did nothing.'

'But you wanted to,' said Isabella, who received an elbow in her ribs. 'Ouch.'

'Okay, that's enough excitement for one night,' said Bea. 'Isabella, get into your own bed.'

She kissed them both goodnight and turned off the light.

'Is Nuala going to be all right?' said Isabella.

'As right as rain. You'll see. Just be kind to her and don't mention it unless she does first.'

After leaving the girls, Bea entered the bathroom and washed the mud from the bath. She picked up the towels from the floor where Nuala had dropped them. A poignant red stain sat in the centre of one of them. She took them downstairs and dropped them into the washing machine. Then she waited for Tom to come home, her back to the Aga, an old shawl wrapped around her, for comfort more than warmth.

Tom got back after half an hour. He crossed the kitchen to where she sat and took her in his arms as she stood up, holding her pressed against him for a long time. A tear fell on Bea's upturned face and ran into her mouth, its saltiness surprising her.

She waited for him to recover before pulling away and wiping his cheek with her hand.

'What's wrong, darling? Didn't you find him?'

'Oh, we found him all right. He'll never talk if he knows what's good for him.'

'Did you hurt him?'

'I didn't have to. He recognised Sean and peed his pants in fright.'

'Sean? But he's only a boy.'

'I guess he knows Brian. Although, whether that drunk would even care about his daughter is debatable.'

'Why are you so upset?'

'It could have been Isabella, or Liz instead. What would we have done? Who would have supported us against this man? Sometimes I regret coming here to a land where religion rules and the Troubles are just getting worse. Will we be safe?'

'You're just upset. We're happy here. The children love Ireland and we have wonderful friends like Mrs O and Maeve. Your shop is a success and people love you.'

'What about Michael? He had to leave. Will he ever forgive me?'

'He's happy too. George looks after him like a grandson. He would never have gone to public school without George.'

'If that Hegarty man had touched my girls, I'd have murdered him.'

'But he didn't. We've got to support Maeve and Nuala through this, whatever happens. That's what's important right now. Where's Sean?'

'I left him at home. He'll be okay now. I told him to come over tomorrow if he wants to talk.'

'Let's go to bed now. We'll make sure the O'Connors don't suffer. They're family now.'

'More than you appreciate. Isabella told me they made a pact to support each other no matter what. Perhaps we should do the same.'

'I think our children are brighter than us.'

'Maybe they are.'

First thing the next morning, Mrs O'Reilly turned up in Bea's kitchen, ears twitching.

'What on earth did you get up to last night? There were comings and goings until dawn.'

Bea did not turn around from the Aga for fear her expression would give her away.

'Oh, Blue was missing,' she said, forcing out a laugh. 'Sean wouldn't go to bed until we found her. She just sauntered in near dawn by herself. We've no idea what she got up to.'

'Really?' said Mrs O'Reilly, parking herself in a chair beside the Aga and looking Bea straight in the eye. 'Your family have a strange obsession with that mangy animal.'

'Well, the children adore her. They couldn't cope if she got lost for good. Michael would never forgive us.'

The truth of what she had said made it easier to lie, and Mrs O'Reilly relaxed.

'Did you hear about the Gogans' horses?'

Chapter 26 – Three Mothers, June 1972

If Nuala's period had arrived on schedule, the awful episode would have faded into obscurity. Nuala reverted to her old self in days, and with the love of all her surrogate and real family members consigned the memory of the assault to her past with alacrity.

'Luckily, Nuala doesn't have any tolerance for alcohol. She's like me that way. She seems to have dismissed the episode as imagination,' said Maeve. 'I don't want to bring it up if she's happy to forget it.'

But about five weeks after the disco, Nuala began to vomit in the mornings, and Maeve's façade of calm crumbled. She lurched into Bea's kitchen, her face stained with tears and pinched with worry.

'What are we going to do?' she said. 'My stupidity ruined my life forever, but if Father Doherty finds out Nuala's pregnant, he'll make her marry that eejit, and end all her chances of a decent life. He's been waiting for the chance to say like mother like daughter ever since I had her.'

'Is Nuala aware she's pregnant?'

'I haven't told her yet. But she's going to guess.'

'Let me talk to Tom. We might be able to help.'

Maeve's visit left Bea in a quandary. She racked her brains for a solution, but nothing occurred to her.

'Perhaps George could take Nuala in, until she has the child,' said Tom.

'But then what? What on earth would Nuala do with a baby? She might not want it adopted, and she can't bring it back here without the entire house of cards collapsing on poor old Maeve,' said Bea.

'I shudder to think what Brian will do when he finds out.'

'He's not going to. We'll think of something.'

'Whatever you do, don't let Mrs O hear about this, she'll broadcast it on RTE.'

Bea had almost admitted defeat when an offer of help came from an unexpected quarter. Marion Edmunds, Darlene's mother, invited Bea to tea. Bea did not recognise the timid voice on the telephone, but she remembered what Liz had said about Marion being shy. It must have been hard for her to make the call. Bea had been dying of curiosity about the Edmunds, their glamorous house, and possibly criminal contacts, but she hadn't been sure how to engineer a visit. Now she had an official invitation.

'How exciting,' she said. 'I feel quite naughty.'

'Don't get seduced into a life of crime,' said Tom.

Bill Edmunds swept up the drive to collect Bea and chauffeured her to the mock-Colonial house, dropping her at the door.

'I've been banished by her indoors,' he said, coming around the car to open her door. 'You're on your own from here.'

Bea walked up the crunchy gravel path, lined by mini copies of famous Greek statues, and reached up to lift the massive brass bulldog knocker. She dropped it onto the door, shocked at the loud bang it made. Marion appeared and checked the front garden, as if for spies, before letting Bea in. They sat down on the white leather sofas. Bea breathed in the stale cigar smoke and leather smell of the room. She sipped her tea, taking in the colour television, and the chrome and glass fixtures. *Liz wasn't exaggerating.* Marion perched on the edge of the seat and took Bea's hand.

'Pardon me for being so frank, but Darlene tells me your friend's daughter is up the duff,' she said.

Bea almost spat her tea over the fluffy white carpet. Liz had told her Marion crept around the house like a ghost, afraid of provoking her husband, but this woman bore no resemblance to the description.

'Um, yes. Nuala, Maeve's daughter.'

'Darlene told me a man raped Nuala at a dance. How old is she?'

'Thirteen.'

'How terrible. That poor little girl. We could have the bastard shot for you if it wasn't for the Provos,' said Marion. 'We're on their territory, and they wouldn't like it if we got involved.'

'Oh, of course, I understand,' said Bea, gulping.

'I have a friend in London called Belle. She's on the game,' said Marion.

Bea choked on her biscuit, and Marion laughed, thumping her on the back and refilling her tea.

'Before I married Bill, I used to work too, as an exotic dancer in the Raymond Revue Bar. Bill watched my act one night, and the rest, as they say, is history.'

'How romantic,' stuttered Bea.

'Yes, it was,' said Marion. 'But he stopped me dancing, and he keeps it secret now, so don't go blabbing.'

Bea shook her head.

'Anyway, your Liz has been a good friend to my Darlene. She's a bit rough around the edges, but Liz never judged her like most people do. She made her feel so welcome and she never tries to make her buy things. It's hard being the daughter of a rich man. You can never tell who your genuine friends are.'

'Liz is a genuine person. Darlene is too. I guess they just clicked.'

Marion nodded.

'Anyway, I'd like to do something for you. I understand Nuala's mother is your best friend here. She must be in a panic about nuns and priests and baby homes and all that.'

'She's afraid the priest, Father Doherty, will make Nuala marry her rapist,' said Bea.

'Listen, my friend in London can get the child an early abortion. Belle has a doctor who looks after women like her when they slip up.'

'But wouldn't it be dangerous?' said Bea, swallowing her inclination to refuse.

'At this early stage, it's quick and painless, like a heavy period. She wouldn't suffer more than some bad cramps. I didn't.'

This candid confession floored Bea. She had always tried not to judge people by her own standards of morality. She hadn't been a virgin when she married Tom, and she refused to judge other people's beliefs or needs by her lack of drama in this sphere. Maeve should have a choice, whatever other people thought.

'I can't imagine what Maeve will say,' she said. 'But I'll tell her.'

'I'll pay for all four girls to go on the ferry and boat train to London. They can stay with Belle in King's Cross, so it will be a cheap trip. We can pretend they are going to the Tutankhamun exhibition as a half-term treat, so no-one outside our families guesses the real reason for the visit.'

Surprised Marion had even heard about the exhibition, Bea hesitated. Her girls had been begging to go, but money was still tight.

'Oh, but I couldn't—'

'Don't be silly. We're rolling in cash. That poor child can't marry her rapist, and the girls will benefit from a trip outside this Stone Age country. I'd like to do this. I never get a chance to help.'

Bea returned home, promising to broach the subject with Maeve. Time was short if they were to abort the foetus before ten weeks. After that, the procedure would be more complicated and traumatic.

'It sounds sensible to me,' said Tom. 'Having a baby after a rape at thirteen would ruin most people's lives.'

'Abortion's still illegal in Ireland, and a mortal sin for Catholics. I'm not sure how to bring up the subject.'

'Darling, Maeve is desperate. This is the only way of minimising the trauma to Nuala. She's not bright. The whole thing would crush her if she went ahead with the birth.'

Bea found herself back in Maeve's kitchen, nursing another cup of strong tea and nibbling a Marietta biscuit.

'What's so important?' said Maeve. 'I could do with some good news. I had to tell Nuala she is pregnant this morning. Do you know what she said?'

Bea shook her head.

'But I thought you couldn't get pregnant if you weren't married. Honestly, the child is so literal.'

'Um, that's what I came to talk about,' said Bea. 'Only…'

'It can't be worse than it is already,' said Maeve. 'She has cried all morning and I can't get her to eat. She keeps saying she doesn't want to marry or have a baby.'

'There are ways to prevent it,' said Bea.

'Like what, shoot Father Doherty?' said Maeve, but she didn't laugh

'She can abort the baby.'

'No, absolutely not, it's way too dangerous. A friend of mine used a coat hanger on herself in desperation. She got sepsis and died.'

'I wasn't suggesting we do it ourselves. Darlene's mother says she knows a doctor in London who'll do it in a clinic. It's not dangerous, unpleasant perhaps, but quick and safe.'

'But Nuala might refuse.'

Bea frowned.

'You could tell her the doctor is checking if she is pregnant. And then say he found she wasn't but had to fix something. To explain the pain.'

Maeve stood up, her hand over her mouth. She swayed. Bea wondered if she would faint.

'No, I'll tell her the truth. She'll realise later if I'm not honest with her. But I can't get the money. Brian counts every penny I spend. He'd kill me and Nuala if I asked him.'

'Darlene comes from a wealthy family. Her mother has a chequered past, and she has offered to help us because Liz and Darlene are such good friends. She'll buy all the tickets and pay for the procedure.'

Maeve sat down again, her head in her hands. She sighed.

'And she says it would be safe and simple?'

'Marion says she had one herself. She worked as a showgirl before she met Bill.'

'Oh, how glamorous. Is she exquisite?'

Taken aback, Bea smiled.

'Yes, she is, still.'

'We have no choice,' said Maeve, folding her arms. 'I won't let priests and religion ruin my child's life. She did nothing wrong, and she doesn't deserve to suffer the consequences of someone else's behaviour for the rest of her life. She'll get over it. Tell Marion I'll be grateful forever, and if there's anything I can do, well, you know.'

'I'll tell her,' said Bea.

Chapter 27 – Spying, June 1972

'Are you going to show me around your house?' said Liam, propping himself up on his elbows and ignoring the throb in his groin. He tried to quell the sexual frustration at being fobbed off at the last hurdle yet again. Darlene had taken him to the gates of heaven and then let him fall through the clouds on a couple of occasions now. It couldn't be long before she acquiesced.

Darlene buttoned up her blouse and tucked it into her flared trousers. She swung her legs over the side of the bed and stuck her feet into in her plimsols. Her cheeks were pink with desire. Liam stroked her face.

'Come on, you know you want to.'

Darlene tutted.

'You're like a broken record. I said no, and I meant it. If you shut up, I'll give you the grand tour.'

Liam grinned.

'Okay, I promise.'

Darlene showed Liam a series of bedrooms, ending with her parents' suite.

'I'll just use the ensuite,' she said. 'Wait here and don't touch anything.'

Who has a jacks in their bedroom? The Edmunds must be loaded. Liam waited until she locked the bathroom door and then pulled open a couple of drawers in the bedside table. Just the usual mixture of reader glasses, aspirins, and hair grips. He couldn't imagine what he should search for.

The wardrobes tempted him with their unseen content, and he peered into one of them. Mr Edmunds's suits and shirts hung from the rail; all spotless and wrinkle free. He looked at the labels; Savile Row. It meant nothing to him, but behind the suits he spotted a safe. The door hung open and inside he could see piles of twenty-pound bank notes stacked high. Just one of those would keep him going for a week. He reached in, but just then he heard the lock click on the bathroom door and leaped backwards to close the door.

Darlene looked up from wiping her hands on her trousers.

'You always look guilty,' she said. 'You'd be a useless villain.'

Liam followed her downstairs, smarting from the insult. *Why didn't I grab a handful of notes?* She took him outside behind the house and showed him the shed full of new, unused gardening equipment.

'Dad doesn't let the gardener use his tools,' said Darlene.

Liam committed the layout to memory.

'I'm sure he's got better things to do than garden,' he said. 'I'm hungry. Is there anything to eat?'

'There's a new restaurant in Kilkenny that I wanted to try out. Do you feel like joining me?'

'Only if your parents don't come.'

Darlene raised an eyebrow. Liam shrugged.

'Is it any wonder I want to spend time alone with you?' he said.

Marion looked up from her magazine as they left, her hair in curlers under a scarf.

'Have a good time, you two,' she said. 'Oh, by the way, Belle says next week is good for her, so I'm going to ring Bea Green and confirm that with her.'

'Great. It'll be brilliant to have a trip to London. Ireland is so boring.'

What trip to London? She hasn't told me anything about a trip. And doesn't she have a boyfriend over there?

Liam didn't like to be left out. He sulked in the car and gave monosyllabic answers to Darlene, who ignored him.

'Enjoy your dinner, love,' said Bill Edmunds. 'I'll pick you up at ten.' He turned to Liam. 'You mind your Ps and Qs.'

'Yes, sir.'

They entered the bistro, and the waiter took them to a corner table with a candle stuck in the neck of a wine bottle. He held the chair out for Darlene, who gave him her best smile and made him blush. Then he handed them each a menu and trotted off to the kitchen. Darlene opened hers with a sigh of contentment.

'Reading a new menu is the best bit,' she said.

'You're going to London without me?' said Liam, looking over the top of his menu and making puppy eyes at her.

'You're not suggesting I take you with me?' said Darlene. 'Don't be ridiculous. Anyway, I'm hungry. What shall we order?'

Liam squinted at the menu. Its gold embossed lettering emphasised the ambition of the restaurant Darlene had chosen for them. He struggled to decipher the dishes, using his limited French vocabulary as his ire increased. Only Darlene could find a faux-French restaurant in Ireland. His impatience with the menu doubled at the delay in getting into her knickers, a treat he had been anticipating since he first met her. There had been some heavy petting, but she had always fobbed him off at the last hurdle. *Tonight would be different.*

'Why do they have poison on the menu?' he said.

Darlene laughed. An earthy sound absorbed into the velvet walls.

'Poisson not poison. That's fish and chips. It's posh to have the menu in French.'

'Why don't they say so? Which one is the steak?'

Darlene sighed. Liam knew that sound. Having fallen for his cool exterior and hints of involvement with certain proscribed organisations, she now found him wanting in most ways. Her relationship with him had caused a rift with Liz, which pained her more than she expected. He blamed Liz, who should have told Darlene the truth about her crush on him, instead of being so vague and hiding her actual feelings. Mind you, he had lied too. He told her that Liz and he were only friends, not even good friends. Liz hadn't disagreed, but she had been quiet on the way back from the cinema when he and Darlene were flirting in the back of the car.

Liam's boorishness ruined Darlene's dinner. She pushed her food around her plate and sulked. Liam finished it for her, eating with his mouth open on purpose to annoy her. He ignored the bill. *Let her pay. Her family were as rich as Croesus.* She paid with bad grace. Maybe he should have offered to pay, but he didn't have any money. *What if she had accepted?*

Afterwards, they waited on the pavement outside the restaurant. Liam tried to French kiss her, to get her interested again, but she moved sideways, wiping her mouth. He jumped back when Bill Edmunds pulled up to the pavement in the Jaguar. Bill didn't get out, but sat waiting in the car, observing them in his mirror and drumming his fingers on the steering wheel, which made Liam feel twitchy.

'Night,' said Darlene.

'Wait a minute,' said Liam, grabbing her arm. 'I thought you, I mean we…'

Darlene smirked.

'Did you now? Well, you were wrong.'

'Are all English girls frigid? Liz wouldn't do it either. She's like the Virgin Mary.'

'Why didn't you tell me you were together? I wouldn't have agreed to go out with you.'

'She's not my girlfriend. She hangs around lusting after me. It's pathetic. I never expected you to be the same.'

Darlene froze. Her eyes narrowed to dark slits like an abandoned pillbox, and fury tightened her chubby face. She shoved him back against the wall.

'I'm fifteen, not ten. I chose who gets me, and it's not an ignorant bastard who left school at fifteen and can't even understand a menu.'

Bill Edmunds opened his car door and got out. He emanated menace.

'You all right, darling?' he said. 'Because if this punk isn't showing you the required respect, I'll rip his limbs off.'

A chill ran down Liam's spine.

'We're only messing around, Mr Edmunds,' he said, straightening his jacket.

'I'll be there in one minute, Dad,' said Darlene. She turned back to Liam. 'Now listen here, you appalling maggot, you stay away from me and my family. I know a grifter when I see one. Our family is royalty in the East End, and we wouldn't let a petty criminal like you within one hundred yards of our territory.'

'And what does that make you?' said Liam.

'Someone you don't want to tangle with,' said Darlene, and she slipped into the door being held open by her father.

The door closed, but not before Liam spotted a handgun between the seats. The proof he needed. He felt a pang of regret for the missed night of passion with Darlene, but now the stakes were higher. No woman dared to reject a member of the brigades. And now he would gain entry to one in Northern Ireland. He didn't bother waving.

As predicted, the arrival of an East End crime family in Wexford made the local branch of the Provos take immediate notice. McClusky came to the phone box on the street corner instead of making him walk miles to a meeting place. He threw the door open with a grunt. Liam checked he was alone before getting in.

'Get on with it,' said McClusky.

'Just following protocol,' said Liam.

'Protocol, my arse.'

McClusky drove them to a car park and turned the car around so it pointed at the exit.

'Did you draw me a plan of the house?' he said.

Liam fumbled in his pockets and pulled out a cream-coloured paper napkin with gold edging.

'And what is this piece of shite?' said McClusky, holding it by the corner. 'You've wiped your gob in it, you filthy fecker.'

'I had to improvise. Do you want it or not?'

McClusky spread it out over the steering wheel.

'Is it to scale?' he said.

'What do you think?' said Liam.

'Don't get antsy with me, boy. It'll do.'

'I want to join the raid,' said Liam, almost shouting in his effort to sound forceful.

'Keep your voice down, you eejit.' McClu[...] looked him straight in the eye. 'Why do you want to join up? Do you even know?'

Liam expected a raft of reasons to flood his mind, but nothing occurred to him. He hadn't ever analysed his choice before.

'Because I hate them. We shouldn't have foreigners governing our land.'

'Do you support De Valera?'

'Of course I do. He's the President.'

'You know he was born in New York and his father is Spanish?'

He didn't know that. He spouted hate and regurgitated stuff his aunt said, believing himself to be a patriot. She told him he had a destiny, like Batman, righting the wrongs carried out by the hated colonisers.

Colm examined him, his cheek muscles working. 'Are you sure about this? There's no going back. What about your mother? That man will kill her one of these days.'

Liam swallowed. *Don't capitulate. This low blow won't weaken me.* He squeezed his eyes shut to stop the images of her pleading face from invading his thoughts.

'She's a slut,' he said, his words threatening to choke him. 'She deserves it.'

He composed himself. 'Are you going to keep your word?'

Colm blew out a long breath.

'I'll keep my word,' he said. 'I'm only worried you may not keep yours.'

Chapter 28 – Termination, June 1972

The girls squeezed onto the narrow landing outside Belle's flat in Kings Cross. Liz rang the doorbell, and the door opened to reveal a middle-aged woman with enormous bosoms and thick mascara.

'You're here,' she said, reaching out to envelop them in a group hug. Her pink boa tickled their faces. Liz sneezed as a piece floated up her nose.

'Come in, you must be tired,' said Belle. 'I heard the ferry is murder.'

'It is for me,' said Isabella.

'We vomited all the way across,' said Nuala.

'I was fine,' said Darlene.

'You're always fine, aren't you love?' said Belle, giving her an extra hug.

Belle's flat had a luxurious if rather tacky interior, characterised by feather boas of many colours draped around the furniture and its owner. A large faded pink sofa dominated the room, which had patterned carpets and lava lamps. Liz sneezed again as the lingering effect of the boa and the smell of cigarettes irritated the lining of her nose.

'Blimey, you don't have a cold, do you ducky? They won't do you if you aren't well,' said Belle.

'Oh, no, it's not me. I'm Liz, and this is my sister Isabella and our friend Nuala. She's the one who needs your help.'

Nuala shuffled forward and before anyone could react, she vomited on the parquet floor. She stared in horror at the lake of sick.

'Don't worry, it happens to the best of us,' said Belle. Liz and Isabella helped Nuala to the sofa, as Belle and Darlene cleaned up the mess with a dustpan and brush, and some paper towels from the kitchen.

'How old are you, sweetheart?' said Belle.

'Just fourteen,' said Nuala.

'Christ, she looks about twelve,' muttered Belle, shaking her head. 'Don't worry, sweety. Aunty Belle's going to save your bacon. We're going to see Dr Gross in the morning, and it will all be over before you can say I'm up the duff.'

'Can Isabella come with me?' said Nuala, sniffing.

'I'm afraid not. We have to go early in the morning so no one will see us, and the location is a secret. But don't worry, you'll be here when the others get back and we can all go shopping as soon as you feel up to it.'

'We don't have any money for shopping,' said Isabella.

'Oh yes, you do. Bill has sent me lots; but on one condition,' said Belle, tapping the side of her nose.

'What's that?' said Liz.

'We have to spend every penny.'

Isabella's eyes almost popped out of her head.

'Do you think there might be enough for a pair of jeans?' she said. 'Real Levis?'

'There just might be,' said Belle.

'Um, we'd like to see the Tutankhamun exhibition tomorrow, if that's okay with you. So we can answer questions about it when we get home to Ireland,' said Liz. 'Is it nearby?'

'You can walk from here. I'll lend you my A to Z. But you must go early. The queues reach around the block. I read in the Standard that you may wait three or even four hours before you get in. Can you please buy me a catalogue? They say it's amazing. I'd like to go, but my clients prefer sex to science.'

She winked at Liz.

'Let's get you settled. I'm afraid I only have one spare room, but there are two double mattresses in there on the floor and the heating is on day and night in this block.'

After supper at the Wimpey hamburger restaurant opposite her block, Belle asked them to shut themselves into their bedroom and not to make any noise.

'I've got a regular coming in. If he hears children talking, it might knock him off his stride,' she said.

'What's a regular?' said Isabella, before Liz pulled her into the bathroom.

'We have to get up at dawn, so brush your teeth and use the loo, so you don't disturb Belle,' said Liz.

'Is this about sex?' said Isabella.

'Most things seem to be when you grow up,' said Liz.

Despite her trepidation about her appointment with Dr Gross, Nuala was already flat on her back, snoring when they entered the bedroom.

'I'm glad she's not on my mattress,' said Darlene.

Liz woke first, stumbling to the bathroom in the still dark flat. Some lurid underwear soaked in cloudy water in the bath. She wiped under her armpits with a flannel and put on some deodorant. Her unruly black curls were tangled, and she had to tug her hairbrush through them. She dropped the hairs into a bin with a foot pedal and noticed an empty Durex envelope on top of the other rubbish. Liam had once waved one at her. He kept in in his wallet, just in case. *In case of what?* She wasn't sure, but once again, sex had reared its head. One of these days, she would find out what all the fuss was about.

Shivering in the cool of the early morning, the three girls stood in the queue outside the British Museum. They had been among the first to arrive but the museum didn't open until ten o'clock so they were in for a long wait. Darlene and Liz left Isabella in the queue chatting to a friendly couple from Lancashire and found a café which served toasted sandwiches and hot chocolate to the all-night cabbies, and early shift bus drivers. They walked back to the queue.

'I'm sorry about Liam,' said Darlene. 'I didn't know he was the guy you fancied. Well, I thought he might be, but you didn't say, and I fancied him too.'

'Oh, that's okay,' said Liz. 'I don't think he's my type.'

'He's not anyone's type,' said Darlene. 'Unless your name is trouble.'

'Well, he's in love with the Troubles, that's for sure.'

'Is he really a Provo?'

'I think he's trying, but they need proof of his abilities before they'll let him join.'

'What sort of abilities?'

'I don't know. My mother's pretty sure he stopped her at a roadblock once, but they didn't tell her who they were looking for.'

Darlene went quiet. She handed out the sandwiches and hot chocolates and then sat by herself 'just for a moment'. When she came back, she seemed pensive and uncertain, but soon her spirits revived once they entered the museum. The tickets were fifty pence each and Liz handed them out with reverence like communion wafers.

'Keep them,' she said. 'This is a once in a lifetime event.'

'I've never seen nothing ancient before,' said Darlene. 'Unless you count your dad's car.'

The sisters couldn't stop giggling.

'I think King Tut may be even older than that,' said Isabella.

They entered the first room, still joshing each other, but even Darlene gasped as they saw the life-size figure guarding the first room with his golden staff in his hand.

'I didn't know history could be so glamorous,' she said.

The pressure of people coming into the museum moved them on faster than they would have liked, but they saw all fifty-five artifacts from the tomb. The young pharaoh's mask entranced all three.

'I can't belief these treasures are almost three thousand five hundred years old,' said Isabella. 'That's way before Jesus.'

They bought four copies of the brochure for the exhibition at seventy-five pence each.

'I hope Belle wasn't joking about the money,' said Liz. 'That's cleaned me out.'

'My father is ridiculously generous,' said Darlene. 'Let's go to Biba first.'

'What's Biba?' said Liz.

'The most beautiful shop in the world.'

Nuala was sitting on the massive sofa in Belle's flat with a hot-water bottle on her stomach when they got home from the museum. Darlene had bought pork pies and other luxuries in Marks and Spencer, and they all tucked into them with gusto.

'Blimey,' said Belle. 'Haven't you lot ever eaten before?'

She oohed and aahed over the brochure for ages, stroking the colour photos with awe.

'Thanks girls, this is magnificent. I almost feel like I saw it too instead of... Well, you know.'

'Was it frightening?' said Isabella.

'Not really,' said Nuala. 'Belle held my hand, and they put me to sleep. When I woke, it was over. I don't even know what they did, but the nurse told me I'm not pregnant any more.'

'How are you feeling about it?' said Liz to Nuala.

'I was a little woozy, but now I feel fine. Belle gave me some pills that stopped the cramps. I don't remember anything to tell you the truth.'

'And neither you should, ducks. Your life is starting fresh from today and you never have to think about any of this again. Are you ready for a bit of shopping? I think we should jump in a cab since Bill's paying, and Isabella needs a pair of patch jeans.'

For two girls who had had to share ill-fitting hand-me-downs for years, the afternoon shopping in London harked back to a time before their flight to Ireland. The fashions and looks in the shop windows brought them right into the nineteen seventies with a bang.

'What on earth are clogs doing on sale?' said Liz. 'I thought they were for Dutch milkmaids.'

'Get a pair,' said Belle. 'They're all the rage. You wear them with flares and a tank top. The girls at school will be so jealous.'

Soon all four girls had bought outfits, shoes, and accessories with Bill Edmunds's largesse.

'If I smile any wider, my face is going to break,' said Isabella.

'We can ring Bill and Marion when we get in. They'll be so pleased to hear you had an enjoyable time,' said Belle.

No-one answered the telephone in the big white house. Belle just shrugged.

'Those phone lines to Ireland are terrible. We can try tomorrow instead. Who wants to go to the Tower of London? Or Madame Tussauds? Or the zoo? We might manage all three. I'm taking the phone off the hook now, so no one can book with me and I can take the day off,' said Belle.

They visited the first two and then returned home to rest and eat cream cakes. Liz wrote copious postcards, while the other girls tried on each other's outfits and watched television.

'Do you want me to post those for you, ducks?' said Belle. 'They'll get home after you do, but I don't suppose anyone will mind. Who's Michael?'

'He's our brother. He's at school in England and he lives with my father's friend George most of the time. I don't think he likes Ireland; he always goes somewhere else in the holidays.'

'You miss him?'

'All the time. He used to be my best friend, before Darlene. But he's only interested in rugby and the cadet corps now.'

'Men,' said Belle.

Whatever she had intended to say, she never finished. The telephone rang, and she picked it up, holding her finger to her lips and winking.

'Hello, this is Belle. What is your delight?'

The girls looked at each other and tried not to laugh.

'Bill, slow down. I can't hear you well,' said Belle, shielding the earpiece. 'Oh my good God. Is Marion okay?'

Darlene jumped up and ran over to Belle, grabbing the phone.

'Dad, what's up. We tried to ring you yesterday but we couldn't get through.'

As white as a sheet, she listened to her father speak, nodding. A tear escaped and ran down her cheek.

'Yes,' she said. 'I'll tell them. I'll go to Auntie Margie's and wait for you there.'

She handed the receiver back to Belle and slid down onto the carpet.

'Whatever's the matter?' said Liz. 'You're as pale as snow.'

'The Provos have burnt our house down.'

Chapter 29 – Homecoming, June 1972

Liz clung on to the railing of the passenger deck and gazed out over the Irish Sea across the foam whipped up by the steel-coloured waves which created the illusion that the ferry navigated stormy skies. Darlene's shocked face hovered in her mind's eye, making her tremble with fury at the injustice of it all. Despite Belle's best efforts, the last evening in her flat suffered from a chill no central heating would remove. If Liz could have taken the other girls and gone to wait at the station, she would have. Somehow, living in Ireland, and being a terrorist, became synonymous, both guilty in Darlene's eyes, who had lost the plot after receiving the news about her home.

'That scumbag boyfriend of yours,' she screeched. 'He did this.'

What was the point in replying? Darlene had stolen Liam from under Liz's nose, and now the pigeons had come home to roost. She had warned Darlene about Liam's dalliance with the Provos, but to tell the truth, she never imagined they would let him join. He struck her as too insecure to kill people, too needy to be chosen as a recruit.

The girls had slunk off under the yellow streetlights to catch the early boat train from Paddington, their rucksacks bulging with contraband from Biba and other fashion emporiums. Liz tried to say goodbye to Darlene, but she moaned and pretended to still be asleep.

'Don't worry, ducks. She'll get over it. I have your address on a postcard so I'll give it to her when she's calmed down,' said Belle.

'You've got to understand. I didn't realise what Liam was capable of. He's just a boy,' said Liz.

'I've seen enough men to know of what they are capable. No one's blaming you.'

Belle gave her a warm hug.

'I don't want to see you again,' she said to Nuala. 'If you get what I mean.'

Euston station loomed shabby in the early light, almost deserted, except for the passengers heading for the boat train.

'Please look after this bear,' said Isabella.

'Wrong station,' said Liz.

They found a compartment halfway down the train and shut themselves in, spreading their bags around the spare seats to discourage invaders on their territory. Nuala lay along one bench, her hands over her stomach, and fell asleep again. Liz and Isabella sat together and gazed out of the window as they pulled out of London.

'There's nothing like a quiet weekend in London,' said Isabella.

'And that was nothing like a quiet weekend in London,' said Liz.

The ferry shuddered as it hit a large swell. Liz tightened her grip on the guardrail, reluctant to go back inside. Isabella lurched across the deck of the ferry and linked her arm through Liz's. Her breath smelled of vomit.

'This bloody rust bucket will be the death of me,' she said. 'A penny for your thoughts.'

'What a bloody mess. I feel like Jonah. First, I lost Michael and now Darlene. I'll be glad to get home. Even the convent will be a relief. A few Hail Marys and a rosary, and I'll feel better.'

'Don't be silly. I can't tell whether Darlene will come around, but Michael loves you,' said Isabella, wrinkling her brow. 'I'm worried about Nuala. She's not reacting at all. It's like nothing happened.'

'She's may be too immature to understand what happened. You can't guess what's going on in her head. She must process it eventually, but perhaps this is her way of coping now.'

'Why can't we do something?' said Isabella. 'He should be in prison.'

Liz sighed and gripped Isabella's arm tighter.

'In a just world, he would be. But Daddy is right.'

'Yeah, life isn't fair. But it should be.'

They stayed there staring into the darkness until a shower drove them back into the smoke-filled lounge smelling of fried eggs and chips. Isabella retched again and disappeared to the toilets. Liz took out the brochure from the exhibition and tried to fill her mind with thoughts of adventure and treasure to drive out the horror.

***

Tom picked the girls up from Kilkenny station and took them home to Dunbell. A torrent of information greeted his questions about London and the exhibition, all the girls trying to outdo each other.

'I heard you bought some nice clothes,' said Tom.

'Mr Edmunds sent Belle loads of money for us to spend. He is a nice man. I can't believe he's a gangster,' said Liz.

'I can't wait to show you my outfits,' said Isabella.

'We're expecting a fashion show,' said Tom. 'Mr Edmunds deserves a medal. I suppose you heard about—'

'We did. Have they gone back to England?'

'I'm not sure. They disappeared after the fire.'

'It's the stupid Provos again,' said Isabella. 'Why can't they disappear instead of the Edmunds?'

'I hope Liam wasn't involved,' said Nuala, knowing he must have been.

'Oh God, I hadn't thought of that,' said Liz. 'I'm sure he wasn't.'

Tom dropped Nuala off at the gate of her house and took the other girls home. She felt shaken by the conversation in the car. It had been easy to forget about the Edmunds on the trip home, but now reality hit home. Her brother seemed a likely culprit after he spent weeks chasing Darlene.

She steeled herself for the reunion with her mother. After pushing the abortion to the back of her mind, she had suppressed any feelings and indulged in their shopping trip. It seemed unlikely now, like a nightmare, or something that happened to somebody else. Her mother would not feel the same.

As she had predicted, Maeve received Nuala with an excess of emotion, suffocating her daughter, who wriggled free as soon as she could.

'How's my precious baby girl?' said Maeve. 'Are you all right? I was so worried about you.'

'I'm fine, Mammy. I had a great time. Don't fret about me.'

A hurt look crossed Maeve's face. Oh God, here we go.

'Are you sure you're okay?' said her mother. 'I'm here for you if you want to talk about it.'

Nuala frowned. 'Mammy, I'll be mortified if you don't forget it ever happened. It's over. I don't want to discuss it, now or ever again. Please?'

Maeve nodded, but the pain lingered in her eyes, driving Nuala up to Sean's bedroom where he was bent over his books.

'Why didn't you come downstairs when I arrived? I got you a present,' said Nuala.

She threw a navy-blue t-shirt with a picture of a London bus over Sean's head so he couldn't read his book. He tossed it to one side without looking at it. Nuala picked it up and put it in front of him again.

'Hey, what's up? Didn't you miss me? Don't you like your t-shirt?'

'You don't get it, do you? You visited London with your friends and saw the Egyptian mummy and bought new clothes. I stayed here on my own, trying to stop Daddy from murdering Mammy. Michael's gone, even Liam's got plans, but I'm stuck here while you all have fun.'

Nuala's mouth fell open.

'She didn't tell you, did she?'

'Who didn't tell me what?' said Sean.

'Mammy.' Nuala hesitated. *No going back now.*

'Tell me.'

'The rape made me pregnant.'

Sean gasped and turned around in his chair.

'Pregnant but –'

Nuala held her hand up.

'I had to visit London to get rid of the baby. The others only came with me to make it less obvious.

Darlene's mother paid for the trip out of the goodness of her heart and her friend Belle recommended a doctor who, you know…'

Nuala avoided Sean's eyes, afraid of what she might see there. He jumped to his feet; his head clamped in his hands as if it might explode. He paced up and down the room, muttering and swearing.

'Jesus, Mary and Joseph,' he said. 'Why didn't you tell me?'

'Mammy didn't want to upset you. It's a mortal sin. I'm going to hell for sure.'

Sean sat down again. He touched her forearm.

'But how—'

'You don't need to know. I promise it didn't hurt.'

'Are you all right now? I mean, about…'

'I don't have a choice. I have to be all right.'

The distress on her face made Sean angry.

'But that man didn't give you one. You didn't ask to be pregnant. He raped you. Surely, he's the one with the mortal sin?'

'Are you so dumb that you haven't noticed? Women get blamed for everything. Even God's against us.'

'I'm sorry,' he said. 'Of course, it's not your fault. I'd like to kill him.'

'Then I'd lose you as well,' said Nuala.

'You'll never lose me, even if you want to. I'm your brother.'

Nuala smiled.

'We all have our burdens.'

***

Despite agreeing not to mention the rape ever again, Sean brooded for days. *How could the church be so wrong about everything? First his mother and now Nuala, the kindest people on the planet, labelled for ever because of one mistake.* He couldn't understand why God picked on them. Even the priest who beat Michael did not act from a holy place. He tossed and turned in his sleep and couldn't concentrate or enjoy in life.

Liam, who came to visit with a rare spring in his step, found his lack of interest irritating.

'For feck's sake. You're moping around here like a wet weekend. Let's take Blue for a walk.'

'You think everything's a joke. I bet it was you that got the Edmunds's house burned down.'

Liam narrowed his eyes.

'I did, but they deserved it. They were criminals trespassing on our territory. The hierarchy got rid of them before they started operations in Ireland. They were a legitimate target,' said Liam. 'Anyway, what's it to you? No one got hurt.'

'What about your sister?' said Sean. 'While you're arsing around the countryside setting fire to people's homes, I have to protect everyone by myself.'

Sean choked, unable to go on.

'What are you talking about? What happened to Nuala?'

'It's not my fault. Da beat the seven bells out of Mammy and he attacked me too. I had to leave the house, so we went to a dance with the Greens. During the dance, a man hurt Nuala.'

Liam grabbed Sean by the shoulders.

'What do you mean hurt?'

'He, he…'

Sean looked at the floor, wringing his hands.

'She disappeared, and I, I couldn't find her. Liz discovered her in a ditch, all dirty with her clothes ripped. We had to hide her from Da. Nobody knows about it. You can't tell anyone.'

Liam's throat constricted, and he gulped.

'Is she all right?'

'She is now,' said Sean. 'But please, don't tell her I told you. She's trying to forget it ever happened, and she'd hate me.'

Liam reached out and tilted Sean's chin up, staring him in the eyes.

'I won't. I promise. But you must do something for me.'

'Of course.'

'Tell me who it was.'

Chapter 30 – Initiation, July 1972

Liam pulled the balaclava down over his ears. He shivered with anticipation, rooting in his pockets for his packet of cigarettes, a habit he could not afford. He pulled one out with icy fingers and stuck it in his mouth, fumbling with the matchbox which he dropped.

'You're not going to light that, are you?' said Colm McClusky. 'For feck's sake, don't you know anything?'

Chastened, Liam put the cigarette behind his ear. McClusky sighed.

'People can smell cigarettes from fields away,' he said. 'You can't sneak up on someone if you are smoking.'

'But isn't this guy in his house?'

'And how do you know he's not in the yard feeding the horses? Presume nothing. Just follow us and keep your mouth shut.'

Liam followed McClusky and his companion, Shorty Finnegan, down the quiet back road. Branches formed an arch over the tarmac, making it look like a tunnel. They entered the short drive to Hegarty's farm, the gravel crunching under their feet. The whitewashed walls of the farmhouse loomed through the gloom. One window threw a beam of light across the yard. They headed for the front door.

Through a half-drawn curtain, Liam spotted a young man playing with his dog while a television flickered behind them. As they edged closer, Liam saw a photograph of an old woman on the mantlepiece. *Pride of place, a mother's boy. Lucky bastard.* Sometimes the injustice of his separation from his own mother tore at his heart. *That moron Brian O'Connor deserved to be taken outside and shot. Maybe once he got established, he would sort Brian out.* He imagined him begging for mercy and smiled.

'What are you smiling for, maggot?' said Finnegan, catching his expression. 'This is serious business.'

Liam wiped the smile off his face, but he saved the image of Brian on his knees for later recall. McClusky pounded on the door with his gloved fist, the sound echoing through the farmhouse. It took a minute for the occupant to twig that someone was knocking. He stumbled through the house and swung the door open, swaying. Seeing the men in balaclavas standing on his door step sobered him up. The man's rosy cheeks drained of colour and his mouth moved, but no sound emerged.

McClusky grabbed his shoulder and frogmarched him into the kitchen. Liam tried to move past Finnegan, but he put his arm across the hallway.

'Let us deal with this,' he hissed. 'Today is watch and learn.'

The three men stood abreast in their black balaclavas, arms folded, staring down Stephen Hegarty who looked like he might faint.

'Are you the pervert who likes little girls?' said McClusky.

'What? No, who told you that?' said Hegarty.

'A little birdy told me you attended the hop at the barn in May.'

'May?' Hegarty scratched his head. 'Yeah, I guess so. I don't under—'

'You didn't rape Nuala O'Connor at that dance?'

'Rape? Wait a minute. Whoever told you that is lying through their teeth. I didn't go near her.'

'She says you did.'

Hegarty looked shocked at this revelation.

'I didn't - she wanted - but she was asking for it,' he stammered.

Liam could not believe what he was hearing. *Nuala was clueless in matters concerning the opposite sex. She had no idea of the affect her adolescent body had on the randy farmers in the area. She couldn't have been asking for it, since she didn't know what it was.* He roared in fury and pain before he could stop himself.

'Kill the bastard!'

Shorty grabbed him around the chest to stop him leaping forward.

'No. Leave it to Mac. He knows what to do.'

'But that bastard raped—'

Shorty clamped a hand over his mouth and whispered in Liam's ear.

'Don't be an eejit,' he said.

Liam realised he had almost given away his identity. He stepped back, panting with fury. McClusky sighed and poked Hegarty in the chest.

'You see how you upset my friend?' he said. 'We don't like rapists.'

'We?' stammered Hegarty.

'The Irish Republican Army, true rulers of this land. You have been found guilty of the rape of a child. We are the punishment squad here to carry out your sentence. Lie on the floor.'

'No, you don't understand. She let me. I thought she wanted it.'

He backed away, crashing into the dresser, and knocking several mugs off their hooks onto the floor where they smashed. Liam winced as they hit the floor.

'Please,' whimpered Hegarty. 'Please.'

He pissed his pants. The acrid odour filled the kitchen, wiping out the aroma of toast that had preceded it. 'I thought she wanted it. I was drunk.'

McClusky gave no sign of hearing him.

'Get him and hold him down on the floor,' he said.

Liam hesitated. The smell of urine had brought him right down to earth. A cold sweat soaked his shirt. He hadn't expected to feel like this. The wailing of the young man, the implacable justice written on the face of McClusky, unnerved him. He wanted to change his mind, to let the man off with a warning, but it was too late.

'Get his legs,' said Finnegan, who sat on Hegarty's chest.

Liam knelt at Hegarty's feet and grabbed his ankles. A piece of bubble gum had attached itself to the sole of Hegarty's shoe. Liam focused on it, trying to imagine what it resembled: *A rhino? A fish?* He stared hard, unable to take his gaze off it, willing the ordeal over. McClusky pulled out an old pistol and aimed it at Hegarty's knees. Liam's blood ran cold as he heard the safety being released.

Two shots rang out. One of Hegarty's legs flew out of Liam's grasp and kicked him full in the face, giving him a bloody nose. He shoved his sleeve under his nose to staunch the blood and put his head back, unable to block out the screaming.

'Mammy, help me. Please, mammy,' said Hegarty, appearing delirious with pain.

'That's the last time you ever touch a girl when you're drunk,' said McClusky. 'Be warned.'

They left Hegarty moaning for his mother and slammed the front door on the way out before heading back up the lane. Finnegan slapped McClusky on the back.

'Great job, comrade.'

'Thanks. You can have that cigarette now,' said McClusky to Liam.

Liam reached up to his ear with trembling fingers, but a tsunami of vomit surged up his throat and he doubled over as his stomach emptied into the ditch.

'What kind of eejit are you?' said Finnegan. 'Everyone knows you shouldn't eat before an op.'

'I'd forget the cigarette if I were you,' said McClusky, pointing to it floating in a sea of sick. 'Come on, let's vamoose.'

Liam nodded, dumb with shock. He shuffled after them as they strode up the lane to where they had parked the car in a gateway. They did not offer to take him home.

'Feck off now,' said McClusky. 'I'll catch you later.'

Liam started walking home to his aunt's house. He couldn't dispel the image of the broken man on the floor of the kitchen wailing for his mother. *The man had raped his little sister, but did that justify a kneecapping?* His head whirled as he remembered the calloused ease with which McClusky dispensed justice.

At least Nuala had some sort of revenge, even if she didn't know who meted it out. No court in Ireland would have convicted Hegarty. The combination of her outfit, 'too short', and the fact she had accepted a drink even though she was under age would have been enough. She, and not him, would have been convicted in the court of public opinion. The charges would never stick.

He hit his thighs with his fists to pump himself up. He couldn't back down now. The Lads had risked their liberty to get justice for him. And he would do the same for them, for Ireland.

***

A few days later, Mrs O'Reilly burst into the Greens' kitchen, panting with her hair askew.

'Did you see the news?' she said.

'We were listening to a comedy on the radio,' said Tom. 'I love the Goon Show.'

'Sit down,' said Bea. 'Will I make you a cup of tea?'

'Yes, of course, although I might need something stronger.'

'What on earth happened?' said Tom. 'Was there another atrocity in Northern Ireland?'

'O God no, nothing like that. No, it's Stephen Hegarty, a young farmer from the next village.'

Tom shot Bea a panicked look, but Mrs O'Reilly didn't seem to notice.

'Have you met him? He's a bit rough,' she said.

'Um, no, I don't think so,' said Tom, rubbing his hands on his trousers.

'A neighbour found him crawling across his yard this morning. The Lads have kneecapped him.'

Bea's hand flew to her mouth.

'That's horrible. Is he going to survive?' said Tom.

'I think so,' said Mrs O'Reilly, glancing at Bea. 'They say he had it coming.'

'How do they know that?' said Tom, effecting calm in the face of this bombshell.

'The Lads called the local paper and claimed responsibility for the kneecapping.'

'What did they say?' said Bea.

'That he's a child rapist,' said Mrs O'Reilly, shaking her head and repositioning a kirby grip. 'I don't often take the side of those scumbags, but if that man raped some poor wee girl, he got what was coming to him.'

'Amen,' said Tom.

Chapter 31 – Joining the Lads, August 1972

'Was it you?' said Liz, leaning on the water trough and observing the water boatmen skim across its oily surface.

'What do you mean?' said Liam, chewing his nail.

'You know exactly what I mean; the farmer who got kneecapped.'

'No, not personally, although I may have seen the bastard get his just deserts.'

He scrutinised her face as she digested this piece of information. It annoyed him he found her attractive. Her dark hair and deep blue eyes set in her porcelain white face made him uncomfortable in a way that Darlene had never managed. He always felt like breaking through her defences and finding out what made her tick, but she never let him breach her studied air of indifference.

He pointed his finger at her chest, brushing her breast on purpose, feeling her flinch under his touch.

'That bastard raped my sister because of you,' he said.

'Because of me? Are you crazy?'

Liz coloured, and he smirked.

'You took her to the dance. She's far too young for that sort of thing.'

Liz shook her head.

'You've got it wrong. Nuala was the one who told us about the dance. I only joined them at the last minute because…'

'Because I chose Darlene instead of you?'

He tried to catch her eye.

'Because Sean did,' said Liz, looking away.

'I don't believe you. He's younger than you. And he's an idiot.'

'I don't care.'

She took a deep breath.

'Did you burn down Darlene's house?'

Liam preened himself.

'I might have. Are you impressed?'

'Impressed? My best friend has left Ireland forever, and a young man will never walk properly again. You're turning into a monster.'

'I'm doing what needs to be done to free my country.'

'By crippling young farmers?'

'You wouldn't understand. The Provos asked me for proof of my loyalty before they would let me join.'

'Why do you want to join so much? To make bombs and kill people in the street?'

'Don't you watch the news? Bloody Sunday will go down in history as a massacre of innocent Irish people by British soldiers. No Irish man worth his salt can stand by and tolerate that.'

'And what about Bloody Friday? How can you justify killing five civilians and injuring more than a hundred others?'

Liam avoided her eyes.

'There were warnings,' he muttered.

'At least twenty bombs exploded in an hour. How could anyone react to that many in time? You're justifying the violence to yourself because you are running away from your life.'

'What life? My mother gave me away, I got thrown out of school, I sleep in a ditch most of the time. The Lads will look after me, they'll be my family from now on. I don't need anyone else.'

'What about your mother, and Nuala and Sean? What will they do if something happens to you?'

'I don't care.'

It sounded hollow, even to him. He cared far too much.

'But you do, I know you do. What about the pact?'

Liam stared at Liz in disbelief. He had not realised how naïve she still was. She had the body of a woman, but she reacted like a girl.

'The pact? Are you insane? Do you really think a juvenile promise means anything to me?'

'It should do. The Greens saved your brother from drowning, and your sister from her rapist. Our mother helped your mother recover from loneliness and rejection. Our father listens to your nonsensical diatribes for hours, so you have an excuse to come to our house and get fed. We keep our promises.'

Liam spat and ground the spittle into the tarmac with his heel.

'Just because there's one weird English family with principles, doesn't mean I should forget mine. I'm going to join them, and no one will stop me.'

Liz sighed. She reached out and touched his cheek, making him jump back as if branded.

'Be safe up there,' she whispered. 'You may not believe in us, but we believe in you.'

Liam strode away down the drive, his hands thrust into his pockets, his chest heaving. *As if he cared about a stupid pact. That's what you get for hanging around with children*. He threw open the metal gate of the O'Connor farmhouse and walked to the back door which hung open. Maeve sat in the kitchen nursing a cup of soup. The rich aroma of boiled chicken carcass filled the kitchen and insinuated itself up his nostrils. She looked up and love leaked from her when she saw who it was.

'Want one?' said Maeve. 'I just finished it.'

He wanted to refuse, but the idea of a last meal with his mother proved too potent. He smiled.

'Grand. Can you cut me some soda bread as well? I'm starving.'

He watched her lay the wobbly table with another setting and carve two big hunks off the soft loaf of freshly baked bread. She placed them on a side plate with a big knob of butter, her fingers worn and calloused from scrubbing the clothes and the floors. Then she spooned out a bowl of soup, so full it slopped over the edges and burnt her fingers.

'Ouch, that's hot,' she said, running them under the ice-cold water from the faucet.

The hot soup tasted like home and he found it hard to swallow over the lump in his throat.

'It needs more salt,' he said.

'No, it doesn't,' she said, frowning. 'You rarely risk bumping into Brian. You can't stay long if you want to avoid him. What's on your mind?'

'I'm joining the IRA,' he said, raising his head from the bowl to see her reaction. 'They want me to train with them.'

Maeve stood up and walked to the far corner of the room, tugging at her apron as if it were strangling her. She shouted across the room at him.

'You can't join those bastards. I won't let you.'

'You can't stop me, Mammy. My mind is made up.'

246

'What about your brother and sister? What if something happens to you?'

'Nothing will happen. The Lads will take care of me.'

'The Lads?'

Maeve's face turned purple with rage.

'The same Lads that blow up people in the pubs. The big-hearted men who murder British teenage soldiers in the streets? Who kneecap farmers? Those Lads?'

She came back to the table and sat down, glaring into his face.

'What would they do if they found out they had an English spy in their midst?' she said, her voice shaking.

Liam stopped eating; his spoon suspended over his bowl.

'What are you talking about?' he said.

Maeve half-turned away, leaning her forearms on the back of the chair. She wiped the stray hairs out of her eyes as if to see into the past.

'It's time you knew anyway,' she said.

Liam put the spoon down and shoved the soup away.

'Time I knew what?' he said, the kitchen suddenly cold.

Maeve turned back to him, a faraway gaze in her eyes, as if she replayed the past in her head.

'When I was sixteen, I took a school trip on a coach to the Burren with my class from the convent. It was the first time I stayed overnight somewhere without my parents. The coach picked us up at school and drove to the Cliffs of Moher. That's where I met him, you know.'

'Met who?' said Liam, but he knew. A shiver ran up his spine.

'Your father. His name was Matthew Harris. We fell in love at first sight. His group stayed at the same hostel as us, so we sneaked away to be together for a few hours. We had one wonderful night together in a shed at the hostel. I remember all the spiders.'

'The spiders? Are you mad?'

Maeve's eyes focused on him again.

'It's not my fault if my brain works like that. Anyway, we said goodbye the next day and promised to stay in touch. I never even considered pregnancy as a possibility. We were so naïve in those days. I wrote to him a few times, but then my mother tore up his address because she didn't approve of me having a boyfriend.'

'But why hasn't he ever come to see me?'

Maeve's look of compassion almost felled him where he sat.

'He never knew about you. When my parents discovered I got pregnant, they called Father Doherty. He offered me a choice, the laundry or marriage to Brian O'Connor. I couldn't tell your father because I didn't have his address any more.'

Liam tried to speak, but the words stuck in his throat.

'No,' he said, shaking his head, eyes wide with horror.

'I chose Brian, because I thought they would allow me to keep you. After the wedding, Father Doherty told me I would have to give the baby away as Brian would not accept a bastard in his family. I'm sorry, I fought for you but they wouldn't let me keep you.'

'Where is Matthew from?' said Liam. 'Could I find him?'

'That's what I've been trying to tell you. Your father is English,' said Maeve. 'If the Provos ever find out, they'll murder you too.'

Liam stood up. 'You're lying,' he shouted. 'You're trying to make me stay. How could you, you bitch?'

He stumbled out into the back yard and roared with anguish. Sean thundered downstairs and ran out into the darkness after him. He found Liam standing in the barn, his eyes wild, smoking a cigarette with long, furious drags.

'My mother is a slut,' he said, bouncing his leg on the ball of his foot.

'Don't you dare say that,' said Sean. 'She's no more a slut than Nuala. Apologise now.'

He lifted his fists up. Liam waved him away.

'Listen, the local cell of the IRA has offered to train me for the brigade, so I came to say goodbye. Mammy's trying to make me stay by telling lies.'

'You're leaving. What about me? I'm too young to take on Da. He will kill Mammy if you don't stop him.'

'She'll get what she deserves then,' said Liam. 'Come with me. Leave all this behind and be a hero instead. I'll tell the lads you're sixteen.'

Sean laughed, a hollow sound.

'I'm not a coward like you are,' he said. 'I'm staying here to keep Nuala and Mammy safe.'

Liam didn't reply. He dropped his cigarette on the dry straw on the ground and while Sean leaped to put it out, Liam disappeared. Sean waited for him to return and apologise, but only the call of an owl broke the silence.

Chapter 32 – Escaping, July 1972

'Green's got a girlfriend,' said Victor Wright, waving the postcard in the air. 'She must be a bluestocking because she's sent him a picture of an Egyptian Pharaoh.'

A chorus of catcalls echoed around the junior common room. Michael lunged at Victor, catching him off guard. He dropped the card on the floor.

'Hey, easy there,' said Victor.

'Cretin,' said Michael, tutting as the card kept sliding from the grasp of his grubby fingers.

He picked it up and examined it, turning it over to read. He stared at the postcard in disbelief. It taunted him with its breathless message about fun and shopping. Liz and Isabella had been in England, and they hadn't come to see him. A crushing revelation.

'Who's Liz then, lover boy?' said Victor.

'She's my sister, you moron,' said Michael.

'That's what you claim, Red.'

The boy sniggered. Michael bridled. *That nickname again. It surfaced soon after the row with Hugo Longford and circulated around school like wildfire. Most boys called each other by their surnames, but everyone called him Red.*

He had tried to remove himself from his Irish connection by joining the Cadet Corps, as recommended by Tarzan, and got a brutal short back and sides so he looked like a soldier. But his ferocious efforts to be the toughest and the best shot produced comments about the fighting Irish. He complained at length, but his friend Dennis Graham refused to sympathise.

'You're famous, or should I say notorious, for decking Longford who was twice your size. You've got a nickname, and every boy in school knows who you are, which protects you from bullies. Then there's me, every bully's dream. I'm fat and dumb. Nobody knows or cares who I am.'

'It's not that. They're just afraid to get squashed,' said Michael, ducking the swinging fist that followed.

As the troubles in Northern Ireland got worse, Michael shunned the common room in the evenings, preferring to study and read in his room. He dreaded the snide comments about his 'Irish friends' as if he could influence the bombers, or stop the shooting. Moving to Ireland had ruined his life, and he loathed it. He couldn't wait to be old enough to move back to England for good. His letters home became shorter, and full of comments on the wonders of living in Brookham with George.

As the summer holidays approached, he searched for a way to avoid going home to Kilkenny. George Kennedy came to his rescue by giving him the chance of travelling to South Africa to visit his grandson, Dirk. Accepting with alacrity, Michael rang home to tell his parents he wouldn't be coming home.

'It's an amazing opportunity, Daddy. George is paying for my ticket, and Dirk lives near Kruger National Park. They have wild animals there like elephants and lions.'

'Lions? Will you see Elsa, the lioness?' said Tom.

'No, that's Meru National Park in Kenya. Anyway, she died of tick fever.'

Tom coughed.

'So, you won't be home at all this summer?'

'No, but I'll come at Christmas instead.'

'I'll send you some spending money.'

'Ben Kennedy is going to pay us to help him so I won't need any.'

'You seem to have it all organised,' said Tom.

'Yes, I'm so excited. I can't wait.'

'Have a great time, let us know when you're back in Brookham with George.'

His father's voice vibrated with hurt and confusion, but Michael refused to acknowledge it. Their move to Ireland had been his father's idea after all. He signed off with a line meant to wound.

'Tell Liz I'll send her a postcard.'

Michael lay under his mosquito net on his massive hardwood bed. Above him, the ceiling fan wobbled and hummed as it spun, making him move to one side in case it fell on him. The sun crept around the sides of the blinds and shot javelins of light into the room. He pulled up the edge of the net and swung his legs off the bed, checking his plimsolls for scorpions before pulling them on. A pile of clean clothes, ironed as flat as leaves of flaky pastry, sat on the rattan chair in the corner.

He shuffled into the bright dining room and helped himself to a plate of fresh fruit, an unheard-of luxury in his home. Pineapple, mango, and melon left trails of juice down his chin as he shovelled it into his mouth. The cook brought him a serving of scrambled eggs and cold meats, which he devoured.

'Wow, you like to eat,' said Dirk, watching him with amusement.

'It's such delicious food,' said Michael. 'You wouldn't believe the catering at school. And the food in Ireland is so boring. Bananas are as exotic as we get over there.'

'When you've finished, we're going to help Dad put up the chicken wire around the bird cages.'

'Okay, give me a minute to drink my tea.'

Dirk left to collect the tools and Michael sat alone in the large room, breathing in the cool morning air, and enjoying the smell of jasmine which wafted through the muslin curtains. The sound of crickets chirping got louder and louder but became a background noise which he didn't hear unless he tried.

The noise of a plate dropping on the floor and shattering made him spin around, his reverie disturbed. A black girl stood behind him; her mouth open in shock. Her unexpected beauty almost stopped his heart. Michael jumped up and collected the pieces, balancing them in the palm of his hand. He held them out to her, smiling.

'Hi, I'm Michael,' he said. 'Who are you?'

Before she could answer, an enraged hippopotamus of a man burst through the door.

'What have you done now, you stupid girl?' he said, his hands on his hips. 'This is the last straw. That's one of the Boss's favourite plates.'

'It was me who broke it,' said Michael. 'I'm sorry.'

The man screwed up his eyes and glared at him.

'Are you sure it wasn't Blessing? She's as clumsy as a gazelle on an ice rink.'

Michael nodded.

'I picked it up from the table to give to her and I dropped it.'

The man took the pieces and rumbled back into the kitchen, puffing, and blowing in indignation. Blessing smiled at Michael.

'Thank you,' she said. 'He just needs one excuse to get rid of me. He can't bear the Makuleke people.'

Before Michael found out who they were, Dirk appeared at the door.

'Let's go then,' he said.

Michael turned around to say goodbye, but Blessing had vanished. He followed Dirk out into the warming air and soon they were pulling and twisting at the wire netting, making it bird-proof. Michael could not get Blessing's smile out of his mind. Dirk caught him daydreaming when he should have been stapling the wire to the framework.

'Oi, keep your mind on your work, the cage nearly collapsed.'

'Sorry, I'm having trouble concentrating.'

'It can't be jet lag, we're on the same time line as the UK.'

'No, the truth is I met a pretty girl this morning and can't get her out of my head.'

'You're hallucinating. There are no women here except for my mother.'

'Her name's Blessing.'

'Are you crazy? She's blik,' said Dirk.

'She's what?'

'Blik, you know, negro.'

'Oh, black.'

'That's what I said, blik.'

'She's still beautiful.'

'Don't be disgusting. They're animals. Why do you think we've got these Apartheid laws?'

Michael did not reply. The Apartheid regime made no sense to him. *Why would you divide people into four groups depending on their colour? What if an Indian was darker than a coloured person? Where did you draw the line between coloured and black?* He had noticed on his journey to Richard's Bay that only white people had cars, and black people lived together in crowded shanty towns while white people had large houses. Ben had been evasive when Michael asked why. 'Because that's how it is here' did not satisfy his curiosity.

Dirk did not suffer from the same reticence. They had brought him up in the Apartheid system and saw nothing wrong with it.

'Africa is a tribal continent,' he said. 'It's governed with brute force. The white men are the strongest tribe in South Africa, so they are the rulers. It's not difficult to understand.'

But it was. Michael did not believe in separating people by race, and his crush on Blessing only grew stronger when it became illicit. She caught him gazing at her several times over the next few days and blushed. Despite his efforts, he did not talk to her again except to thank her for clearing the plates. Dirk made sure of that.

'We're going to the Kruger National Park today,' he said. 'Dad says we've earned a day out. Lekker?'

'Lekker,' said Michael. 'I'll get my camera.'

They entered the park through the gates on the northeast corner and soon passed by several abandoned villages of mud huts with palm-leaf roofs.

'Why does nobody live here?' said Michael.

'Because they'd get eaten by lions,' said Dirk.

'This area of the park used to be Makuleke tribal land, but they moved the tribe to Ntlhaveni about two hundred kilometres away when they expanded the park boundaries,' said Ben. 'Speaking of lions, I know a patch of acacias trees where one pride takes their afternoon nap. Let's go down there and see if we can find them.'

Chapter 33 – Blessings, August 1972

Several days later, Michael found Blessing sitting under a mango tree eating a piece of biltong, tearing the meat with her pristine white teeth. She looked around in alarm as he approached her.

'Do you need something, boss?' she said, scrambling to get up.

'Michael, my name's Michael.'

'I can't call you that.'

'There's no one listening.'

'They'll call you a Kaffir-boetie,' she said. 'Don't you care?'

'What's that?'

'A white person who likes black people.'

'I've been called worse. Am I allowed to ask you a question? You said you were Makuleke, and I think we drove through one of your villages in the National Park.'

'They're not ours any more. The government moved us from our ancestral lands, rich in game, wild fruits, and fish, onto a plot of dry savannah which we did not know how to farm. It was not big enough to sustain us all, so many people had to leave and look for work far from home, like me.'

'How old are you?'

'Fourteen. Why?'

'I am too. I can't imagine having to leave home and work.'

'Where do you live?'

'Ireland, but --'

Blessing's face lit up.

'You're Irish? How wonderful. My teacher told me about Ireland. She's a missionary from Cork. You also know what it's like to be oppressed. We are the same, despite our different skin colours.'

She reached out and squeezed his hand. Michael's heart sank. How could he tell her he belonged to the oppressors, not the oppressed?

'You're right. The British pushed the Irish farmers off their land and exiled them to the poor soil in the West of Ireland,' said Michael. 'They gave the farmers small plots which served only for subsistence farming, sustaining their families on a diet of potatoes.'

'See, just like us.'

'Except the crops failed because of a potato blight, causing the people to die of starvation. Many people left for work in America and never returned.'

Her shoulders sagged. 'Like me,' she said.

'Blessing, where the hell are you?'

Chef's voice roared out from the kitchen and she skipped past Michael, heading for the back door. She blew him a kiss before disappearing into the house.

Michael couldn't get the conversation out of his mind. The parallels with the British treatment of Ireland worried him. To his shame, he remembered laughing at a sign he had seen in a bed-and-breakfast hotel in Brookham – No Coloureds, No Dogs, No Irish. *How would it feel to be treated like that? He had had a brush with prejudice at school, but nothing compared to this.*

Michael managed to get Ben alone one evening when Dirk went to bed early with mild sunstroke. As he did every night, Ben read a chapter of his book and drank a gin and tonic out on the veranda. He smoked a cigarette to keep the mosquitos away, blowing the smoke over his clothes to distance them. Michael offered him some repellent.

'No thanks. The ciggies work pretty well. How are you getting on? Are you missing home?'

Michael shrugged.

'I don't know where home is. I can't get used to Ireland, but people in England judge me because I live there.'

Ben took a deep drag on his cigarette.

'I know how that feels. South Africa is great in lots of ways, but I've never felt like I belong. The Apartheid system grates on me every day.'

'Why don't the black people throw the white people out?'

'And where would they go? They've lived here for hundreds of years. This is their home too.'

'But the system is disgusting, how can people justify it?'

'Apartheid will disappear soon. There's a lot of opposition to the system outside Africa. Sporting sanctions are biting hard here. We can't take part in the Olympics, and they called off the cricket tour of England. It can't be long before governments use economic sanctions against South Africa too.'

'So, you'll stay?'

'If they let me. You can't change things by running away. I try to treat all my black staff with respect and pay them decent salaries. I hope they'll remember that when things change.'

'What about Dirk? He seems pretty happy the way things are.'

'His school is full of Boers, a lot of whom are strong supporters of Apartheid. It's only natural he picked up their attitude. I try to reason with him, but I guess he'll learn the hard way. It's never easy to be on the wrong side. Someone has to make the first move.'

'I'd like to contribute something to your staff while I'm here,' said Michael. 'They've been very good to me.'

'For all of them, or just one of them?' said Ben. 'I've seen the way you look at Blessing. Oh, don't worry, if I was your age, I'd be staring too. She's exquisite.'

Michael grinned.

'I had planned to refurbish the staff quarters,' said Ben. 'They're looking a bit tatty, and I'm worried about the wiring. Do you fancy helping me with that?'

'Of course.'

Michael sat without speaking for a while as his head whirled with ideas. Finally, he stood up, leaving Ben reading his book.

The next morning, Blessing gave Michael a wink at breakfast, making him blush and drop his spoon into his porridge. He wiped the splashes off his khaki shirt, trying not to laugh. *How do I tell her the truth, when she might shun me for being English? And yet, I can't face lying to her again either.* He resolved to stick close to Dirk, avoiding any tough conversations with her.

Instead of banishing his woes, his visit to South Africa had brought them out into the open and made him examine his own motives. Life had become a booby-trapped maze of contradictions, but one fact shone crystal clear, the only place he could count on unconditional acceptance was with his family, no matter where they were. He could hardly bear to remember his father's hurt tone on their last phone call.

Ben took the boys to the beach for a week of fishing and sailing where Michael's buzz cut bleached almost blond. He had grown a couple of inches too, and his clothes became tight on his expanding frame. His reflection surprised and thrilled him when he glimpsed himself in a full-length mirror at the hotel. *Few boys at school are big enough to insult me now and get away with it.*

When they got back to the game lodge, Michael devoted himself to fixing up the staff quarters and improving their living conditions with Ben and Dirk. They stripped out rotting window frames and rewired the housing to modern standards. They even put proper showers into the bathrooms, replacing the rusty buckets with holes in them with shower heads.

Ben threw a party for the staff to celebrate the upgrade and as a farewell for Michael. The chef cooked a massive braai with ten different types of meat, all liberally sprinkled with chilli sauce. Michael had to drink a flagon of water after his first brush with the South African idea of 'spicy'. He sat outside with his eyes running while he stopped sweating. A pair of cool hands covered his eyes and made him hold his breath. Blessing giggled in his ear.

'I hear you're leaving us tomorrow. Were you going to take off without saying goodbye?'

'Of course not. Dirk is like the apartheid police though; he watches me like a hawk in case I try to talk to you.'

'Well, I'm here now.'

She leaned in and kissed his lips with her own plump cushions. He pulled her closer, and they fell onto the grass laughing. She smelled of fried onions and garlic, and her lips stung his with their chilli lip gloss of beef fat. His first kiss, and he prolonged it, marvelling in the whole-body experience of his arousal.

They managed five minutes together before Ben called them back indoors for the speeches. Michael floated into the dining hall, changed forever from the child he had been when he arrived. Life seemed to offer infinite possibilities. It was time to take sides.

Chapter 34 – Training, October 1972

After the success of the campaign to hound the Edmunds family out of Ireland, and his blooding at the Finnegan kneecapping, Colm McClusky did not hesitate to recommend Liam to the hierarchy.

'I didn't think you had it in you,' he said to Liam. 'Training starts on Monday next week.'

Liam beamed. Finally, they had taken him seriously. He shelved his doubts as his pride took over. He'd soon prove himself worthy of membership. He couldn't wait to get started.

'I won't let you down,' he said. 'Where do I go?'

'You know the woods up behind the quarry? Someone will pick you up at the stile beside Gogan's farm and take you through to the headquarters. Make sure nobody follows you.'

'I won't disappoint you,' said Liam.

'You'd better not. I stuck my neck out for you,' said McClusky.

Liam coughed and hesitated.

'Spit it out, son.'

'Thanks for dealing with the rapist.'

'We believe in justice, you know. He got what was coming to him.'

'Thanks anyway. My family means the world to me.'

'No bother. Good luck.'

Mrs O'Reilly did not express surprise when she opened the back door of her house to find Liam standing outside in the unlit yard, with his rucksack over one shoulder. She shooed him into the kitchen, looking around before shutting the door.

'Look what the cat dragged in. Are you expecting a bed?' she said, trying, and failing, to be stern.

'I need somewhere to stay,' said Liam. 'I'd be grateful if you could put me up for a while. But you can't tell anyone I'm here.'

'Is it hiding from Brian you are? That man is a liability. He martyrs your poor mother when he has the drink taken.'

'She's well able for it. One of these days Sean will be big enough to knock him down, and then he'll stop. My aunt threw me out. It seems I'm not flavour of the month around here.'

'You can stay in Fintan's room at the side of the house. The window is almost covered with ivy and faces over the driveway, so only the rooks will see into your room.'

'Thanks, Mrs O.'

'I'll cook enough food for both of us, and you can help yourself when there's no one around.' She frowned, bringing her bushy eyebrows together. 'Do I have your word you're not up to anything illegal?'

'Cross my heart and hope to die.'

'Right, I'm going to watch the news. Make yourself at home but be sure no one spots you.'

Liam lay on the mattress in Fintan's room, looking at the damp patch on the ceiling. He quivered with anticipation for the start of training. *How many others would be there? Would they allow him to shoot a gun?* He'd been reading up on his history, and he itched to get revenge on the British for their brutality during the era of the Black and Tans. McClusky remained unconvinced of his motives for joining, but he would show them all.

The next morning Liam set off early, before Tom left for work, trotting down the drive and turning right on the road toward Gogan's farm. The cool air smelled of cow dung and newly mown hay as he skirted the ditch with his cap pulled down over his eyes to avoid identification by passing motorists. In his jacket pocket, the heavy shape of a slab of buttered barm brack slapped against his thigh. His tongue smarted from trying to gulp down a cup of tea too hot to drink.

In the silence of the early morning, the unmistakable sound of a dog's nails clipping the tarmac made him turn around. Blue had followed him from the farmhouse. She wagged her tail and came towards him, head lowered in anticipation of a scolding. He wanted to send her back, but stroking her warm body gave him courage and the companionship he craved. *She couldn't be any trouble. I'll tie her to a tree if necessary.*

'Come on, girl,' he said.

Blue trotted ahead of him on the road, nose to the gravel. They got to the stile at the same time as a tall, thin man with dentures that moved around his mouth like barrels in a waterlogged ship.

'You mushed be Liam,' he slurred. 'I'm Donal. Wash the idea of bringing your dog? Is it for target practish or what?'

Liam blanched.

'No, she followed me. I'll leave her at home tomorrow. I promise.'

'I was only codding. She's a beautiful animal. Did you get her off the travellers?'

'Yes, she's half greyhound, half Irish Wolfhound, I think.'

'Let's see how we go. If she's a pain, you must take her home. This training is deadly serious, and any distractions could be fatal.'

They walked up a muddy path along the stone wall behind where Sean had almost drowned in the slurry pit. Liam stopped in his tracks, staring at the square patch of innocent-looking bright green grass. The memory of Sean's frantic face dissolving into relief as he realised his big brother would save him cut through his upbeat mood. *He'll never survive Brian's temper without me. What the hell am I doing here?*

'Are you all right? You look like you've seen a ghost,' said Donal.

Liam shook himself.

'Yes, grand thanks. I just remembered something, that's all. Nothing important.'

They entered the woods and climbed up the side of the hill, always taking the right fork of the path. After half an hour, Donal stopped in front of a large, well-camouflaged Nissen hut. If Liam hadn't been with Donal, he would have walked right past it without a second glance.

'HQ,' said Donal. 'If you ever tell anyone its location, we reserve the right to shoot you, and your dog.'

'I would never –'

'Nobody is accusing you of anything. You've been told. Bring the dog inside so she doesn't bark and attract attention.'

Donal opened the door and Blue pushed past him, running up to a young man with sandy hair and freckles who sat at a Formica table. After having a lick and a sniff, Blue curled into a ball in the corner of the room and dozed off. Donal gestured at the youth.

'Liam, this is Fergus Walsh. Fergus, this is Liam O'Connor.'

Liam bit his tongue to stop himself from disagreeing. *Are you going to call yourself Harris now, you gombeen? How much more English could it sound?* He had wrestled with the knowledge about his father without cease since Maeve had told him the truth. There seemed to be no alternative but to reject it, as if she had never told him. He pretended she had lied to stop him going, and his father was doubtless one of the Lads too. But the revelation had destroyed his long-held convictions, and it took all his bravado to continue down the path he had chosen without turning back.

Donal slapped a green book onto the table in front of him, making him jump out of his skin.

'Wakey, wakey, it's time to acquaint yourselves with the training manual. This is the famous Green Book. Disclosure of its contents will result in a court martial. We expect you to read and absorb all the information contained within. Got it?'

'Yes, sir,' they chorused, and grinned at each other.

'Right, let's get started.'

After a couple of hours, Donal went up the hill to check on something, leaving the two youths to get acquainted. They completed a cursory review of each other's family background. Then, they leafed through their copies of the green books, pointing out fascinating facts and old-fashioned phrases.

'It says 1956 version on mine,' said Fergus. 'It's quite literary. I found a quote on tactics from Lawrence of Arabia.'

'No wonder it's so restrained, except for the bits about killing people,' said Liam.

'By the way, whatever you do, don't volunteer for the explosives section.'

'Why not?'

'My Dad told me there have been a few fatalities this year.'

'Isn't that the point of bombs?'

'The members of the units blew themselves up.'

'But how –'

'Premature detonation. Shh, he's coming back.'

Donal appeared with leaves in his hair and claggy mud clinging to his wellingtons. He didn't comment on his absence.

After a morning spent learning about circuitry and timers, Donal called a halt for lunch.

'Did you bring anything with you?' he said.

'I've got some barm brack,' said Liam. 'I couldn't find anything else at my digs.'

'They've locked the food away so you can't steal it,' said Donal.

'I've got some ham sandwiches. I'll swap you one for a piece of the barm brack,' said Fergus. 'I'll tell my Mam to make sandwiches for two from now one.'

'Oh, I couldn't ask you to do that,' said Liam.

'It's no bother. Anything for the Lads.'

'Now that's the right attitude,' said Donal.

In the company of Fergus and Donal, Liam's worries evaporated. He had a mechanical bent, so nothing they were learning struck him as too academic. During the afternoon, Donal produced an Armalite rifle.

'The AR eighteen. Isn't she a beauty? The Yanks gave us donations for arms procurement and the top brass bought us these.'

He stripped it down to its component parts.

'Watch me carefully now. You'll be putting it back together.'

The matte-black, oily pieces left shapes on the newspaper, mesmerising Liam who couldn't wait to caress them and slide them back together. They spent the afternoon taking turns and timing each other.

'This gun will change the balance in our favour,' said Donal. 'Who wants to try out their shooting?'

He led the boys to a flat piece of ground dug out of the hillside behind the Nissen hut, striding ahead of them in his long tweed coat.

'I cleared this earlier for us to use. We need to cover it up again when we finish,' he said.

Streaks of bright orange had leaked from the clay and run down the target painted on the hillside, like drizzle on a rainbow cake. Donal reached into a bush and took out a Lee-Enfield rifle. He took a clip from his pocket and showed them how to load it.

'Down-up-down-up-down,' he said, showing them the bullets arranged in the clip. 'That stops them jamming.'

He opened the breech by pulling back the bolt and shoved the clip in using his thumb. Then he slid the bolt back into place and handed the rifle to Fergus, whose lip curled.

'Aren't we going to use the Armalite?' he said. 'These yokes are ancient.'

'The Armalites are for the veterans of the fight. You'll be lucky to get an ancient handgun at this rate. Anyway, you're unlikely to be shooting for a while,' said Donal.

'What will we be doing?' said Liam.

'You'll see soon enough. Now, who can get five bulls-eyes?'

Chapter 35 – Photographs, October 1972

Michael shifted his weight to free his arms and let his breath out slowly. Three hundred yards away, the target came in and out of focus as he screwed his eyes up to stop a drop of sweat falling into one of them. His index finger rested on the cold metal trigger and his cheek on the worn barrel. *One more shot would do it. The Ashburton Shield and his name on the honours board at Whittingham were at stake.* He shut his eyes to concentrate as he waited for his turn. A woman walked by downwind of the shooters and her perfume wafted over them. Michael breathed in its sweetness, and Blessing's face invaded his thoughts, making the stress of competition fall away.

Since returning from South Africa, a whole new world of possibilities had opened up for Michael. A second skin of imaginary armadillo scales now covered him and deflected the petty comments of the anti-Irish lobby at school. They were pathetic. He pitied them, locked up with their prejudices and unable to admit they might be wrong. His resentment at being dragged to Ireland still simmered, but he shelved it for another time.

He had written a long letter to Blessing on the flight home and posted it in the airport. George paid to develop his films in the Kodak outlet when he realised Michael had spent all his money on holiday.

'If I wait for you to have enough cash, I'll never see them,' he said. 'I want to see my son and grandson.'

Grateful, Michael picked the fruit from the trees and mowed the lawn in the back garden without being asked. He shared George's impatience to see the photographs, but for a different reason. When the prints were ready, they collected them and ripped open the envelope. They sat together in the car park, passing them between each other.

'Goodness, isn't Dirk tall now?' said George. 'Is he good company?'

Michael hesitated, searching for the right words.

'Yes, he is, but I prefer Ben,' he said. 'I can see why he's Daddy's best friend.'

'He inherited a lot of Lee's wonderful qualities,' said George. 'And who is this exquisite young woman who appears in a lot of the photos?'

Michael blushed and grinned.

'That's Blessing,' he said, stroking the photo with his fingers, lost in contemplation.

George tapped the side of his nose.

'Oh my, you've fallen hook, line and sinker for her, haven't you?'

'She's the most wonderful person I've ever met,' said Michael. 'You can't imagine how wise she is, despite her age. I'm going to marry her, you know.'

George guffawed.

'You're a one-woman man, just like your father. But don't you think it's a bit too soon to decide?'

Michael frowned.

'Is it because she is black? Because if that's—'

'No, never think that. I don't care what colour she is, if she makes you happy. You are like a different person since you came back from South Africa. She has done wonders in a short time. Have you written to her?'

'Yes, I sent a letter from the airport.'

'Excellent, I'll give you extra money this term for stamps and a phone call or two. These long-distance relationships are expensive.'

'Thank you. I knew you'd understand.'

To Michael's relief, it wasn't long before letters started arriving from South Africa filled with news and love. George dropped them up to the school when they arrived and collected Michael's letters to send to her. It gave him an excuse to visit the boy at school, which he always enjoyed.

Michael kept his relationship a secret, even from Dennis, who could always come up with a derogatory comment for most minorities. *Would Dennis even understand the passion that has invaded my life?* He couldn't risk an adverse reaction. It's not as if he revelled in popularity at Whittingham. His thin skin and maturing physique made him less easy to tease, and less of a safe target.

One day a beautiful portrait of Blessing fell onto the floor of the common room and to Michael's distress fluttered to Victor Wright's feet. He picked it up and looked at it in astonishment. Michael steeled himself for the torrent of abuse and racism likely to result in his choice of girlfriend. To his surprise, Wright handed it back to him without comment, only raising his eyebrows in surprise.

Later, Wright sat beside him at supper.

'Is she your girl?' he said.

Michael nodded.

'My girlfriend is a Hindu,' said Wright. 'I can't tell anyone in my family about her because they wouldn't agree with me seeing her.'

'Do you love her?' said Michael.

'Don't ask dumb questions, Green.'

The target sharpened in his sight and he squeezed the trigger. He knew before they told him he had hit the inner circle.

'Just outside the bullseye, my boy,' said the Colonel, giving out the prizes. 'Courage under pressure. My sort of chap. Have you thought about joining the army?'

Michael smiled inwardly. He could just imagine the outrage from Sean if he 'joined the other side' in such an overt manner.

'The Cadet Corps will do me for now, sir.'

'You already look like a soldier. How old are you?'

'Fifteen, sir.'

'Hmm, yes, still a little wet behind the ears. I'd be glad to welcome you into the Royal Anglians when you are older.'

'Thank you, sir, but I live in Southern Ireland and I understand it isn't possible for soldiers to go there right now. I'd like to visit my family and see my friends. Perhaps when the Troubles are over.'

The Colonel tried to stare him down, but Michael did not flinch.

'Damn shame,' said the Colonel, moving on to the next boy.

George welcomed him home at half term with a hug.

'Your father must be so proud of you,' he said.

'Um, I haven't told him,' said Michael, blushing under George's intense gaze.

'Why ever not? Have you had some sort of fight? Is that why you didn't go home this summer?'

Michael sighed.

'No. It's hard to explain.'

'I'm listening.'

'It's about Ireland.'

'Ireland, again?'

'No, still. You don't understand. He took us all there without asking, just because he wanted an adventure. It ruined my life, and Liz's. We hate it over there. He didn't think about us. It's hard to forget.'

He shrugged. George's eye's opened wide.

'You mean he hasn't told you yet?'

'Told me what?'

'Why you moved.' George slapped his forehead. 'That man is an idiot. No wonder you are so stubborn. You inherited it from him.'

'I don't understand.'

George gestured for him to sit down. What on earth could have justified his father's behaviour? Would he know if George lied to him?

'Your father had a thriving business which he built up from scratch with his partner, Henry Faversham. They started door-to-door selling vacuum cleaners and other new household products. As the idea caught on, and business increased, they opened a shop in the high street.'

'I remember Henry. I don't know why Daddy abandoned him.'

'Well, they moved to a bigger shop after a few years, and your father wanted to take money out to buy a caravan as a surprise for your mother. He asked Henry to draw down the funds from the bank, but Henry kept putting him off despite there being a large profit in the account.'

The hairs on Michael's neck prickled.

'What happened?' he said.

'Your father left for work one day and found the shop sealed shut. He searched for Henry, but he had run away. Only his wife remained. She told him that Henry had gambled away the business and the properties guaranteeing the loans, including your house.'

'All of it?'

'Yes, your father was made bankrupt and had to hand over the house and everything in it to the bank. That's why you moved to Ireland, taking no furniture or belongings. And why the major gave your parents his car.'

Michael pictured them all standing outside his grandparents' house and his feelings of resentment when they had to squash into Grandpa Joe's car. He felt sick.

'If they make you bankrupt in England, you can't open a new business for six years. So, Mrs O'Reilly offered to help because of her friendship with Lee.'

The lump in Michael's throat threatened to choke him.

'Why didn't he tell us?'

'I don't know. Maybe he thought you were too young to understand?'

Michael didn't answer. He stared at his knees, unable to articulate the combination of relief and misery he felt. George patted him on the shoulder and went to make the supper.

They posted Michael's name on the school honours board and the school photographer took a picture of him holding the shield standing beside his name. He ordered three copies of the photograph and gave one to George. He sent one to his parents and sent one to Blessing. The boys at school left him alone after his name adorned the board, and he settled down to work on his O-levels with the rest of his year.

Chapter 36 – Secrets, December 1972

Michael looked up from bulling his boots to a mirror shine. He dropped the cotton cloth and rubbed his bicep, grimacing.

'Are you looking forward to coming to Ireland?' he said.

Dennis spat on his boot and avoided Michael's inquiring glance.

'My mother won't let me go with you any more. She says it's too dangerous because of all the bombing and shooting.'

'But that's in Northern Ireland. I live in Ireland, which is a separate country. It's not dangerous in southern Ireland.'

'She didn't object until those two car bombs exploded in Dublin, but that decided her and I can't budge her now,' said Dennis.

'I heard someone on the news blame the UVF for planting the bombs,' said Michael.

'Why would they do that? Wouldn't that make the Troubles worse?'

'They wanted to influence the Irish government debate on enforcing stricter measures against the IRA.'

'My mother doesn't watch the news,' said Dennis. 'She listens to Women's Hour and Gardeners' Question Time on the radio. She's not keen on reality.'

'I only asked you out of politeness, anyway. I didn't really want you to come,' said Michael, receiving a dead arm for his remark.

Stormy seas turned his ferry into what a fellow passenger described as a vomit bucket, so Michael stayed on deck as much as he could bear, braving the salty spray as he sat on a bench sheltered from the worst of the wind. His childhood travel sickness had disappeared, and he now had a good pair of sea legs as long as he didn't catch a whiff of vomit, which still had the power to set him off.

Despite his disappointment at Dennis crying off at the last minute, he looked forward to Christmas with genuine longing. If he shut his eyes, he could catch the smell of his mother's cooking and hear the excited squeaks of Isabella ransacking her stocking. His trip to South Africa had put a lot of demons to rest in a way he couldn't explain to himself. The knowledge about his father's bankruptcy had made him feel guilty, but had also dispelled his doubts about Ireland. No wonder his parents were so determined to look forward and not back.

The lights on the quay at Dun Laoghaire beckoned the ferry to its side from miles out, and it chugged through the waves like a shepherd through snow drifts onwards to safety. Michael fell asleep on the train to Kilkenny and would have missed his stop, had a man sitting opposite not woken him up.

'I saw the black cats' scarf,' he said.

Michael grinned and wrapped the scarf, a present from Sean, around his neck. He thrust his arms into his wool overcoat and pulled his suitcase from the alcove at the end of the carriage, heaving it and himself out on the platform just before the whistle blew for the train to leave again. After watching it go, he stood outside on the pavement until his father drew up in the car.

'Jump in,' he said. 'This thing is on its last legs so I don't dare stop the engine.'

Michael chucked his suitcase into the back seat and sat up front, breathing in the familiar leather odour of the battered seats.

'It's time you thought about replacing it,' he said.

'But it will soon count as vintage,' said Tom. 'It could be a valuable antique.'

Michael laughed. His father's sense of humour never changed.

'Tell me about the trip to South Africa,' said Tom. 'How was Ben? Did you get on with Dirk?'

'Ben's business is doing well. He has a superb chef so people come to stay just to eat his food.'

'And Dirk?'

'We got on, but we had little in common. He's a real Boer.'

'At least he wasn't a bore.'

'I think I would have preferred that.'

'Did you take any photos?'

'Yes, I'll show them to you later when everyone is there.'

'George told me you met a girl.'

Michael spluttered.

'You two are worse gossips than Mrs O,' he said.

'No-one is a worse gossip than her, although…'

'Although what? Come on, tell me now.'

'Okay, but keep it to yourself. I think she's harbouring her own secret right now.'

'What do you mean, harbouring?' said Michael.

'Liam's staying in her house, but she has told no one. I saw him from the kitchen window one morning sneaking off down the drive.'

'Where's he going?'

'Who knows? That boy is a law unto himself. Perhaps he's working on a farm nearby, but I don't see why he has to hide.'

'I'm sure we'll find out.'

Michael cleared his throat. His father raised an inquiring eyebrow.

'Spit it out,' he said.

'George told me. About the bankruptcy, I mean. I can't believe you haven't told us.'

Tom stared ahead at the road, his cheek muscles working.

'I had my reasons. We didn't want people to treat us differently, to tease you at school. It's hard enough being in a new country without giving people reasons to reject you.'

'But I thought you came here on a whim. I blamed you for the things that happened to me. You should have told me.'

'You were too young. I felt responsible. I thought I should have noticed that Henry was a gambling addict.'

Michael shook his head.

'I'm sorry, Daddy.'

Tom squeezed his leg.

'I'm sorry too. I never knew you felt this way. You hid it well.'

'Whenever we complained, you told us life was unfair. I gave up trying to find out the truth.'

Tom sighed.

'No wonder you didn't want to come home. When did George tell you?' said Tom.

'When I came home from South Africa.'

'Are we friends again now?'

'I'd like that.'

The rain fell in sheets as Michael jumped out to open the gate to the yard at Dunbell. Cold drops crept down his neck, soaking into his shirt as he leaned into the back seat to grab his suitcase. Isabella and Liz waved through the rivulets on the window panes from the kitchen. He hardly recognised them after so long apart. Tom opened the kitchen door, and they entered to a hug-storm made more intense by Blue leaping up on her hind legs to lick Michael's face of the tears that escaped despite all his efforts.

The aroma of roast lamb made his head whirl.

'I could eat a horse,' he said, tasting the mint sauce with a spoon.

'You must make do with a sheep,' said Bea, ruffling his hair. 'It's so short and you're so tall, you don't look like my little boy any more.'

'And his voice,' said Isabella. 'He sounds like Roger Moore.'

'Roger Less, more like it,' said Liz, beaming.

Long after the children had gone to bed, Bea and Tom sat together on the sofa in the little sitting room, reminiscing about their time in Ireland.

'I never realised how much they cared. I feel responsible,' said Tom.

'The only villain in this piece is Henry Faversham. It's not your fault.'

'I know. We should have told them though.'

'Time ran out. So much has happened, and yet nothing has changed,' said Bea.

'Let's go to bed now, Mrs Green,' said Tom. 'I've got to get a tree tomorrow from the market, and there may be a scrum to get the best one.'

Tom, Bea, and Isabella left for Kilkenny early without waking the others. Liz had to finish a history assignment, and she wanted to get it out of the way before Christmas 'so I can relax'. Michael slept like the dead most of the morning. When he woke, his head ached from dehydration and he stumbled into the kitchen for a glass of water. Sean also entered the kitchen, carrying a small present which he shoved into his coat pocket.

'Mick, you're back.'

Sean could not disguise the delight in his voice. The two young men gave each other an embarrassed hug.

'I've got to go upstairs and get dressed. I'll be down soon,' said Michael.

'You've got to tell me everything,' said Sean.

'How long have you got?'

After Michael took himself and another glass of water back upstairs, Sean scratched his head and looked around at Liz working at the kitchen table.

'Did you forget something?' said Liz.

Sean reached into his pocket.

'I got you this, for Christmas,' he said.

'For me? But I didn't get you anything. I wasn't expecting –'

'It's only a small present, to say thanks for helping with my studies. I don't know what I'd do without you.'

Sean blushed beetroot to the roots of his hair, matched by Liz, who played with the small red bow on top of the present to distract herself.

'Open it, go on,' said Sean.

'Now? But it's not Christmas.'

'I won't be here on Christmas day, please open it.'

Liz pulled the bow open and took the lid off the box. A layer of tissue paper hid the contents. She held her breath and pushed it aside. A silver chain with a heart-shaped locket sat underneath the paper.

'Well?' said Sean. 'Don't keep me in suspense.'

Liz took it out and gazed at it.

'It's the most beautiful thing anyone's ever given me,' she said. 'I–'

'It's my heart,' said Sean. 'I want you to have it.'

He stepped closer to her and the warmth of his body made her giddy.

'I don't understand,' she said, but she did.

Sean touched her face with his rough hand.

'Will you be mine, Liz Green? I've waited so long.'

Liz shut him up by kissing him awkwardly.

'I know,' she said, and kissed him again as he wrapped her into his coat.

'What's all this then?' said Michael, who had reappeared and stood watching them from the door.

They jumped apart, speechless.

'For feck's sake, Mick. Your timing is appalling,' said Sean.

'That's my sister you're kissing,' said Michael, but he smiled. 'It took you two long enough. It was like a sequel of Gone with the Wind.'

'You knew?' said Sean.

'For ages, maybe years.'

'I didn't,' said Liz.

'Know what?' said Tom, as he burst into the kitchen with the tree.

'Nothing,' said Michael. 'Christmas secrets.'

Chapter 37 – Lansdowne Road, January 1973

Michael rubbed his eyes, the crusty rheum flaking off under his knuckles. He resisted the temptation to scratch his face despite the siren call of his pox scabs. As his vision cleared, he noticed someone perched on the chair beside his bed.

'Am I hallucinating?' he said.

Liam examined his pox covered face.

'Jaysus, you look manky,' he said.

'Thanks, I'll recover, but you'll always be a scabby bollix.'

'Now that's no way to speak to your future brother-in-law.'

Michael guffawed. His chest crackled, and he coughed, pulling himself upright on the pillows.

'What are you doing here?' he said. 'I thought you'd have travelled north by now.'

'I'm leaving today, but I wanted to check on you before I left. You've been delirious, you know. You had us worried for a while.'

Michael pulled his eyebrows together as he tried to recollect the passage of the illness, but could only dredge up vague memories of people coming in and out of his room and forcing him to drink through a swollen throat.

'What happened?' he said.

'Your chicken pox developed pneumonia,' said Liam.

'Am I better now?'

'You're talking bollix again, so I guess you're on the mend. Listen, I want you to mind my family for me while I'm gone.'

'Me? But you're off to kill English soldiers. Why would I do anything for you?'

'I won't kill anyone. They don't let junior foot soldiers go to Belfast. I'll be working on the border smuggling supplies across.'

'For the IRA? Please don't go. You have nothing to prove.'

'I've completed the training and taken an oath. It's not like a football club. Once you've joined, you can't just leave.'

'We could take you to England. George Kennedy would find you a place to stay, and a job if you want one.'

Liam stood up, shaking his head.

'It's too late. Mind them for me, won't you please?'

'With my life.'

Liam left Michael wondering if he had imagined the whole thing. He lay back against the pillows, wheezing. Despite Liam's insistence on joining the Provos, Michael could not hate him. He recognised parallels with his own alienation and to his surprise, felt quite emotional about Liam's departure. *Stupid bastard.*

Sean came to see Michael later in the day, and a wide grin broke out on his face when he saw him sitting up in bed.

'For feck's sake, Mick, you had us all worried sick.'

'What happened? I can't remember.'

'I heard you went gob first into your food on Stephen's Day. Maybe you couldn't face any more turkey. You had the doctor worried too. Chicken pox can be quite dangerous at our age.'

'What are you doing here then?' said Michael.

'Oh, I had it years ago. See this round scar on my forehead. That's a pockmark. You get them if you scratch the scabs.'

'Yuck, okay, I'll keep that in mind.'

The door of the bedroom opened and Tom put his head around it.

'Hi lads,' he said. 'Good to see you're on the mend. I've got a proposition for you.'

'What's the craic?' said Sean.

'Well, the doctor recommended Michael doesn't go back to school until the end of January –'

'The end of January?' said Michael. 'What about my lessons?'

'It can't be helped. The school says you'll get extra tuition when you return. Meanwhile they asked if you can read ahead in your textbooks.'

Tom sat on the edge of the bed.

'Anyway, there's a rugby match on the twenty-seventh of January at Lansdowne Road; Ireland versus England.'

'They're coming?' said Michael. 'Isn't that dangerous? Scotland and Wales refused to come last year.'

'Well, they asked the English players one by one if they would play, and enough of them said yes to raise a team. I'd like us to be there if you're up to it. And Sean, of course. What do you think?'

Sean hesitated.

'I'm not sure,' he said. 'I've never been to a rugby match. What if I don't like it?'

Then he laughed at Tom's expression.

'I was only codding. Of course, I'll come. It'll be brilliant.'

No-one got left out. Both families and Mrs O'Reilly piled onto the train to Dublin full of rugby fans who were drinking bottles of Guinness and eating Taytos. Nuala and Isabella sat with Mrs O'Reilly who glared at anyone brave enough to approach them. Maeve, looking festive in a bright green tweed coat and a hand-knitted pair of gloves and matching bobble hat, sat with Tom and Bea. She had even put on some lipstick. Michael looked around at his extended family and a warm sensation invaded his heart.

'Your mother looks pretty,' said Liz to Nuala.

'It's great to see her having an adventure without Brian,' said Michael.

'He's having his own adventure at the pleasure of the Gardai. They found him drunk at the wheel a couple of days ago,' said Sean. 'He had already refused to come and watch a foreign game, anyway.'

'Any chance of them keeping him?' said Mrs O'Reilly.

Maeve tried not to laugh, her cheeks pink with happiness.

They survived the drinking and singing on the train, and staggered out onto the street from Westland Row station. They walked to the bus stop to wait for the bus to the Lansdowne Road rugby ground. Crowds of people wrapped up against the biting wind surged up the street, talking and laughing. Despite the crush, they got on the first bus as the men in the queue made way for the family group.

'It's about time someone showed a bit of solidarity,' said Mrs O'Reilly, resplendent in her moth-eaten fox-fur coat, clutching her crocodile handbag like a weapon.

'There isn't a rebel anywhere who wouldn't be terrified of Mrs O in full flight,' Tom whispered in Bea's ear.

The bus swept round the front of Trinity College and down Grand Canal Street onto the Shelbourne Road. Liz gazed over the walls into the grounds of the University and crossed her fingers for the future. Sean noticed and winked at her, nodding. For the first time, Michael felt at home as they motored down the streets of Georgian houses with their excited crowds. On a seat ahead of him, he saw his parents kissing like shy teenagers.

The bus dropped them right beside the ground. Despite the crush of people waiting to get into the game, they got tickets for the South Stand and found a standing space in front of one of the metal barriers.

'We can avoid the crowd surges by keeping our backs to the barrier,' said Tom.

They stood in a tight group, stamping their feet to keep warm. Soon the ground filled up and swelled with noise, which rose to a climax as the English team ran onto the pitch. All around them were people shouting bravo and clapping.

'Where's the Irish team?' said Sean.

'I guess they're staying back in the changing room for a minute,' said Tom.

The loud cheering turned into a standing ovation of five minutes.

'Not a dry eye in the house,' said Mrs O'Reilly, dabbing her face with a handkerchief decorated with shamrocks.

The match had a predictable result, given the weakened state of the England team, but every play generated massive cheers from the enthusiastic crowd.

'It's a pity we couldn't give you a better game,' said Tom, after England had lost. 'But at least we showed up.'

As the crowd swept out of the stadium after the match, the barrier came down at the railway crossing. Tom, ever alert, pulled most of the group to the left of the gate where there was space to stand, but Liz got tugged into the crush on the right and carried along panic-stricken. She turned her pleading face to her family. Noticing her distress, Sean ploughed in after her. He had filled out during the year and had the strength of a young bullock.

'Stay here. I'll get her,' he said.

His red mop of hair moved through the crowd and, somehow, he arrived at Liz's side. He sheltered her from the crush with his feet planted on the ground, trying to move her back towards Tom and the others. Just when it appeared the crowd would overwhelm them, the train whistled through the crossing, and the barrier lifted, releasing the pressure. The crowd streamed past them as they waited for the pressure to dissipate.

'You saved me,' said Liz.

'I'll always save you,' said Sean. 'I'm going to marry you.'

Liz laughed.

'Don't you think that's a bit premature?' she said.

'I'm serious,' said Sean. 'I'm just waiting for you to be.'

'Can I go to university first?'

'I'm coming with you.'

Chapter 38 – The North, February 1973

The van drove over a pothole and bounced on its axle, causing Liam to lift off the floor and back down with a thud that rattled his kidneys. He groaned, clasping his knees. Fergus grinned at him.

'You need to put on some weight,' he said. 'It's that skinny arse of yours, no shock absorbers.'

'At least I don't have one like an ice skater.'

'Have you been looking again?'

'Feck off,' said Liam, throwing an old shoe at him.

Fergus picked it up.

'That's a fine shoe,' he said, turning it around. 'It's a pity the other is missing. I…'

'You what?'

'There's blood on it,' said Fergus, throwing it to the far corner.

'Don't be an eejit. It more likely engine oil or something.'

'It's definitely blood.' Fergus gazed at the floor of the van and rubbed the back of his neck. 'Do you ever have any doubts?' he said, without looking up.

Was this a trap? He sounded sincere, but Fergus lived and breathed the IRA. Liam found it hard to believe this Fenian could be serious.

'Of course not. Do you?'

'No, it's just –'

The van hit another pothole, throwing the two young men to one side of the van. The shoe landed in Liam's lap. He held it up in the light leaking through the panel separating them from the driver. A blob of congealed blood sat on the toe, making him drop it.

'It's blood, isn't it?' said Fergus. 'I told you.'

'What were you expecting?' said Liam. 'This is a war.'

'I don't know,' said Fergus.

He reached out and put his hand on Liam's arm. 'You won't tell them, will you?'

'Tell them what?' said Liam. 'Shut up, amadan.'

After what seemed like an eternity, the van shuddered to a halt and the back doors were thrown open. Liam and Fergus slid out and stood blinking into the pitch-black moonless night.

'I can't see a fecking thing,' said Fergus.

'This way,' said the driver, switching on a torch with failing batteries.

A weak beam of light illuminated a footpath which led to a large cottage backing onto a yard with outbuildings of various sizes, set in a dip in the landscape. Ancient trees loomed over it, giving it a sinister air.

'I feel like we're Hansel and Gretel,' said Fergus.

'You're Gretel,' said Liam. 'Ouch.'

He had caught his foot on a tree root and fell to earth with a thump.

'Are you okay?' said Fergus

'Stop fooling around,' snapped the driver.

Liam got up, rubbing his knee, and stumbled after them, trying to follow the fading torch light without falling down again. The driver pushed open the door, which creaked theatrically. He dropped a bag of provisions on the floor.

'There's food, batteries and torches in the bag, and beds with sleeping bags upstairs. Sort yourselves out. Someone will be over to check on you and give you an assignment this week.'

He paused at the door.

'By the way, they use this place for punishments, so keep clear if they bring someone in.'

Before Liam could ask him what he meant, the man left, slamming the door, which almost fell off its hinges.

'What was that about?' said Fergus.

'No idea. There's a gas cooker over there. Let's get a kettle on,' said Liam.

'It's freezing. Is there any turf for the fire?' said Fergus.

'I can't see any in here. I'll go outside and see if there's any in an outbuilding. Hand me a torch.'

Liam opened the back door and stepped into the cobbled yard surrounded by low buildings. He shone the torch in a circle before heading for the nearest entrance on the side of a long, low barn. He had to duck under the light switch dangling in front of him as he entered. Reaching back, he stopped it swaying and clicked it with caution. Long fluorescent bulbs flickered into life under metal canopies, illuminating several cross beams with ropes hanging from them. There were brown stains on the concrete floor and a reek of iron hung in the air.

Liam's hackles rose as he surveyed the sinister scene. He swore under his breath. *What on earth happened in here?* It looked like a cameo from a horror film. A shiver ran up his spine. The electric cord swung away from him as he tried to grab it again, his hand shaking. He caught it with two hands and clicked the switch, lunging at the open door and back out into the yard. He shut the door and leaned against it, his heart thundering in his chest.

'What's keeping you?' said Fergus, standing at the open back door which shot a dagger of light across the yard.

'Nothing. Leave the back door open so I can see my way back in and make the tea. I'll be there in a minute.'

Liam retched as the image of the blood stains filled his mind. He shook himself and tried the other doors in the yard, wincing with fright at the shadow within. To his relief, a small shed on the left of the house contained piles of dry turf. He loaded up with as many as he could manage and pushed the door with his foot, striding across the yard using the light from the kitchen window to find his way.

'Great, you found some. I've built a wigwam of twigs and newspaper, so we should be okay now.'

'I hope you've got good lungs,' said Liam, taking refuge in humour.

Once the fire got going, they pulled up a couple of decrepit armchairs and stretched their legs towards the flames. The bulb had blown, so they sat in the dark, the warm light thrown by the fire playing on their faces.

'What did you find out there?' said Fergus.

'Nothing.'

'Don't cod a codder. I know you saw something in one of those sheds. Your face turned as white as snow out there. I could see you shining in the dark.'

Liam picked his cuticles.

'Remember what the driver said about punishments? I found a shed with blood on the floor. Not just drops. Pools,' he said.

'Christ, what is this place?' said Fergus

'I don't know. I thought we would smuggle goods across the border, not bodies.'

'Maybe they killed a sheep for meat. There can't be many shops around here.'

'Probably.'

The single beds upstairs each had a bundled up sleeping bag lying on them. Liam picked up one and sniffed it, holding it away from his nose in disgust.

'For feck's sake, this thing is rank. What's the other one like?'

'What's worse than rank,' said Fergus, screwing up his face.

'And the window's broken,' said Liam. 'This place is a palace.'

Fergus cut a piece of cardboard from a box he found in the kitchen, and they pushed it into the window frame as a glass-substitute.

'Good as new,' said Fergus.

Despite the repair, an icy wind blew around the bedroom, forcing the boys to abandon it and go back downstairs.

'Let's sleep in the chairs by the fire. That way we don't have to get inside the sleeping bags,' said Liam.

'Grand plan. I'll get some more turf.'

'It's the shed on the left. Don't go into the barn on the right unless you want nightmares.'

After an uncomfortable night, Fergus made porridge for breakfast. Liam scoffed his with a layer of sugar on top, luxuriating in the warmth generated by the hot food.

'We've got to do something about those sleeping bags,' said Fergus. 'I didn't sleep a wink even with the fire.'

'Why don't we wash them? I saw a metal bath in one shed,' said Liam.

'Are you sure that's possible? Won't they shrink or something?'

'My mother washed mine with no problem. Let's give it a go.'

The two men used all the saucepans to heat water on the stove and filled the metal basin with soapy water. They dropped the sleeping bags into the water and pummelled them. At first, they didn't notice the water changing colour. Then Fergus jumped back.

'Jaysus, the water's turning pink. Do you think it's the dye coming out?'

Liam scratched his head. He let out a long breath, trying not to let nausea overcome him.

'Let's change the water.'

After a few rinses, the bags smelt almost clean.

'Let's hang them up to dry,' said Fergus. 'Oh no, typical.'

The clouds opened and heavy rain blew into the yard.

'We can hang them in the barn,' said Liam. 'Don't freak out though.'

'Why would I freak out? Come on.'

Fergus grabbed one of the sleeping bags and ran into the barn. Liam ran behind him, stopping to empty the metal basin. Fergus stood like a statue with his jaw hanging open.

'What are those ropes for?' he said.

'Laundry,' said Liam. 'Let's use them for the sleeping bags.'

'But this must be where—'

'Shut up. Just hang up the bags.'

'This must be where they punish the hostages.'

'Don't think about it. We won't be involved in anything like that. Anyway, the prisoners deserve everything they get.'

'How do you know that?'

'Because the Lads are human like us. They don't go around torturing innocent people.'

Liam couldn't help remembering Hegarty's face as he pleaded for mercy before the kneecapping. He shook his head to dislodge the memory. He couldn't get distracted now. Fergus finished tying up the sleeping bag, which hung over a patch of dried blood, dripping into it, and cleaning a patch in the middle of it. He couldn't look Liam in the eye. Reality had set in and neither man wanted to articulate their disillusion. Liam shut his eyes, trying to picture the kitchen at Dunbell with the aroma of Bea Green's cooking.

'Come on,' said Fergus. 'Let's get back to the house.'

Chapter 39 – The Delivery, June 1973

Liam shivered in his damp clothes as he waited, hidden in a ditch under a giant beech hedge. He shifted his position to ease his stiff legs and moved the bag he carried on to his left shoulder. A car drove past through a puddle, showering him with muddy water. He swore and shook his jacket to stop the water soaking in. *So much for the glamorous life of a terrorist. He hadn't seen a woman for months.* Fergus was good company when they were in there together, but time in the cottage dragged with nothing to do except wait for orders.

Liam had sneaked across the border unseen, carrying the bag of detonators and clocks for the explosives team to assemble, while the van crossed the checkpoint several fields west of him. The pouring rain ensured an easy crossing as the British Army patrols sheltered from the deluge, but his cheap bomber jacket did not provide any protection from the rain or the east wind that whipped across the fields. *Should he ask for better gear?* Liam had not yet dared to broach the subject before he had gained the respect of the local cell.

Just when he couldn't crouch any longer, the van trundled up the road and stopped for him to get in. He scrambled out of the ditch and opened the back, crawling in with his bag. The calf muscle in his right leg cramped, and he grabbed it, dropping the bag on the floor.

'Watch those detonators. You don't want to end up like Jack McCabe,' said the driver.

'He had bad luck in spades,' said his companion, slapping his thigh.

Liam cracked a fake smile at the grim joke and pushed the bag into the corner.

'Where are we off to, lads?' he said.

'The Crumlin road,' said the driver. 'You're going to deliver the bag to a safe house while we wait on the corner.'

Belfast, the epicentre of the troubles. He had not done a drop there before. Most of his duties had involved smuggling arms across the border by crossing the fields with Fergus in the dead of night. They had become adept at feeling their way along in the pitch dark of the countryside, down now familiar back routes and hidden pathways. So far, they had avoided bumping into a British Army patrol, but their luck might run out at any time.

'Where's Fergus gone today?' he said.

'Oh, don't worry, your fellow faggot will be back soon. He's taking a trip to Armagh with the local cell.'

Liam flinched at the insinuation, but he did not engage in banter with the driver, a crude man with no empathy and ferocious halitosis. *Probably a psychopath, definitely a sadist.* Liam had never asked him his name. They referred to him as the death beetle when he wasn't around. Fergus had taken an almost pathological dislike to the man and had to be restrained from attacking him on several occasions.

By the time they got to the centre of Belfast, the malfunctioning heating system in the van had almost dried Liam to the bone.

'You need to get that fixed,' said the passenger. 'You could roast a chicken in here.'

'Stop fussing,' said the driver. 'Oi, you in the back, get out and walk up the road behind us. Keep going until you reach the house on the left with the boarded-up windows. It's about one hundred yards from here. Knock three times, pause, and then knock twice. We'll collect you in one hour from the front of the Holy Cross Church. Is that clear?'

'Crystal,' said Liam.

'Okay, wait a minute and I'll give you the all clear to get out.'

As Liam left the vehicle, he felt the hairs on his arms stand on end and a prickle at the base of his neck. He tried to appear nonchalant, like he delivered a bag of explosives most days of the week. He didn't glance back at the van, but kept walking as if he knew the place.

A British Army patrol emerged from a side street in front of him and turned into the road. They carried self-loading rifles or SLRs, instantly recognisable to Liam, and their youthful faces were stretched with fear. The man on the front pointed his gun forward, the two men at the sides pointed left and right, and the man at the back aimed his gun behind them. Liam stepped off the pavement to let them past, but the soldier on the left shoved him into the middle of the road with a grunt. He avoided being run down by a driver who stared at the patrol from his Ford and didn't notice Liam until the last moment.

Liam jumped back onto the pavement, his heart battering his ribcage. He resumed strolling towards the house which loomed ahead of him. The echo of his knocks reverberated throughout the house as his desperation to get off the street translated into extra force. An old woman opened the door, her face raisin-like under her salt and pepper hair, done into braids that hung to her waist.

'Are ye trying to knock the door down, or what?' she said. 'Go up to the roof. Seamus is waiting for you. There's a pot of fresh tea up there, take a cup with you if you want some.'

'Yes, please, and can I use your toilet also please?'

The old woman smiled at his politeness and jerked her thumb towards a cupboard under the stairs.

'It's in there, pet. I'll get you a cup.'

The toilet was tiny. Liam sat rather than stood to prevent banging his head on the steps above him. He dropped his head into his hands, feeling the weight on his elbows as he tried to calm himself. Afterwards, he washed his hands in the tiny basin, splashing water onto his trousers and leaving a tell-tale trail of drops. He sighed and squeezed back out into the hall where the old woman handed him a cup, smiling at the drops on his trousers. He rolled his eyes at her and climbed the stairs.

Liam pushed the trap door into the loft with his head as he climbed the narrow folding stairs upwards, struggling with the bag and sweating with anxiety. His head popped up into the loft and he stared down the barrel of a sniper's rifle.

'And who the blazes are you?' said Seamus. 'Identify yourself or I'll shoot.'

'I'm Liam, from the Inishkeen cell. I've brought some supplies for the bomb guys.'

'The bomb guys?' Seamus chuckled. 'You're new, aren't you?'

'Relatively.'

'I was only pulling your leg. Thanks a million for the delivery. I spotted you on the street earlier, impeding that patrol. You've got some balls. I'll give you that.'

Liam shrugged. He hadn't done it on purpose, but he didn't intend telling him.

'How did you spot me?' he said.

'Through here,' said Seamus, lifting a slate. 'I had hoped they would march this way, but no such luck. Have a peep.'

While the sniper held the slate, Liam gazed down on the street.

'Which one of those men is an undercover soldier?' he said.

None of the men looked remarkable. All had short hair and bomber jackets. Liam shook his head.

'No idea,' he said.

'Do you see that man pushing a pram?' said Seamus. 'That's a squaddie. No Irish man would be seen dead doing that.'

He laughed.

'It's his lucky day. I can't shoot him now you've delivered the gear. I've got to take it to the lads and I can't risk having a patrol on my arse. Help yourself to tea.'

He took the bag and opened the skylight. Liam heard him slithering over the slate roof, but when he peered out, Seamus had disappeared. The thought of him laughing as he talked about shooting a man pushing a baby in a pram gave Liam the chills.

The death beetle pulled over and waited as Liam got back into the van.

'All good?' he said.

'No problem,' said Liam, stretching out his legs, which hit something that wriggled under a blanket and uttered a grunt.

'Don't kick the traitor,' said death beetle.

Liam snapped his legs back in alarm. His eyes adjusted to the gloom, and a pair of legs stuck out from the blanket tied around the person's body. There were a pair of women's slippers on the feet and some thick nylon tights with a ladder running up them. A wave of revulsion came over him as he realised that they had kidnapped a housewife.

So much for enemy combatants, words, just words. Misery blanketed him. *Doubts? Fergus had been right. These people were cold-blooded killers. Men with prams and housewives?* Not the targets he had in mind when he joined. Disillusion had been slow in coming, but now it hit him like a slap in the face. *Why hadn't he listened to his family?* Even Tom Green's pragmatic attitude made sense now.

After an uncomfortable journey, they pulled up to the cottage and the death beetle sent Liam, and Fergus who had already arrived, up to their room, while he and his companion carried the prisoner through the house kicking and screaming.

'Who is it?' whispered Fergus.

'Some poor woman they dragged out of her house.'

'What did she do?'

'I don't know. She's a housewife, for God's sake, with laddered stockings. She didn't resemble a criminal mastermind to me.'

Muffled thuds came from the back yard. Liam chewed his fingernails to the quick, his nerves shredded by the events of the day. Fergus paced the room, muttering to himself.

'Are you praying?' said Liam.

'It's a rosary. I don't know what else to do.'

'Should we rescue her?'

'They'll shoot us.'

The retort of a pistol made them both jump.

'Jaysus, Mary and Joseph,' said Fergus. 'They shot her.'

'Fecking bastards,' said Liam, shaking his head.

'I don't know what I'm doing here any more,' said Fergus. 'I thought it would be fun to fight for your country. I didn't realise we'd be shooting women and children.'

'What happened today?'

'They kneecapped a young lad for selling marijuana in Belfast,' said Fergus, who trembled.

'Did you watch it?'

'No, but I heard him screaming for his mammy afterwards. I vomited, but they didn't notice.'

Liam recognised the details from his experience. What were they doing there? Fergus sniffed and swallowed his tears.

'What are we going to do, Liam? I can't stay here.'

'Me neither. Let's get out of here. As soon as they go tomorrow, we'll make a break for it.'

'But we've no money. They made sure of that. I can't ring home. They'd be too ashamed to take me back. And how will we travel? What if they come looking for us?'

'I've got friends who'll help us. Trust me.'

Chapter 40 – Byrne's Folly, July 1973

The phone rang just as Tom got halfway up the stairs with a breakfast tray for Bea. He reached up to leave it on the landing and trotted downstairs to the sitting room where he picked up the receiver. He waited for the pips to finish before answering.

'Hello? Tom Green here.'

The sound of panting came over the crackling line.

'Tom, it's Liam. You've got to help me.'

'Liam, what's going on? Where are you?'

'Please, I didn't know…to call.'

'Calm down. Of course, we'll help you, but you have to tell me what you need.'

'I ran away. They killed…a widow…five children… pool of blood. Gave me a mop. I couldn't…'

'Explain later. We need to get you out of there. Where are you?' said Tom.

'Castletown Cross…edge of Dundalk near the border. I'm in a phone…, but I can't…here.'

Tom racked his brains.

'Is there somewhere to hide nearby?'

A hollow laugh followed by more pips and swearing.

'Hello, can you hear me?' said Tom.

'Yes, but I have no more money for the phone. I saw the ruin of a castle nearby,' said Liam. 'It's one of those old towers.'

'Okay, go there and hide as best you can. I'll drive up there. It will take me about four hours so make sure they can't find you first. Is there a graveyard?'

'Yes.'

'I'll honk my horn twice and wait for you with the engine running. What road—'

But the pips sounded again, and Liam had gone. Tom rubbed his face and tried to focus. *He couldn't go alone; he had no hope of finding the castle. Mrs O'Reilly would know where it was. She had an encyclopaedic knowledge of Irish history.*

He ran upstairs, narrowly avoiding falling head first over the tray. He picked it up and burst into the bedroom.

'What's the rush?' said Bea.

'It's Liam. He rang from a phone box in a complete panic. He's run away.'

'Run away? But won't they hunt him down?'

'I'm not sure, but we can't leave him there. I'm going to drive up and rescue him.'

'What about Maeve?'

'Do you think that clown she married will let her go? It's better if I do it. Anyway, she doesn't have a car and Sean is in bed with flu.'

'Don't go on your own. Take Mrs O.'

'You read my mind.'

Mrs O'Reilly opened the door with curlers in her hair, and the habitual cup of tea in her hand.

'Tom. What a surprise. What can I do for you?'

'I need your help, Jacinta. Liam's got himself in a fix.'

Mrs O'Reilly rolled her eyes and tutted.

'What now? That boy's middle name is trouble.'

'It's serious this time. I had a call from a phone box about ten minutes ago. He's run away from the IRA and is hiding near Dundalk, at an old tower at Castletown Cross.'

'Oh, that'll be Byrnes Folly. It's built on top of Dun Dealgan Fort.'

Tom's mouth dropped open.

'How did you know that?'

'Oh, it's the birthplace of Setanta or Cu Chulainn who's a famous character in Irish legend. I visited it in my youth with Mr O'Reilly when we were courting.'

She blushed as some piquant memory of the place came to mind.

'Will you come with me?' said Tom. 'I need a co-pilot and people will respond better to you near the border.'

'I will. Give me five minutes to take out these curlers and I'll be out. By the way, we should take my car. Yours is too conspicuous.'

'Okay, I'll get Bea to make some sandwiches. Can you do the tea?'

Fifteen minutes later, they were on the road. Tom had still not recovered from the fact that Mrs O had come out holding a shotgun and a box of cartridges, as well as the flask of tea. *Lee sure knew how to pick her friends.*

'What are ye gawping at?' she said. 'These lads won't be carrying flowers. We need a deterrent, just in case.'

'But what if the Gardai stop us?'

'I've got a licence. I'm taking the gun to my nephew in Dundalk.'

'Do you have a nephew in Dundalk?'

'Probably, I have nephews everywhere. My eight siblings have forty children between them. You drive and let me deal with it.'

Mrs O'Reilly put the gun into the boot and got into the car with the flask of tea. She folded her arms over her ample bosom and Tom knew it was fruitless to discuss any further. Instead, he took comfort from having the Irish equivalent of a cruise missile in his vehicle.

The Irish countryside flew past as Tom opened up the throttle and made the most of the empty roads as the population got their lie-in before Sunday mass. Mrs O'Reilly chattered away and pulled a constant stream of snacks from her straw bag, passing them to Tom as he motored along. They stopped for Mrs O to use the toilet in a pub as she refused to go in a hedge.

'You must be codding me,' she said, when Tom suggested it.

They took advantage of the stop to refuel the car and check the tyre pressures.

'Just in case,' said Tom.

They pulled into Dundalk around lunchtime, driving down empty streets that echoed with the sound of the engine.

'It's like a ghost town.'

'Everyone's eating their Sunday roast,' said Mrs O'Reilly.

They drove through the town centre and out the other side into countryside divided by lush hedgerows into bright green squares like a leprechaun's patchwork quilt.

'We're close now,' said Mrs O'Reilly. 'It should be on the left.'

Tom slowed the car as they gazed through the trees.

'That's it. Over there,' shrieked Mrs O'Reilly, pointing at a square tower set on a mound surrounded by mature oak, beech and ash trees. Tom turned the car around and parked it in front of a battered van which someone had left outside the metal gates.

'Why would anyone park here?' said Tom.

'Maybe they're having a picnic. It used to be a popular spot for courting in my day.'

Tom shielded his eyes and peered into the driver's side window. A coil of oily rope sat on the passenger seat beside some gaffer tape.

'I don't think they're here for fun,' he said.

Mrs O'Reilly gasped as she saw the contents of the van.

'Right,' she said. 'Time to get serious.'

She took the shotgun from the boot and reached into her straw bag for a handful of cartridges. She shoved several in the pockets of her tweed jacket and cracked open the gun, sliding two cartridges into the barrel. Tom put out his hands, but she shook her head.

'I'm Irish and I have a licence. If I hit anyone, I'm just a batty old woman with poor eyesight.'

'And are you?' said Tom.

Mrs O'Reilly guffawed.

'I can knock the head off a pigeon at one hundred yards.'

Tom shrugged. He wasn't much of a shot anyhow. It remained a mystery to him how Michael had won all those trophies with the Cadet Corps. *What on earth would he think of his father's mission of mercy?* He hoped he would be proud of him.

'Here, take these,' said Mrs O'Reilly, holding out some bolt cutters. 'We might need them.'

They started down the gravel path leading to the entrance, their feet crunching despite their efforts to sneak along. They came to a ramp running between two stone walls leading up to the top of the mound, which had a protective bank around it. Tom held Mrs O'Reilly back as a shadow fell over the top of the wall.

'We'll find you, toe rag. And when we do…'

A man's voice, followed by the sound of hawking. A large gob of phlegm flew over their heads and dropped on the path. Mrs O'Reilly brought the gun to her shoulder, but Tom shook his head, pointing out the path wending its way around the mound.

'There must be another way in,' he whispered.

They inched their way along until the trees hid them from the top of the hill fort. Sure enough, there was a pathway leading up to the folly.

'That's too steep for me,' said Mrs O'Reilly.

'No problem. You stay down here and cover our escape route. I'll find our boy.'

Mrs O'Reilly secreted herself in the opening to a sealed tunnel under the mound from where she could watch the road on both sides without being noticed. Tom set off up the path, his leather-soled shoes slipping on the mud as he grabbed at roots to stay upright. His bravado evaporated as he mounted the path. *These people are trained killers. I must be out of my mind.*

But he crested the hill, keeping a large oak between him and the line of sight. In front of him, the square tower with long window slits loomed over the rest of the ruins, which were almost at ground level. A metal gate blocked the arched entrance to the tower, but Tom spotted movement inside, as if someone glanced outside and then withdrew their head. *Liam. But where were the others?* A twig cracked to his right and a rough looking man passed by with a pistol. He disappeared into the wood. Tom let out his breath and lowered the bolt cutter he had lifted. He sprinted to the gate, intending to open it, but someone had locked it by using a padlock.

'Liam,' he hissed. 'Let me in. Quick, before they see me.'

Liam's pale face appeared, and he struggled to insert the key in the lock. Tom lifted the bolt cutters and cut it open, grunting. He slipped into the tower, shutting the gate.

'Thank God,' hissed Liam. 'I thought my time was up.'

'It still might be. We've got to leave now. There's a path over there that leads to the bottom. Mrs O'Reilly is down there, so let her know it's you or she'll blow your head off.'

'She's armed?'

'And dangerous.'

'But what about you?'

'I'll be right behind you.'

A cough alerted them to someone's presence outside the tower. A man's silhouette appeared outside the gate with a pistol in his outstretched hand. He bent down and picked up the lock.

'Over here,' he shouted, and pushed the gate open.

Tom jumped out of the shadows and brought the bolt cutter down on the man's wrist.

He swore and dropped the pistol, jumping around in pain.

'Run,' said Tom.

They pushed the man to the ground where he lay moaning, holding his wrist. Liam picked up the pistol. The death beetle came around the tower, shooting as he ran.

'Don't stop. Keep going to the treeline,' said Liam. 'They've only got ancient pistols. They couldn't hit a barn door on the run with those.'

When they reached the trees, Tom leant against a trunk, gasping for breath. Liam fired towards the oncoming man, who threw himself behind a low wall.

'Come on,' said Tom. 'We're coming down, Mrs O.'

They slithered down the hill, landing beside Mrs O'Reilly who had the shotgun on her shoulder.

'Let's get out of here,' she said.

They ran to the stile, Mrs O'Reilly laboured behind them, wheezing and limping. After helping her over the stile. Tom jumped into the car and started the engine. Liam threw himself into the back seat. To Tom's dismay, Mrs O'Reilly walked behind their car.

'Oh my God. She's not going to take a leak right now?' said Liam.

A massive bang, followed by another, and Mrs O'Reilly appeared at the passenger door.

'What are you waiting for?' she said.

They screeched away as the death beetle vaulted the stile. His screams of rage were audible. Liam flipped him a bird through the back window.

'You can slow down now,' said Mrs O'Reilly. 'They won't be following us.'

'What did you do?' said Tom.

'They won't get far on two wheels.'

Chapter 41 – Blue Morning, August 1973

Michael wandered downstairs, following the smell of bacon to find his father over the frying pan, whistling.

'I'm starving. Can I have some of that?'

'I'll make you a bacon butty if you'd like?' said Tom.

'Yes, please. Can you wrap it for me? I thought I'd take Blue for a walk in the woods up by Gogan's farm.'

'Okay, don't go too far. Mummy wanted you to go to Kilkenny with her.'

Tom dropped three slices of sizzling back-bacon onto a slice of fresh brown bread and shook some tomato ketchup onto it. He covered the bacon with another slice of bread and cut the sandwich in half. Then he wrapped it in greaseproof paper.

'There you go.'

'It smells delicious. Thanks Dad. Blue. Walkies.'

Michael set off with Blue, who gambolled at his side, sniffing his pocket with longing. For once the clouds had cleared, and the sky was an azure blue. The slanting morning sunshine threw massive shadows across the lane and butterflies flirted with the jasmine on the tops of the hedgerows. He took a deep breath, enjoying the freedom from studying and exams, and Cadet Corps.

When he got home from boarding school, Liam had been using his bedroom.

'It's only for a night or two,' said Tom. 'We've got to ship him off to England before the lads figure out where he is, and come looking.'

This peculiar sentence did not remain mysterious for long. Mrs O'Reilly couldn't wait to tell him about their adventures. Michael was left open-mouthed by the hair-raising exploits of the unlikely dynamic duo.

'She did what?' he said. 'That's amazing.'

'She shot out the tyres of their van,' said Liam, creased over with mirth. 'You've never seen anyone so surprised.'

'The IRA man or Mrs O?'

'Both.'

'What are you going to do now?'

'George has offered to find me an apprenticeship.'

'Good old George. He is our guardian angel.'

'Well, I can't stay here, so there's no choice,' said Liam.

'You're lucky to have an option,' said Michael.

Michael walked up the Gogan's field past the slurry pit, giving it a wide berth. Blue pricked up her ears and trotted ahead of him, looking back to make sure he was coming.

'Where are you going, girl?' said Michael. 'We don't go that way.'

But she appeared determined, so Michael humoured her. There was plenty of time.

Tom had parted Mrs O'Reilly from her copy of the Irish Times and had his head down, devouring its contents, when Liam came down for breakfast.

'Hey there, sleepyhead, you missed Michael. He's gone for a walk with Blue.'

'Where did he go? Maybe I can find him.'

'He told me he was going to the woods behind Gogans' farm. He hasn't been there for ages. I—'

Liam had turned white as a sheet.

'What's wrong?'

'Nothing. I forgot something. I'll get Michael, and I'll be back.'

'Don't you want any breakfast?'

But Liam had headed out of the back door. He broke into a run as soon as he left the house, a rising panic in his throat. *No, no, no.* He sprinted down the road, his lungs bursting, and leaped over the fence into Gogan's field. Almost faint from the effort, he struggled up the hill into the woods and turned right. Faint imprints of Blue's paw prints told him he had guessed correctly. She was leading Michael to the training grounds.

His heart screamed at him, but he kept running through the leaves and mud, pushing himself to the limit. Low-hanging branches whipped his face. *Will I be too late? Why have I insisted on being so bloody macho?* He had almost arrived at the hut. Then he spotted Michael and Blue up ahead. He stopped and grabbed a breath.

'Wait there,' he shouted. 'You're going the wrong way.'

'What?'

'The wrong way. You're going—'

A man stepped into the road, wearing a balaclava, and holding a pistol.

'What the hell are you doing here, you traitor? And why have you brought a soldier with you?'

'A soldier? No, you don't understand. He's a cadet, and he's still at school.'

'He looks like a soldier to me. The English accent and the army haircut are a giveaway.'

Up ahead, Michael had stopped moving. His face registered shock.

'Let's ask him, shall we?'

The man waved his pistol at Liam, who walked towards Michael and Blue.

'Keep walking,' he said. 'Let's go to the training ground.'

The two young men walked ahead of the man with the pistol. Michael glanced at Liam for reassurance but found none. A second man stood in the clearing, also wearing a balaclava.

'Look what I found.' said the first. 'A traitor and a soldier out for a walk, so they say.'

Blue stood between the two pairs, wagging her tail uncertainly. Michael held out his hand, and she placed her head into it. He rubbed her ears, trying to figure out what to say.

'What have you got to say for yourselves then?' said the first man.

'I'm not a soldier,' said Michael. 'I live here, at Dunbell farm. I'm sixteen and I go to cadet corps at school in England. I have to have my hair short. It's school rules.'

'And I suppose you're not a traitor,' said the second man, waving his gun at Liam.

'I'm a coward, but I'm not a traitor. I couldn't do those things; killing women and kneecapping boys. I made a mistake.'

'I don't believe you. Your little friend in Inishkeen squealed on you both before we shot him. We know all about you.'

'Fergus?'

'Dead as a doornail,' said the first man, laughing.

Liam launched himself at the man with a yell of fury. A gunshot ran out, and he fell to the ground, mortally wounded. Michael knelt over him, trying to staunch the blood.

'What have you done? He did nothing bad. He was afraid. That's all.'

'I'm afraid we don't have time to find out,' said the second man and aimed his pistol at Michael, who shut his eyes.

Suddenly, Blue launched herself at the man and the gun flew out of his hand, landing at Michael's knees. He grabbed it and shot at the man, getting him in the shoulder. The other man fired off a shot and Michael slumped to the ground.

'Is he dead?' said the injured man.

'He soon will be. I shot him in the heart.'

'Let's go.'

'Can you walk?'

'What about the dog?'

'Don't waste any more bullets. It's only a mongrel.'

Epilogue – London, May 2011

The doorbell rang, and Isabella opened it to find her sister Liz standing outside in the street. Her knee-high black boots were polished to a brilliant shine. The stiff breeze had released some of her greying hair from her bun and it danced about her head. Her blue eyes watered in the wind.

'You're here' said Isabella.

'I am,' said Liz 'I wouldn't miss it. Sean's just parking the car.'

Liz took off her coat and hung it in the hall while Isabella bustled around her. Unlike her sister, Isabella worked at home and she wore old jeans and a scruffy sweater. She looked much younger than her sister. She had no grey in her tawny hair and her face was unlined and plump.

'Nuala's here already.'

'Will you have a cup of tea?' asked Isabella.

'No thanks, I'm grand,' replied Liz.

'Are you sure?'

'I'm grand thanks.'

'Go on, go on, go on, go on.'

They both sniggered. They loved the Mrs Doyle character from Father Ted. She reminded them of their time in Ireland. They were as close as only sisters could be, sharing jokes that need no further comment between them. Sometimes they used Gaelic words incomprehensible to their friends. They had become more like twins than sisters, despite their age difference.

Sean knocked on the door about five minutes later, panting from exertion.

'Jaysus, I had to leave the car miles away,' he said. 'How's it going there, Isabella?'

'Not bad. Come in quick, it's starting in five minutes.'

'Is Nuala here?'

'She is.'

They crammed onto the three-seater sofa, wiggling into the tight space.

'This reminds me of the back seat of the Morris Minor,' said Liz.

'I'm still sitting on the crack,' said Isabella, getting a dig in the ribs.

The broadcast started, and they leaned forward in unison as the commentator started describing the scene in great detail. Most of the time, the camera focused on a little old lady in a cream outfit with an olive-green laced border and buttons.

'Doesn't she look great?' said Isabella.

'She does' replied Liz.

The old lady was standing beside another woman, a generation younger than her, also smartly dressed in a sober black outfit. The women walked up some steps to a monument, leaving behind them their husbands, two men in dark suits, one older and slightly bowed. There was an air of great solemnity.

'Isn't it great to have two women in charge for a change?' said Nuala.

'Yes,' said Liz. 'It should happen more often.'

'I'm outnumbered so I'm saying nothing,' said Sean.

The two pairs of siblings sat entranced by the scene playing out in front of them. They watched as the soldiers gave wreaths to the two women which they laid at the bottom of the monument and then stepped back, swaying in the strong breeze. Some speeches in Gaelic followed, with no English translation offered, by a soldier in a dark green uniform of rough looking moleskin. A long and intense silence, broken only by the Last Post, had a huge emotional effect on the siblings. Isabella sneaked a peep at Liz. There were tears streaming down her cheeks.

'Who'd have believed it?' she said. 'Isn't it quite brilliant?'

For once Nuala was lost for words. She nodded.

'It is quite astonishing. The Queen in Dublin as the guest of the female president of Ireland? A warm Irish welcome extended to the reigning British monarch,' said Sean, quoting the commentator. 'I can't quite believe it myself.'

His voice caught in his throat and Liz grabbed his hand, squeezing it tight.

The telephone rang, breaking the spell.

Isabella picked up the receiver.

'Hello?' She smiled. 'Yes, we're all here. I'll put you on speaker phone.'

'Is it yourself?' said Sean.

'It is,' said Michael. 'I'm here with Blessing. Have you heard from our parents yet?'

'Didn't I tell you?' said Liz. 'They went up to Dublin to the ceremony with Maeve.'

'How wonderful. Wasn't it amazing? We cried,' said Blessing.

'I didn't,' said Sean.

'Liar,' said Liz.

'Whatever would Liam have made of this?' said Nuala, dabbing her face with a tissue.

'He'd have gone out for a walk with Blue,' said Isabella.

'Dear old Blue. But Mickey was the actual hero. He's the one who found me,' said Michael. 'If it wasn't for him—'

'We'd be rid of you,' said Sean.

'That's not very nice,' said Isabella.

'Who wants a cup of tea?' said Liz.

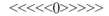

I hope you enjoyed this book.

Please leave a review if you would like to.

Thank you for supporting me

PJ

The second book in the Green Family Series, Africa Green, is now available on Amazon and at all online retailers.

Acknowledgements

I would like to acknowledge the help of Una Willers in the writing of this book. Her sharp brain and eagle eyes spotted many time clangers and information gaps which I did not. We surfed the lockdown together and I am very grateful for her support.

Also, I would like to thank Kevin Causey, my editor, for forcing the second draft out of me with razor sharp comments about the shortcomings in my manuscript. Editing is a bit pointless without someone who knows how to tighten and lengthen in equal measure.

Finally, a word for my cover designer, Jared Shear, who waited patiently until I was ready and has produced a haunting cover that encapsulates the story.

The Green Family Series

Africa Green – Book 2

Will a white chimp save its rescuers or get them killed?

Journalist Isabella Green travels to Sierra Leone, a country emerging from civil war, to write an article about a chimp sanctuary. Animals that need saving are her obsession, and she can't resist getting involved with the project, which is on the verge of bankruptcy. She forms a bond with local boy, Ten, and army veteran, Pete, to try and save it. When they rescue a rare white chimp from a village frequented by a dangerous rebel splinter group, the resulting media interest could save the sanctuary. But the rebel group have not signed the cease fire. They believe the voodoo power of the white chimp protects them from bullets, and they are determined to take it back so they can storm the capital. When Pete and Ten go missing, only Isabella stands in the rebels' way. Her love for the chimps unlocks the fighting spirit within her. Can she save the sanctuary or will she die trying?

Fighting Green – Book 3

Coming soon

The Sam Harris Series

Set in the late 1980's and through the 1990's, the thrilling Sam Harris Adventure series navigates through the career of a female geologist. Themes such as women working in formerly male domains, and what constitutes a normal existence, are developed in the context of Sam's constant ability to find herself in the middle of an adventure or mystery.

Sam's home life provides a contrast to her adventures and feeds her need to escape. Her attachment to an unfaithful boyfriend is the thread running through her romantic life, and her attempts to break free of it provide another side to her character.

The first book in the Sam Harris Series sets the scene for the career of an unwilling heroine, whose bravery and resourcefulness are needed to navigate a series of adventures set in remote sites in Africa and South America. Based loosely on the real-life adventures of the author, the settings and characters are given an authenticity that will connect with readers who enjoy adventure fiction and mysteries set in remote settings with realistic scenarios.

Fool's Gold - Book 1

Newly qualified geologist Sam Harris is a woman in a man's world - overlooked, underpaid but resilient and passionate. Desperate for her first job, and nursing a broken heart, she accepts an offer from notorious entrepreneur Mike Morton, to search for gold deposits in the remote rainforests of Sierramar. With the help of nutty local heiress, Gloria Sanchez, she soon settles into life in Calderon, the capital. But when she accidentally uncovers a long-lost clue to a treasure buried deep within the jungle, her journey really begins.

Teaming up with geologist Wilson Ortega, historian Alfredo Vargas and the mysterious Don Moises, they venture through the jungle, where she lurches between excitement and insecurity. Yet there is a far graver threat looming; Mike and Gloria discover that one of the members of the expedition is plotting to seize the fortune for himself and is willing to do anything to get it. Can Sam survive and find the treasure or will her first adventure be her last?

Hitler's Finger - Book 2
The second book in the Sam Harris Series sees the return of our heroine Sam Harris to Sierramar to help her friend Gloria track down her boyfriend, the historian, Alfredo Vargas.

Geologist Sam Harris loves getting her hands dirty. So, when she learns that her friend Alfredo has gone missing in Sierramar, she gives her personal life some much needed space and hops on the next plane. But she never expected to be following the trail of a devious Nazi plot nearly 50 years after World War II ...

Deep in a remote mountain settlement, Sam must uncover the village's dark history. If she fails to reach her friend in time, the Nazi survivors will ensure Alfredo's permanent silence. Can Sam blow the lid on the conspiracy before the Third Reich makes a devastating return?

The background to the book is the presence of Nazi war criminals in South America which was often ignored by locals who had fascist sympathies during World War II. Themes such as tacit acceptance of fascism, and local collaboration with fugitives from justice are examined and developed in the context of

Sam's constant ability to find herself in the middle of an adventure or mystery.

The Star of Simbako - Book 3

A fabled diamond, a jealous voodoo priestess, disturbing cultural practices. What could possibly go wrong? The third book in the Sam Harris Series sees Sam Harris on her first contract to West Africa to Simbako, a land of tribal kingdoms and voodoo.

Nursing a broken heart, Sam Harris goes to Simbako to work in the diamond fields of Fona. She is soon involved with a cast of characters who are starring in their own soap opera, a dangerous mix of superstition, cultural practices, and ignorance (mostly her own). Add a love triangle and a jealous woman who wants her dead and Sam is in trouble again. Where is the Star of Simbako? Is Sam going to survive the chaos?

This book is based on visits made to the Paramount Chiefdoms of West Africa. Despite being nominally Christian communities, Voodoo practices are still part of daily life out there. This often leads to conflicts of interest. Combine this with the horrific ritual of FGM and it makes for a potent cocktail of conflicting loyalties. Sam is pulled into this life by her friend, Adanna, and soon finds herself involved in goings on that she doesn't understand.

The Pink Elephants - Book 4

Sam gets a call in the middle of the night that takes her to the Masaibu project in Lumbono, Africa. The project is collapsing under the weight of corruption and chicanery engendered by management, both in country and back on the main company board. Sam has to navigate murky waters to get it back on course, not helped by interference from people who want her to fail. When poachers invade the elephant sanctuary next door, her problems multiply. Can Sam protect the elephants and save the project or will she have to choose?

The fourth book in the Sam Harris Series presents Sam with her sternest test yet as she goes to Africa to fix a failing project. The day-to-day problems encountered by Sam in her work are typical of any project manager in the Congo which has been rent apart by warring factions, leaving the local population frightened and rootless. Elephants with pink tusks do exist, but not in the area where the project is based. They are being slaughtered by poachers in Gabon for the Chinese market and will soon be extinct, so I have put the guns in the hands of those responsible for the massacre of these defenceless animals

The Bonita Protocol - Book 5
An erratic boss. Suspicious results. Stock market shenanigans. Can Sam Harris expose the scam before they silence her? It's 1996. Geologist Sam Harris has been around the block, but she's prone to nostalgia, so she snatches the chance to work in Sierramar, her old stomping ground. But she never expected to be working for a company that is breaking all the rules.

When the analysis results from drill samples are suspiciously high, Sam makes a decision that puts her life in peril. Can she blow the lid on the conspiracy before they shut her up for good?

The Bonita Protocol sees Sam return to Sierramar and take a job with a junior exploration company in the heady days before the Bre-X crash. I had fun writing my first megalomaniac female boss for this one. I have worked in a few junior companies with dodgy bosses in the past, and my only comment on the sector is buyer beware…

Digging Deeper - Book 6
A feisty geologist working in the diamond fields of West Africa is kidnapped by rebels. Can she survive the ordeal or will this adventure be her last? It's 1998. Geologist Sam Harris is desperate for money so she takes a job in a tinpot mining company working in war-torn Tamazia. But she never expected to be kidnapped by blood thirsty rebels.

Working in Gemsite was never going to be easy with its culture of misogyny and corruption. Her boss, the notorious Adrian Black is engaged in a game of cat and mouse with the government over taxation. Just when Sam makes a breakthrough, the camp is overrun by rebels and Sam is taken captive. Will anyone bother to rescue her, and will she still be alive if they do?

I worked in Tamazia (pseudonym for a real place) for almost a year in different capacities. The first six months I spent in the field are the basis for this book. I don't recommend working in the field in a country at civil war but, as for many of these crazy jobs, I needed the money.

Concrete Jungle - Book 7 (series end)
Armed with an MBA, Sam Harris is storming the City - But has she swapped one jungle for another?

Forging a new career was never going to be easy, and Sam discovers she has not escaped from the culture of misogyny and corruption that blighted her field career.

When her past is revealed, she finally achieves the acceptance she has always craved, but being one of the boys is not the panacea she expected. The death of a new friend presents her with the stark choice of compromising her principals to keep her new position, or exposing the truth behind the façade. Will she finally get what she wants or was it all a mirage?

I did an MBA to improve my career prospects, and much like Sam, found it didn't help much. In the end, it's only your inner belief that counts. What other people say, or think, is their problem. I hope you enjoy this series. It was written to rid myself of demons, and it worked.

You can order these books in paperback at your favourite retailer.

Please go to the PJSKINNER.com website for links and the newsletter

Connect with the Author

If you would like updates on the latest books by PJ Skinner or to contact the author with your questions please click on the following links:

Website: www.pjskinner.com

Facebook: https://www.facebook.com/PJSkinnerAuthor

Twitter: https://twitter.com/PJSkinnerAuthor

Amazon Author page; https://www.amazon.com/PJ-Skinner/e/B01ABVE7J2

About the Author

PJ Skinner is the author of the Sam Harris Series of adventure-thriller novels. A geologist who has spent thirty years roaming the planet and collecting tall tales and real-life experiences, she now writes fact-based novels from the relative safety of London. She still travels worldwide collecting material for the series and having her own adventures.

The Sam Harris Adventure Series is for lovers of adventure thrillers happening just before the time of mobile phones and internet. It has a unique viewpoint provided by Sam, a female interloper in a male world, as she struggles with alien cultures and failed relationships.

Rebel Green was written with the inspiration of her childhood spent in Ireland. It deals with themes of alienation and belonging.

The author has written a sequel to Rebel Green, following the adventures of Isabella Green. Other projects in the pipe line include a series of Cozy Mysteries, or a book about… You'll have to wait and see.